INSIGHT CITY GUIDE

OXFORD

Discovery CHANNEL

APA PUBLICATIONS
Part of the Langenscheidt Publishing Group

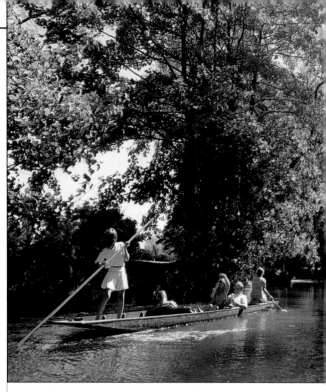

![INSIGHT GUIDE]

OXFORD

Editor
Brian Bell
Art Director
Klaus Geisler
Picture Editor
Hilary Genin
Production
Kenneth Chan
Cartography Editor
Zoë Goodwin

Distribution

UK & Ireland
GeoCenter International Ltd
Meridian House, Churchill Way West
Basingstoke, Hampshire RG21 6YR
Fax: (44) 1256-817988

United States
Langenscheidt Publishers, Inc.
36–36 33rd Street, 4th Floor
Long Island City, NY 11106
Fax: (1) 718 784-0640

Canada
Thomas Allen & Son Ltd
390 Steelcase Road East
Markham, Ontario L3R 1G2
Fax: (1) 905 475 6747

Australia
Universal Publishers
1 Waterloo Road
Macquarie Park, NSW 2113
Fax: (61) 2 9888 9074

New Zealand
Hema Maps New Zealand Ltd (HNZ)
Unit D, 24 Ra ORA Drive
East Tamaki, Auckland
Fax: (64) 9 273 6479

Worldwide
**Apa Publications GmbH & Co.
Verlag KG (Singapore branch)**
38 Joo Koon Road, Singapore 628990
Tel: (65) 6865-1600. Fax: (65) 6861-6438

Printing

Insight Print Services (Pte) Ltd
38 Joo Koon Road, Singapore 628990
Tel: (65) 6865-1600. Fax: (65) 6861-6438

ABOUT THIS BOOK

The first Insight Guide pioneered the use of creative full-colour photography in guidebooks in 1970. Since then, we have expanded our range to cater for our readers' need not only for reliable information about their chosen destination but also for a real understanding of that destination. Now, when the internet can supply inexhaustible (but not always reliable) facts, our books marry text and pictures to provide that much more elusive quality: knowledge. To achieve this, they rely heavily on the authority of locally based writers and photographers.

Insight City Guide: Oxford is carefully structured to convey an understanding of the ancient university town and its culture, as well as to guide readers through its sights:

◆ The **History** and **Features** sections, indicated by a yellow bar, cover the history and culture of the city through informative essays.

◆ The main **Places** section, indicated by a blue bar, is a complete guide to all the sights and areas worth visiting. Principal places of interest are cross-referenced by number to the colour maps.

◆ The **Travel Tips** listings section provides easy-to-use information on how to get around, hotels, shops, restaurants and much more. Its contents are listed on the back flap.

fellow at St Edmund Hall, he chose to go on living in Oxford after leaving the university "partly through lethargy but mostly because it is such a pleasant place to live."

Another Oxford resident, **Tony Halliday**, a senior managing editor with Insight Guides, was consultant on the book and took many of the photographs. **Clare Peel**, another Insight managing editor and an Oxford graduate, updated the profiles of Oxford colleges, originally written by **Simon Veksner**.

The chapter on Warwick in the excursions section was written by **Michael Ivory**, and the feature on architecture by **David Horan**. The Travel Tips listings section was compiled by **Richard Carmichael**.

This edition has retained much of the work of the original contributors, including **Christopher Catling**, who wrote many of the Places chapters, **Roland Collins** and **Helen Turner**, who wrote the history section, **Ray Hutton**, who traced Oxford's history as a car-manufacturing centre, **Mark Davies**, who lived on a canalboat and wrote the feature Canal Life, **David Leake**, a gardener at Corpus Christi College who wrote about the city's elusive gardens, and **Yvonne Newman**, a Headington resident who wrote several of the one-page boxes.

Much of the evocative photography is by **Chris Andrews**, who publishes books, calendars and even playing cards featuring Oxford scenes. Other important photographic contributors include **Glyn Genin** and **Caroline Jones**.

The contributors

This edition of *Insight City Guide: Oxford* was edited by **Brian Bell**, Insight Guides' editorial director, who lives just 20 miles from the city – or, more significantly, 18 miles from the nearest Park and Ride bus terminus since trying to find a convenient car parking space in Oxford is as unlikely as winning the lottery.

That isn't a problem for **James Ferguson**, who lives in the city and has fully updated and revised the text for this edition as well as writing new pieces on Literature, Alternative Oxford, and Oxford Brookes University. A graduate of Pembroke College and a former junior research

CONTACTING THE EDITORS

We would appreciate it if readers would alert us to errors or outdated information by writing to:

**Insight Guides, P.O. Box 7910, London SE1 1WE, England.
Fax: (44) 20 7403-0290.**
insight@apaguide.co.uk

www.insightguides.com
In North America:
www.insighttravelguides.com

LEFT: the famous dreaming spires, seen from Boars Hill.

Travel Tips

THE BEST OF OXFORD

Setting priorities, saving money, unique attractions...
here, at a glance, are our recommendations, plus tips
and tricks even the students won't always know

ONLY IN OXFORD

● **May Morning** A true Oxford tradition when choristers sing from the top of Magdalen College Tower and revellers celebrate the advent of summer.

● **Punting on the Thames** Hire a punt for an hour or two as an ideal way to see the city's riverside scenery and learn to steer in a straight line. *Page 200.*

● **The View from the Tower** The 188-ft tower of the University Church of St Mary the Virgin is a great place for surveying spires and quadrangles. *Page 91.*

● **Book Lover's Paradise** Blackwell's Bookshop is a venerable Oxford institution and welcomes browsers and buyers from around the world. *Page 137.*

● **Hogwarts Hall** Christ Church's impressive dining hall, with its hammerbeam roof, was used to film scenes from the Harry Potter films. The college opens to visitors almost every day. *Page 153.*

● **Port Meadow** Oxford's great expanse of flood plain makes for an atmospheric walk among grazing horses and birdlife. *Page 202.*

● **The Bodleian Library** Dating from the 15th century, the Divinity School is one of Oxford's most spectacular historic buildings, complete with an ornate vaulted ceiling. *Page 177.*

● **The Sheldonian Theatre** As well as being one of Sir Christopher Wren's architectural gems, this is a major concert venue. *Page 84.*

BELOW Magdalen choristers greet May Morning.

OXFORD FOR FAMILIES

These attractions are popular with children, though not all will suit every age group.

● **The Oxford Story** Featuring the sights, sounds and smells of 900 years of Oxford history, this automated tour is a hit with children. *Page 130.*

● **Take a Bus Ride** Open-top bus tours come with commentary and are a good way of seeing the main sights. *Page 250.*

● **Take a Boat Trip** Get on the water with a Thames excursion up to Iffley or beyond from Folly Bridge. *Page 251.*

● **Hinksey Park** Just south of the city centre down Abingdon Road, the park has an open-air swimming pool with splash feature. *Page 206.*

● **The Castle and Prison** The newly renovated prison complex will appeal to the ghoulish with tales of executions and ghostly hauntings. *Page 187.*

● **Botanic Garden** Familiar to fans of Philip Pullman's children's books, the garden also has a steamy and colourful tropical hothouse. *Page 116.*

BEST PUBS

- **The King's Arms** The city-centre student haunt *par excellence*, with real ales and extensive menu. *Page 145.*
- **The Turf Tavern** Low ceilings, intimate bars and walled gardens provide unforgettable atmosphere. *Page 145.*
- **The Rose and Crown** Traditional pub set in a charming North Oxford street. *Page 183.*
- **The Eagle and Child** Once the haunt of Tolkien and other literary luminaries, it has avoided modernization. *Page 169.*
- **The Head of the River** Great views of the Thames and especially popular in summer with its expansive outdoor seating. *Page 155.*
- **The Trout Inn** A riverside pub in the nearby village of Wolvercote, the Trout is a perennial favourite with drinkers and diners alike. *Page 203.*
- **The Perch** Close to Port Meadow, this is an Oxford summertime institution, with large garden, good food and a healthy walk nearby. *Page 203.*
- **The Fishes** An up-and-coming gastro-pub with a strong wine list and sophisticated menu. *Page 203.*

ABOVE: The Head of the River pub is well located on the Thames.

ABOVE: pub lunch al fresco.

COLLEGE HIGHLIGHTS

- **Christ Church**: its Quad, Tom Tower and Cathedral. The largest and best-known college. *Page 151.*
- **Magdalen**: its bell tower, Chapel, Deer Park, Addison's Walk. *Page 102.*
- **Merton**: its Chapel with remarkable stained glass, and Mob Quad. *Page 112.*
- **Exeter**: its splendid High Gothic chapel by Sir George Gilbert Scott and the Fellows' Garden where Tolkien walked. *Page 135.*
- **St John's**: its expansive gardens and the statues in Canterbury Quad. *Page 171.*
- **Trinity**: more fine gardens and a baroque chapel. *Page 132.*
- **Brasenose**: its famed door knocker and the startling views of the Radcliffe Camera and St Mary's from the Old Quad. *Page 90.*

TOP EVENTS

- **Eights Week** The annual drama of the fiercely competitive inter-college boat races, taking place over four days in late May. *Page 196.*
- **Encaenia** A colourful piece of academic pageantry held each June when visiting dignitaries walk through the streets to be awarded honorary degrees. *Page 126.*
- **Cowley Road Carnival** A day-long and often raucous celebration of East Oxford's cultural diversity that takes place on multi-ethnic Cowley Road in mid-June. *Page 67.*
- **St Giles' Fair** All the fun of the fair, with every type of hair-raising ride, in normally stately St Giles. *Page 164.*
- **Christmas Music** Carols are beautifully sung in the 12th-century Christ Church Cathedral in the run-up to Christmas.

RIGHT: rowing at Oxford is fiercely competitive.

8

BEST WALKS

●**Christ Church Meadow** Oxford's city-centre rural retreat takes you into a surprisingly peaceful world of lush pasture land and Thamesside paths. *Page 195*.

●**University Parks** The "green lung" of North and wild flowers. *Page 104*.

●**The Thames Towpath** The stretch of towpath between Folly Bridge and Iffley is ideal for watching aspiring boat race contenders at practice. *Page 197*.

●**Mesopotamia Walk** Named after the land between the Tigris and Euphrates, this scenic walk follows the Cherwell over a number of bridges. *Page 198*.

●**Canal Walk** Leave busy Hythe Bridge Street to discover a picturesque world of prettily decorated canal boats and placid waterside gardens. *Page 192*.

BEST MUSIC VENUES

●**The Sheldonian Theatre** Occasionally used for concerts, Christopher Wren's magnificent auditorium seats 2,000, with unobscured views of the stage.

●**Holywell Music Room** Sympathetically restored, this venerable 18th-century concert hall is famous for its chamber music.

●**The New Theatre** The city's most spacious venue stages mainstream pop concerts as well as opera, comedy and an ever-popular Christmas pantomime.

●**Jacqueline du Pré**

ABOVE: taking a stroll in Worcester College gardens.

Oxford boasts a rich array of trees and shrubs as well as pleasant walks by the banks of the Cherwell. *Page 179*.

●**Addison's Walk** A tree-lined circuit within the grounds of Magdalen College gives views of the deer park, Cherwell

ABOVE: the Covered Market offers shopping as it used to be.

TOP SHOPPING

●**The Covered Market** The ideal antidote to high street uniformity with traditional butchers, stylish craft shops and pleasant cafés. *Page 123*.

●**The Wednesday Market** A weekly outdoor event in Gloucester Green, offering good value for money.

●**Farmers' Market**

Music Building A modern purpose-built auditorium in the grounds of St Hilda's College, it hosts an eclectic mix of medieval, classical and avant-garde performances.

●**The Jericho Tavern** Associated with Oxford bands such as Radiohead and Supergrass, this lively pub has a long association with local rock and folk music.

●**The Zodiac** The city's premier night spot provides a high-octane mix of big-name acts and local talent together with regular club nights.

Emphasis on local organic produce.

●**Little Clarendon Street** Arguably the trendiest shopping street in Oxford, also featuring a good selection of restaurants and bars.

●**Cowley Road** A multi-ethnic cornucopia of Asian outlets and European delicatessens, punctuated by every sort of eatery. *Page 67*.

●**Turl Street** A medieval car-free lane, where you can browse in second-hand bookshops and consider buying top-quality shoes from Duckers.

BELOW: Cowley Road Carnival.

THE BEST OF OXFORD ◆ 9

BEST MUSEUMS AND GALLERIES

●**Ashmolean Museum**
Breathtakingly eclectic
mix of archaeological,
sculptural and artistic
treasures, with work
by Michelangelo,
Raphael and Impres-
sionists. *Page 157.*

●**Pitt Rivers Museum**
Eccentric temple of
ethnological exhibits
where you'll find an
amazing array of
weird and wonderful
objects from all over
the world. *Page 177.*

●**University Museum**
This Gothic pile con-
tains an eye-catching
range of dinosaur
skeletons and Savery's
famous Dodo paint-
ing. *Page 175.*

●**Museum of Oxford**
A permanent exhibi-
tion traces the devel-
opment of the town
rather than the univer-
sity, with fascinating
architectural exhibits.
Page 147.

●**Modern Art Oxford**
Oxford's own avant-
garde modern art
gallery has perma-
nently revolving exhi-
bitions of cutting-
edge work. *Page 149.*

●**Christ Church
Picture Gallery** Over
300 paintings on show
in the college's private
collection, with work
by Veronese, Holbein
and Van Dyck. *Page
154.*

ABOVE: Richard Burton introduced Elizabeth Taylor to Oxford.

BEST THEATRES AND CINEMAS

●**Oxford Playhouse**
The city's most cele-
brated theatre, with
many illustrious past
members, still offers a
good range of drama,
dance and opera.

●**Burton Taylor
Theatre** A 50-seater
annex to the
Playhouse, this studio
theatre specializes in
student productions
and experimental
small-scale drama.

●**Pegasus Theatre**
Located in East
Oxford, the Pegasus
runs a varied pro-
gramme of events
with an emphasis on
youth theatre and
community education.

●**Old Fire Station
Theatre** With 170
seats, this is bigger
than the Burton
Taylor but stages a
similar programme of
student-oriented per-
formances.

●**Ultimate Picture
Palace** Cowley
Road's relaxed art-
house cinema shows
films from around the
world to a largely stu-
dent audience.

●**The Phoenix Picture
House** Bohemian
Jericho's fashionable
cinema, where an
intelligent range of
mainstream and elu-
sive films draws a
faithful clientele.

BELOW: the University Museum's herd of dinosaurs.

INSIDE TRACK

Access to the colleges The 39 colleges
that make up the University of Oxford
have very varied policies regarding visitors, ranging from the welcoming to the
unfriendly." 'Closed" signs are a common sight, especially in the mornings,
and some colleges charge an entrance
fee of up to £4.50. Groups are advised
to book a visit in advance. The University website (www.ox.ac.uk/visitors)
contains useful information. As a general rule it makes sense to use an official guide. Knowledgeable guides can

be booked through the Information Centre (see p.259) or can usually be found
in Broad Street, near Blackwell's Bookshop. Disabled access is sometimes a
problem in particular colleges.

University buildings Apart from the
colleges, the University offers some
stunning architectural and cultural
treats in the form of libraries, museums
and galleries. These are usually much
more accessible to visitors than the colleges and often do not charge entrance
fees. You should not miss the Ash-

molean Museum, the Museum of Natural History and the Pitt Rivers
Museum, all of which testify to the
extraordinary richness of the University's artistic and scientific legacy.

The Oxford Story For those who prefer
their history served up in a digestibly
themed format, the Oxford Story (see
p.130) provides an entertaining overview of the University's development
across the centuries. Children will enjoy
the indoor ride through the past and the
interactive facilities.

A TALE OF TWO CITIES

While tomorrow's leaders are shaped within the University, today's cars roll off BMW's production lines. The historical tension between these two sides of Oxford – Town and Gown – is still potent

It is small wonder that Oxford is one of the world's most anthologised cities. Many famous writers, having attended its university, have tried to recapture on paper an experience that profoundly affected their lives. Often their feelings recall the relationship between child and parent: a complex cocktail of love and resentment, admiration and disdain.

Matthew Arnold, whose poetry immortalised Oxford as "that sweet City with her dreaming spires", captured this ambivalence in a letter to his mother in 1861: "I always like this place, and the intellectual life here is certainly much more intense than it used to be; but this has its disadvantages too, in the envies, hatreds, and jealousies that come with the activity of mind of most men."

In *Wealth of Nations* (1776), Adam Smith was less equivocal, dismissing Oxford as "a sanctuary in which exploded systems and obsolete prejudices find shelter and protection after they have been hunted out of every corner of the world". A century later, George Bernard Shaw was just as beastly: "It is characteristic of the authorities that they should consider a month too little for the preparation of a boat-race, and grudge three weeks to the rehearsals of one of Shakespeare's plays."

Those writers, of course, are equating Oxford with the university, and it is certainly the aura of learning that draws most visitors to the city. But there are many other sides to Oxford: it is a thriving market town, for example, as well as a pioneer of the latest bio-tech research. John Betjeman, an influential architectural critic as well as a poet, once lamented that the car factories "could have been a model for the rest of England, so that visitors to the university, instead of trying to pretend no industrialism was near and bathing themselves in a false twilight of grey Gothic things, would have naturally hurried to see the living beauty of industrial Oxford after the dead glory of university architecture." The failure of such hopes led another poet, W. H. Auden, to moan: "Oxford city is sheer hell. Compared with New York, it's five times as crowded and the noise of the traffic is six times louder."

Yet even the complainers keep coming back, forgiving the city its foibles as they would forgive a venerable but wayward parent. Its allure is elusive, but its myths are powerful, offering visitors what the writer Peter Ackroyd called "a clutter of broken images" that demand to be seen again and again. ❏

PRECEDING PAGES: student line-up; the interior of the Sheldonian Theatre.
LEFT: meeting of minds in an Oxford quad.

THE MAKING OF OXFORD

The site was first settled in Saxon times, and was named after its oxen ford. In the 1640s Oxford played a central role in the Civil War, and through the centuries a less bloody civil war continued between Town and Gown

Oxford was a late starter. Shunned by Stone-Age tribes and avoided by the Romans, it had to wait on the Saxons, who always lived and moved by water, to launch it in importance as one of England's great defensive and cultural centres. If that is a simplistic view of local history, then the evidence to the contrary is thin on the ground – and, indeed, in the museums. A few axe-heads, some bronze tools and perhaps the burial mounds of farmers and cattle herders in Port Meadow by the river and in the University Parks are all that remain to span thousands of years.

It is not difficult to see why the site of Oxford was unattractive to settlers. It was low-lying and traversed by the deep streams of the Thames and Cherwell. The Romans, who hated clay soil for their roads and never settled at fords, bypassed the site to the east and north, building their villas away from the rivers.

The Middle Ages

Assorted worthies were credited with founding Oxford – a legendary King Memphric in 1000 BC, Brutus bringing Greek scholars after the fall of Troy, and, more credibly, Alfred the Great. Offa, King of Mercia from 757 to 796, may have built the oxen ford across the river that gave the settlement its name.

Those dates are narrowly beaten for the founder's stakes by the persistent legend of St Frideswide. Daughter of a Mercian king, the

virginal Frideswide seems to have resisted the unwelcome attentions of a princely suitor by blinding him with the aid of a well-aimed thunderbolt. Relenting, she restored his sight with water from her own private holy well by the river. At Binsey, to the west of the fringes of Oxford, that well still exists in the churchyard, and is credited by a notice posted on the church door with being "the very beginning of anything at Oxford".

Frideswide, vowed to celibacy, went on to found a priory on a site near the present cathedral. The time: the early 8th century. The place: a gravel spit near where the Thames and Cherwell rivers meet. Nothing except an obit-

---

LEFT: one of the many 10th-century illustrated manuscripts kept in the Bodleian Library.
RIGHT: King Alfred defended Oxford against the Danes.

uary is recorded of the 400 years of the priory's existence. It was burned down during a massacre of the Danes in 1002.

In the cathedral that replaced the priory, between the choir and the north aisle, is the shrine of St Frideswide. Stand near it and you are at Oxford's heart and Oxford's beginning. From the fragmented canopy of stone, faces peer through sculptured leaves of ivy and sycamore, oak and vine, a medieval mason's interpretation of the virgin princess's escape from her tormenter to the safety of the forest.

Fact or fiction, St Frideswide is remembered every year on 19 October in a service at the cathedral attended by both Town and University. The body of the saint is no longer there; it disappeared during the upheavals of the Reformation in the 16th century.

The town developed as a sort of Saxon conference centre, and even became attractive to monarchs in spite of St Frideswide's curse on royalty after her misfortune. At Henry I's great palace of Beaumont, just beyond where the Ashmolean is now, Richard the Lion-Heart and probably King John were born. Henry had also built a palace – or, more likely, a hunting lodge – at Woodstock, 8 miles (13 km) from Oxford in the forest of Wychwood.

Trade brings prosperity

Following a decline in the 11th century, the fortunes of the town were rescued by the growth of the trade in wool and cloth. This brought the formation of trade guilds, of which the weavers and corvesers (shoemakers) were the earliest, and provided the embryo of civic rule. The right to produce, sell and buy goods was strictly controlled. No one could set up a loom within 15 miles (24 km) of Oxford or sell leather without the guild's consent. The weekly market was held under a similarly strict protectionism.

The scholars arrive

The university was the product of spontaneous combustion, the pursuit of knowledge fusing with the convenience of physical and spiritual community that Oxford provided. From the early 12th century, English scholars, all of them clerks in holy orders, customarily went to the University of Paris to complete their

INVASION AND CONQUEST

The natural barriers of the Thames and Cherwell rivers helped Oxford develop as a strategic frontier town in England's battles against Danish invaders. Gradually, some Danes settled in the town, but this uneasy integration was brought to a bloody conclusion in 1002 by the king's order to massacre all those living in Oxford. Seven years later the Danish army sacked the town as a reprisal, which may account for the derelict condition of much of the town and its suburbs outside the walls.

The Norman Conquest in 1066 ushered in an even bigger physical change. Robert d'Oilly, the town's governor, upgraded the defensive works by building a castle which destroyed an entire western suburb and involved the diversion of the road to the west. Keep and mound were raised and a moat fed from the Thames. Walls were extended to include the castle and the eastern suburb near the River Cherwell. As with the Tower of London, the Normans believed in symbolising their power in stone.

It is also likely that d'Oilly built Grandpont, the first stone bridge (where Folly Bridge now stands). Within the castle walls d'Oilly erected a chapel to St George, one of the first-known dedications to the patron saint of England, and in the founding of the Secular Canons of St George we can anticipate the beginnings of the university itself.

education, but, following an unresolved quarrel with the king of France in 1167, King Henry II ordered them home.

Oxford was a natural place for these outcasts to settle. There were already centres of learning in the Augustinian monasteries of St Frideswide's Priory and Osney Abbey, and they were close to power. Henry, from his palace at Beaumont could readily select public servants from this pool of academic talent.

Life for the early students at Oxford was organised along the lines of the tradesmen's guilds. Like apprentices, they lived and studied for seven years with their Masters in "Halls". After four years they took their Bach-

either. The first colleges were founded by bishops, catered only for graduates and were exclusively for the wealthy. They were organised like monasteries, with a hall, chapel, lodgings, kitchen and quarters for the Master; the pattern is the same today.

The atmosphere of a medieval college is most nearly captured in Merton. Founded in 1264 by Walter de Merton, it shares the "oldest" title with University and Balliol.

A cuckoo in the nest

From the 13th century, Oxford's 6,000 people became increasingly dependent on the growing university. The most important trades –

elor of Arts degree, and at the end of the course their Master's degree, which entitled them to lecture. Those who chose to do so hired houses, boarding and teaching their students under one roof. Beam Hall in Merton Street is one of these halls. Most disappeared as colleges gradually took their place.

The first colleges

As the university had no buildings, Congregation, the governing body, met in the church of St Mary the Virgin. There were no students

LEFT: the Battle of Hastings decided England's future.
ABOVE: an 11th-century haymaker.

TOWN VERSUS GOWN

Tensions between the scholars and the citizenry have a long history. In 1209 a woman was killed by scholars, and two of them were hanged in revenge. Traders were often accused of overcharging scholars. Town and Gown took their differences into the 17th century, spilling less blood but spending more money on legal arguments over an ever-increasing number of issues. In 1609 the city complained of proctors' high-handed treatment of citizens, the excessive number of alehouses licensed by the university and the drunkenness and bad manners of its members. Little was resolved, but legal fees accounted for half the city's income.

weavers and cloth merchants, shoemakers, masons, metalworkers, artists in stained glass, manuscript painters and scribes – prospered.

As the university's star moved into the ascendant, so that of the town waned. Relegated to the status of a country and market town, it became more and more subservient to the university's needs. As a cuckoo in the town's nest, puffed up with self-importance and royal patronage, the university forced trades and residents out as more and more sites in the central area were acquired for colleges. Houses were demolished wholesale.

The plight of the Oxford townsfolk is vividly illustrated in the fortunes of the

weavers, whose guild was one of the earliest in England. In the 12th century there were 60 members. By 1270, 15 remained. Fifty years later there were none.

Poverty and poor living conditions bred disease; in 1348 a quarter of the town's people succumbed to the plague. Labour became scarce and an attempt was made by both Chancellor and Mayor to control wages. Widespread dissatisfaction led to popular demonstrations against authority.

Building the colleges

For the next 200 years, the history of Oxford is the history of the university. New colleges were founded by bishops investing in learning as an insurance for the future power and influence of the Church, king and realm. "Men of learning, fruitful to the Church" was the prescription of William of Wykeham, Bishop of Winchester, for his students when founding New College in 1379. With the land went part of the 12th-century city wall and an obligation to keep it in good repair that still conserves this valuable link with the city's past.

A clutch of colleges followed: Lincoln in 1427, founded by the Bishop of Lincoln; All Souls, by the Archbishop of Canterbury with Henry VI as co-founder in 1438; Magdalen in 1458 by another Bishop of Winchester. The aims were always the same: to sustain the material superiority of the aristocracy.

Brasenose was founded by another Bishop of Lincoln in 1517, and Corpus Christi by the Bishop of Winchester in 1525. Trinity was set up by a civil servant in 1555, and St John's,

THE OXFORD MARTYRS

In 1549 the first Book of Common Prayer was issued and Protestants could now worship in their own faith. But it was a short honeymoon. When the boy king Edward VI died, his successor, Queen Mary brought what can only be described as a burning zeal to the re-introduction of Roman Catholicism. Between 1555 and 1558, following the repeal of anti-papal legislation by a compliant parliament, 300 people were burnt at the stake for heresy.

Mary chose the streets of Oxford for the public humiliation of the three most influential and resistant of the Protestant leaders – Bishops Ridley and Latimer and Archbishop Cranmer. At first held in the Golden Cross Inn, then

in the Bocardo Prison by Northgate, Latimer and Ridley went to the stake in Broad Street. Cranmer, it is said, was forced to watch from his cell as attempts were made to get him to recant. This he did, but when fastened to the stake his courage and his faith returned, and he thrust into the flames the hand that had signed the recantation.

Oxford's memorial to the martyrs today faces the threat of traffic in St Giles in a Victorian Eleanor Cross that has Cranmer in a niche holding his Bible. A cross in Broad Street marks the scene of the burnings, and in Balliol College nearby a door blackened by the fire that consumed the flesh of three brave men is preserved.

also in 1555, by a Lord Mayor of London.

Because colleges were by now accepting undergraduates as well as graduates, rich men could buy their sons a university education, and clever scholars could get assisted places.

Henry versus the Church

The severing of the link between the established Church and the Pope in Rome by Henry VIII's assumption of leadership of the Church of England brought the university itself to the brink of destruction. The wealth of the colleges and their essentially ecclesiastical nature made them a prime target when parliament authorised the dissolution of the monasteries

urged that the university should follow the same fate as the monasteries, but Henry was a scholar and had a personal reason for wishing to see it survive. In 1532 Wolsey, his Chancellor, had founded Cardinal College on the site of St Frideswide's Priory.

After Wolsey's dismissal Henry refounded it as Henry VIII College and after the suppression the college re-emerged as Christ Church. The remnant of the priory church became Oxford Cathedral and went on to enjoy a double life as the college chapel. Henry's epitaph on the outcome was to be: "No land in England is better bestowed than that which is given to our universities."

in 1536, and their property and revenues were made over to the Crown.

As Franciscans and Carmelites, Cistercians and Benedictines were expelled, the door closed on medieval Oxford. Their property was dispersed among the colleges, and the sites were greedily developed.

The pressure on Henry grew as his advisors

LEFT: an early university procession, painted by the celebrated artist Rudolph Ackermann.
ABOVE: Sir Thomas Bodley, a diplomat whose efforts founded the Bodleian Library in 1602.
RIGHT: Richard Foxe, Bishop of Winchester and founder of Corpus Christi.

The age of privilege

The spread of the New Learning and the Protestant Reformation continued under Henry's son, Edward VI. Translations of the Bible into English began to appear in churches and the services themselves were conducted wholly in English.

Mary's death brought the burnings to an end in the cooling-off period of Elizabeth I's reign from 1558 to 1603. The Church became Protestant again, this time permanently.

In this climate of tolerance, learning flourished and the city's population and prosperity increased. While theology was still predominant, other subjects became popular as careers in public life and the professions led well-off parents to choose the university for their sons' education. The age of privilege had arrived.

The university's power

In the early 17th century came the last of the great charters reinforcing the university's powers and incidentally breeding fresh disputes. The university gained the right to appoint its own coroners and the Chancellor was given the right to veto new building in the town. Dunghills and poor paving would attract fines, and the right to police the streets was bandied about between Mayor and Chancellor.

Behind the walls of their colleges, garden-ers drew their battle lines with spade and fork. On the banks of the Cherwell, opposite Magdalen tower, they created in 1621 Britain's oldest botanic garden, called "Physick" Garden because it produced herbs and plants for medicine and was linked with the scientific studies of the Faculty of Medicine.

Civil War capital

In the struggle ahead Oxford was to be the stage, and King and Parliament merely players. Charles I's connection with Oxford thrust it into the forefront of the conflict between Crown and State that erupted in civil war in 1642. The miracle is that the city emerged vir-

tually unscathed from the extensive works undertaken to put its defences in readiness for assault, and from the siege that subsequently took place but which was abandoned, without the expected battle ever happening.

The King already had strong support at the university. Nearly all the dons and scholars were sympathetic to the Royalist cause. But the townspeople deeply resented the university's control over their affairs and so supported Parliament.

A surprise visit in 1642 from a troop of

ABOVE: Ackermann's *Kitchen at Christ Church.*
RIGHT: Oliver Cromwell, who overthrew Charles I.

Royalist cavalry under Sir John Byron brought the citizens out on to the streets and a half-hearted attempt was made to close the gates. After some confusion the Royalists were welcomed in by the scholars. Eleven days later the cavalry went, leaving a divided city to receive a Parliamentary force with Lord Saye at the head. The university was disarmed, the townspeople armed, the head was shot off the Virgin on the porch of St Mary's, and the troops left for what was to be the first great battle of the Civil War.

The Battle of Edgehill made Charles look for a new headquarters, now that London was in the hands of Parliament. Oxford's central position, natural defences and accessibility to areas of support in the west and north made it an obvious choice, and an accommodating Christ Church provided a good substitute palace for the King.

The King departs

The Parliamentarians seem to have made rather ineffectual attempts to contain Charles in Oxford. The elusive King was able to escape after the decisive battle of the war at Naseby, returning to Oxford and a hoping to plan a renewed siege. Looking for guidance in his predicament, he decided to borrow a book on other civil wars from the Bodleian Library, sending a peremptory note. His request was refused: the Library *never* lends books, not even to kings.

The last Oxford saw of Charles, who had decided on escape and surrender to the Scots, was as a humble servant with short hair on horseback riding out over Magdalen Bridge in the middle of the night. For the garrison, surrender was near. With the King's assent, conditions were formally agreed and the soldiers marched out on 25 June 1646. The war was over and Oxford was saved.

War wounds

Picking up the pieces was not easy for the university. There were few scholars, but the college buildings and the churches were undamaged. Farmers and landowners in the immediate vicinity of Oxford complained of damage by Royalist troops to their houses, woods and cattle, and of the loss of income from not being able to grow crops. They found the university inflexible, however, as did those in the city who had suffered during the occupation, and negotiations were abandoned.

Business in Oxford settled down slowly to its only real trade: selling to the university. With this obvious limitation, small shopkeepers were kept small and the only growth was in poverty. The city persisted in its attempts to extend its powers but made little progress.

Idle students

After the monarchy was restored, the Puritan influence evaporated from Oxford and serious scholars, as so often in subsequent years, be-

Theatre, and a place for the bell from Osney Abbey in Tom Tower. The Clarendon Building found a new home for the Oxford University Press, and the fantastic curiosities collected by Elias Ashmole joined experimental science in the Old Ashmolean Museum.

There followed Gibbs' masterpiece, the Radcliffe Camera, the world's first library in the round, and the unique evocation of the Tower of the Winds in the Radcliffe Observatory. Sir Nicholas Hawksmoor contributed the twin towers of All Souls' College, Gothic outside and classical within. Palladian architecture jostled medieval, and stone replaced brick.

The glory of Oxford was assured; the uni-

moaned the behaviour of their students. Anthony Wood, in his *Life and Times, 1631–95*, wrote: "Why doth solid and serious learning decline, and few or none follow it now in the university? Answer: because of coffee-houses, where they spend all their time; and in entertainments at their chambers, where their studies are become places for victualers, also great drinking at taverns and ale-houses (Dr Lampshire told me there were 370 in Oxford), spending their time in common chambers whole afternoons, and thence to the coffee-house."

But the university also began devoting its attentions to building. A place for grand ceremonial was provided in Wren's Sheldonian

TRANSPORT CONTROVERSIES

Opened in 1790, the Oxford Canal, which brought cheap coal from the Midlands, survived competition from the Grand Junction Canal but was killed off by the railway, suffering a final indignity when its terminal was filled in for Nuffield College in 1937. The city and university were less inviting to the railway pioneers. A proposed terminus for the Great Western Railway at Magdalen Bridge in 1837 was rejected. Opponents feared what might happen if the lower classes could move about more freely and said that students' morals would be corrupted. Concessions were made, however, and the railway steamed into Oxford in 1844.

versity's academic achievement anything but. Student sons of the wealthy drank much and learned little. Exams became a farce. The seeds of 19th-century reform and revival were sown in this climate of stagnation.

Housing boom

New enterprises brought workers to the area and a consequent demand for new housing. When the Oxford University Press moved to Walton Street in 1830 it became the principal employer, its employees finding homes nearby in the new suburb of Jericho.

Towards the end of the 18th century the main streets around Carfax were still cluttered with

19th century it doubled to 24,000. The character of shopping was also changing. Earlier restrictions on the sale of goods other than those produced locally were abandoned. Factory-made goods were being brought in from London and the Midlands by railway and canal, ousting the work of all except for the specialised craftsmen. Choice became wider, credit was no longer given, and price fixing and tickets replaced bargaining.

Unfortunately for the growing number of retailers, the student population halved in the first half of the 19th century and many shopkeepers found themselves in economic difficulties as a result.

market stalls, just as they had been in medieval times, impeding the free movement of traffic, unhygienic and untidy. Both city and university agreed that a market building was the answer, and in 1774 meat, fish and vegetables were moved to an area behind High Street.

The new market, open every day, was extended and roofed over in the Victorian "iron" age, then as now the preponderance of butchers a barometer of prosperity. It was also an indication that Oxford's population was increasing rapidly. In the first 40 years of the

ABOVE: an Oxford book auction in 1747, painted by William Green Jnr.

A time of change

Between 1830 and 1850 one question engaged members of the university to the exclusion of everything else. In the words of a contemporary scholar, Mark Pattison, it "entirely diverted our thoughts from the true business of the place". Such was the Oxford Movement, which started with a church sermon and left Oxford, with its protagonists, to be debated elsewhere.

It all began on 14 July 1833 when John Keble, Fellow of Oriel and Professor of Poetry, preached the Assize Sermon in the University Church. It stimulated the publication of the controversial *Tracts for the Times*, which gave the Movement the alternative title of "Tractarian". The main thrust of the arguments put forward was in support of a "Catholic" church, but not Roman Catholic, and the most tangible outcome was the revival of ceremonial in Anglican churches.

One in particular, St Barnabas, built to serve the growing working-class suburb of Jericho, was visited by the Rev. Francis Kilvert in 1876. He noted in his celebrated *Diary* that the priest wore "a biretta and a chasuble stiff with gold. The poor humble Roman Church hard by is quite plain, simple and Low Church in its ritual."

Of the leading churchmen associated with the Movement, John Newman, vicar of St

At the beginning of Queen Victoria's reign in the 1840s, the collection of rarities of the dubiously acquired inheritance of Elias Ashmole was still installed, neglected and deteriorating, in the Old Ashmolean building in Broad Street. Thanks to two timely bequests, a suitable home was found for the display of these and the university's treasures and works of art. In 1841 Charles Robert Cockerell designed the neo-classical Ashmolean Museum which so magnificently today introduces the wonderful diversity of its contents. The most compelling of the exhibits is the Alfred Jewel *(see page 159)* – the Alfred who could have been the university's founder.

Mary's at the time, addressed his readers of the first Tract as "Fellow-Labourers". After the last Tract appeared he left Oxford, embraced the Roman Catholic Church, and was made a Cardinal in 1879.

John Keble's posthumous contribution to Oxford was the college named after him in 1870. The intention was to provide people of small means with an academic education based on the principles of the Church of England. The chosen architect was William Butterfield, a follower of the Movement, who produced a building in Gothic Revival style.

When the sun fell on its patterned brick, John Betjeman thought it appeared at its worst. Norman Shaw saw Butterfield as "paddling in a boat of his own". His building is certainly unique and striking.

Diversity is the essential element of the growth of Oxford throughout the 60 years of Queen Victoria's reign, a diversity of demand from an expanding city that ranged from books to breweries, marmalade to melodrama and town houses to trams.

The tram to North Oxford

There is a romantic idea that the development of the area north of the Martyrs' Memorial that is North Oxford came about when the university allowed dons to marry. The need for large family housing, however, was earlier felt by the city's wealthy merchants and traders.

No doubt St John's College, which had acquired the land as early as the 16th century, was alive to its potential for development as well. Gothic was the flavour of university architecture; red and yellow brick its chosen medium; gables and gardens characterised the style. Keble College and the Parks' Museum welcomed the villas like hens with chickens. By 1880 most of the houses had been completed, and after 1877 the dons began moving in with their families.

Five years later North Oxford's first trams followed them up the Banbury Road all the way from Carfax for one penny. The horse-drawn single deckers on 4-ft (1.3-metre) gauge rails also ran from east to west over a specially

LEFT: Ackermann's *The Astronomical Observatory.*
RIGHT: a dead-heat at the end of the
1877 Oxford–Cambridge Boat Race.

widened Magdalen Bridge, up the High Street and out to Jericho via Walton Street. Speed was limited to 13 km (8 miles) an hour and further restricted if confronted with a herd of cattle. Worse, a flock of sheep called for a dead stop.

It was the turn of the century before an electric tramway was mooted, and 1913 before the idea was effectively scotched by the motorbus. William Morris, later Lord Nuffield, was refused a licence by the city to run these, but tickets for a ride could be bought in shops. The Tramway Company followed suit, but with buses instead of trams, and eventually won exclusive rights to run Oxford's first official bus service.

Books and boats

Blackwell's bookshop *(see page 137)* is such an Oxford's institution that you expect it to go back further than 1879, yet it was only then that Benjamin Henry Blackwell started his business at his house in Holywell Street. Bigger premises were soon needed.

Down on the river at Folly Bridge, Salter Bros had been quietly contributing to Oxford's sporting prowess and public pleasure since they established the firm in 1858. Boats and college barges were built here, including the eights that took the university to victory over Cambridge, and in 1886 they began the steamer trips that have opened Oxford's waters to millions. ❑

WOMEN? WHO LET *THEM* IN?

The seeds of the slow and grudging acceptance of the equal right of women to higher education were sown not by the university authorities but by central government through the Parliamentary Commissions of 1850 and 1874. Oxford came a conspicuous second to Cambridge in admitting women more freely. As early as 1863 examinations had been open to girls at Cambridge, and Girton became the first residential college for women in 1869.

But it was nine years before Oxford followed suit with Lady Margaret Hall, for Church of England girls, and Somerville College, the first to place no religious requirements on its entrants (both are now mixed). St Hugh's

joined them in 1886 and St Hilda's Hall in 1893, founded by the Principal of Cheltenham Ladies' College for women going up to Oxford from that college.

Concessions were slow in coming. Examinations were opened to women in 1894, but degrees and equal status for women's colleges had to wait until the 20th century.

Male chauvinism took many forms. At Brasenose College, the Moosehunters were a group of young men who strapped antlers to their heads and crashed around in pursuit of young maidens. One Junior Common Room debated a motion that: "Women should be hired out on the same basis as college punts."

OXFORD'S MOTORING HERITAGE

Given its current traffic problems, it's ironic that
the city helped pioneer motor manufacturing in
Britain. The much loved Morris Minor was built
here, and so is today's BMW-produced Mini

The career of William Richard Morris, Viscount Nuffield, has been described by British industrial historians as the biggest success story of the 20th century. His achievement had a profound effect on Oxford and the surrounding area, for it was through Morris's efforts that a major industry – motor manufacturing – was added to what had been a predominantly academic city. He was also one of the great benefactors of his time, distributing some £30 million to various charitable causes before he died in 1963 at the age of 85.

Morris cars were made in the district from 1912 and today the sprawling Cowley factory complex, on the ring road to the southeast of the city, is owned by Germany's BMW.

The William Morris story

William Morris was born in Worcester in 1877, but his parents were from Oxford and the family moved back to the city when he was a young child. He attended the Church School in Cowley, leaving at the age of 14 to become apprenticed to a bicycle repairer. Within months, and with just £4 capital, he had established his own cycle repair business in a shed behind his parents' house in James Street, Cowley St John.

Rebuilding old bicycles soon led to building new ones, the first order being for an abnormally large frame to suit the towering rector of nearby St Clement's Church. Next came Morris motorcycles, or what would today be called mopeds.

Morris became an agent for a number of British car and motorcycle manufacturers. By

1910 he had given up making two-wheelers and built a new garage on the Longwall site. He began to consider producing a car of his own. It would be a small car of high quality, made in large numbers and sold at a low price. The way to achieve that, he concluded, was to reduce the cost of design, tooling and manufacture by purchasing all the major components from outside companies and simply assembling the cars in Oxford. Longwall was not big enough, so Morris moved out to the suburb of Cowley.

Appropriately this first car, delivered in 1913, was called the Morris Oxford. It cost £175 and became famous as the first of the "Bullnose"

Morrises, so-called because of the rounded shape of their brass radiators. Morris sold 393 Oxfords in the first year and over 900 in 1914; this represented the beginning of mass production in Britain. After World War I, production increased sharply but so did costs and therefore prices. Then came the slump. By 1921, 60 cars a week were coming out of Cowley – but sales had reduced to a trickle. Faced with a stockpile of cars, William Morris took the bold step of slashing prices by as much as £200 a car – a lot of money then. While others scoffed, he said that sales would double – and he was right. By 1923 Morris was selling 20,000 cars a year; in 1925 demand reached 55,000.

converted a generation of young Americans to lightweight British sports cars.

As the company grew, the original idea of assembling from mostly bought-in components became less attractive and Morris started to make more of the vehicles themselves. The Cowley factory kept on expanding. It even had its own railway halt.

Money for medicine

Lord Nuffield (as he became in 1938) and his wife Elizabeth had no children and he was determined not to leave his fortune to be decimated by death duties. Medicine was a lifelong interest and in the 1920s he donated sums of

New blood

One of Morris's managers, Cecil Kimber, also had ambitions as a car-maker and designed special, more rakish, bodies for the Morris Oxford and Cowley which were then sold as MG (for "Morris Garages") and carried the distinctive octagonal badge. The MG Super Sports models were so successful that by 1929 a separate MG factory was set up, first in Cowley and then Abingdon, from where the best-selling Midget sports cars emerged. It was the T-series successors to these that, 20 years later,

LEFT: Lord Nuffield in his later years.
ABOVE: Morris manager Cecil Kimber with a 1923 MG.

WILLIAM MORRIS

Though rich beyond dreams, he was a man of simple tastes. He used the same small and modestly furnished office upstairs in the old school building at Cowley for 50 years. His desk had a pile of neatly sliced used envelopes to use as notepaper and he would unknot string from parcels for future use – habits inherited from his father and his own poorer days as a child. Asked to comment on his wealth, he once said: "You can only wear one suit at a time." His own luxuries were specially made cigarettes and long sea voyages to distant lands – a taste he acquired when he visited America to study Henry Ford's production methods.

money to various hospitals. In 1937, he put up £900,000 to establish a new university establishment, Nuffield College, to the west of the city. However, World War II intervened and the foundation stone was not laid until 1949.

Although he loved Oxford, William Morris had not, in his earlier years, enjoyed friendly relations with the city authorities or the university. He was suspicious of graduates in business and for a long time would not employ anyone who had been through the university. Disagreement with the city council went back to 1913, when he had proposed buses as an alternative to trams to replace Oxford's horse-drawn trams. The council rejected the idea, so

Morris bought a fleet of six buses and put them into operation illegally. His audacity paid off, for the bus service was popular, the city was spared ugly and disruptive trams, and he eventually sold the vehicles to the council.

Merger mania

During World War II, the Cowley plant produced battle tanks, repaired aeroplanes, and made Tiger Moth trainers, as well as engines for military aircraft. An airstrip was built on the factory site.

In 1952 the company merged with its arch-rival, Austin, to form the British Motor Corporation. Lord Nuffield, by then 75, was appointed chairman but retired after just six months. In 1968, after further mergers, BMC became British Leyland.

The unremarkable 1971 Morris Marina was the last car to carry the Morris name. Eventually, after a troubled period of heavy losses which led to government control, British Leyland became the Rover Group and, in 1988, a division of British Aerospace. The new owners concentrated Rover executive car production in the Cowley body plant and shut down Cowley North and South, which included Morris's original buildings. With the help of Honda, Rover's fortunes were reversed. But the Japanese, after heavy investment, were shocked when British Aerospace abruptly sold the company to the Bavaria-based BMW.

The BMW years

BMW's arrival at Cowley in 2000 sparked a further revival in Oxford's car-manufacturing fortunes, as the German company decided to base the new Mini production line there. Investment totalling £280 million between 2000 and 2004 saw employment at the plant rise to 4,500 after years of decline. By 2005 Cowley was turning out some 4,000 Minis a week, making it the third most productive car plant in the UK, and a new streamlined version of the car was unveiled in 2006.

Much of the old car factory has been obliterated, but Oxford remains a significant presence in British motor manufacturing. Visits to the car plant can be arranged by telephoning 01865-825842 *(see page 207)*. ❑

THE MINI

In August 1999, 70,000 people and 5,000 Minis from all over the world converged at Silverstone racing circuit to celebrate the 40th anniversary of their legendary car. The Mini was reputedly designed on a restaurant tablecloth by Sir Alec Issigonis as a blueprint for the smallest car for four adults. At its launch, it cost a mere £500. Since then over 5.3 million have been sold. It became a fashion icon in the 1960s, associated with such stars as Twiggy and Peter Sellers, and starred with Michael Caine in the 1969 film *The Italian Job*. Production stopped at Cowley in 1968, but the car was restyled and brought back to Cowley by BMW in 2000.

LEFT: the early Mini became a 1960s fashion icon.

Oxford University Press

Oxford University Press, known widely as OUP, is the world's largest university press. It publishes more than 3,000 new titles a year, employs some 3,000 people worldwide and has a turnover of over £300 million (US$480 million).

Among its most influential publications is the *Oxford English Dictionary*, first published in 12 volumes and dedicated to Queen Victoria. Today it has four supplements and has been republished in combined form in 20 volumes (£1,650). It also comes in a much-praised CD-Rom version.

As the beginning of each of its books reminds us, "Oxford University Press is a department of the University of Oxford. It furthers the university's objective of excellence in research, scholarship and education by publishing worldwide."

OUP has no board of directors but is controlled by a body of senior Oxford scholars – the Delegates of the Press – and a finance committee. Like any university press, it serves education and research, but unlike others it has to pay its own way.

OUP is very international in its outlook, maintaining branches and promotion offices in over 50 countries, many with their own substantial publishing programmes. It also publishes in many languages, chiefly in the Indian subcontinent and Africa.

It is more than 500 years since the first book was printed in Oxford, though the date in Roman numerals on the title page actually reads 1468 instead of 1478 – an unfortunate beginning for a press renowned for its high standards of accuracy.

The guardians of OUP were often highly eccentric characters, from Archbishop Laud and Dr Fell in the 17th century to Henry Frowde, the first to bear the title "Publisher to the University", in the late 18th and early 19th centuries. His successor, Humphrey Milford, had notoriously unpredictable instincts but seemed invariably to be right, leading to considerable expansion at home and overseas.

OUP has had a succession of homes, including the Sheldonian Theatre and the Clarendon Building, the latter partly financed by the profits from the first edition of Lord Clarendon's *History of the Great Rebellion*. In 1830 it moved to its present home in Walton Street, a series of elegant buildings grouped, in true Oxford fashion, round a quadrangle complete with ornamental pond, lawn and copper beech. It has frequently had a London presence, too: a Bible warehouse in Paternoster Row, and later offices in nearby Amen House. All publishing is now based in Oxford.

One of OUP's unusual features is a large

and flourishing music department. This not only publishes sheet music and major editions of classical works, but promotes the performance, recording and hire of the work of over 20 contemporary composers.

Although OUP played a major role in the history of printing, including being the first printers in Britain to use the beautifully designed "Fell types", brought over from the Netherlands by Dr Fell, its own printing works closed in the late 1980s. It now outsources all printing, although many artefacts and papers relating to its history are preserved in the OUP Museum (visits by appointment only, tel: 01865-556767). ❑

RIGHT: the days when OUP printed its own books.

MODERN OXFORD

As Oxford developed in the 20th century from
a sleepy market town into an important
industrial centre, it faced a new range
of social and economic problems

Vera Brittain, author of *Testament of Youth*, went up to Somerville College in 1914, an innocent former debutante who had been born into "that unparalleled age of rich materialism and tranquil comfort", as she describes the Edwardian age. The Oxford that she discovered in the first year of World War I still basked in that mellow security even a decade into the new century.

This was the Oxford of Zuleika Dobson, the eponymous heroine of Max Beerbohm's novel who caused titled undergraduates, besotted with her, to drown themselves in the Isis. Colleges dominated the university, and the university controlled the city that existed to service it. Around the stately quadrangles were narrow, medieval streets containing small businesses and close-knit communities. Public transport was still by horse-drawn trams that were advertised as meeting every train at the sleepy, non-mainline station. In the North Oxford suburb, built to house the large Victorian families of the dons, croquet was played on the lawns, and afternoon tea was served with ceremony.

Death in the trenches

In 1915, Vera Brittain left Oxford to train as a nurse. In 1919 she returned to Somerville. "It seemed unbearable that everything should be exactly the same when all my life was so much changed." She had lost her brother, her lover, and many friends; 2,700 Oxford men had died in the trenches.

LEFT AND RIGHT: Oxford women at work in World War I as ticket collectors and unpaid social workers.

It is invidious to select one name from these thousands, but H.G.J. (Harry) Moseley, who was killed at Gallipoli in 1915, had graduated from Trinity College, and was the most promising physicist of his generation. His work on atomic structure using the relatively new X-rays was in four years already enough for a Nobel prize to be confidently predicted. His classic equipment has an honoured place in the Museum of the History of Science.

In every college the memorial slabs went up, and the ancient buildings were haunted for those who had survived. The great eccentric William Spooner, Warden of New College (*see page 141*), had a plaque erected in the chapel to record the names of college members who had died fighting on the enemy side: "In memory of the men of this college who coming from a foreign land entered into the inheritance of this place and returning fought and died for their country in the war 1914–1919".

But life went on, and for many the top priority was to live it as on a roller coaster, for as much excitement and risk as possible. Between the wars, Oxford University, so often an exaggeration of the contemporary mood, experienced the excesses of hearties and aesthetes.

Evelyn Waugh's 1945 novel *Brideshead Revisited* offered the fictional version of this lifestyle, and Vera Brittain wrote of her contemporaries: "One and all combined to create that 'eat-drink-and-be-merry-for-tomorrow-we-die' atmosphere which seemed to have drifted from the trenches via the Paris hotels and London nightclubs into Oxford colleges."

Tenacious traditions

The invasion of Oxford by women *(see panel)* made little impact on male undergraduate life in the inter-war years. Traditional sports and clubs continued. Eights Week still brought throngs of families and girlfriends to cheer on the boat races and socialise on the picturesque college barges lining the riverbank.

Many of the clubs remained exclusively male, notably the Oxford Union debating society that was founded in 1823 and by mid-century occupied its own premises between Cornmarket and New Inn Hall Street. Its debates were the nursery of a glittering succession of politicians, lawyers and clerics, the most famous of whom were always ready to return in later life as guest speakers. The Union resisted admitting women as members until after World War II. The many other clubs were gradually opened to women, but the majority of male undergraduates had little contact with their female counterparts.

Equally far-reaching changes had been happening to the city of Oxford. By the 1920s, it was no longer a sleepy market town, but an important industrial centre. As early as 1898, William Morris had opened his garage, and the first Morris car came off the line in 1913. By 1923, the Cowley factory's production was over 20,000 vehicles a year *(see pages 28–30)*.

The area east of Magdalen Bridge had become a town in its own right, owing no allegiance to the university. The industrial age in Oxford had finally arrived.

Between 1911 and 1951, the population of Oxford grew from 62,000 to 97,000, mostly due to the immigration of industrial workers. Many of these came from the Welsh valleys,

of New College, was the prime mover in establishing the Oxford Preservation Trust, whose first act was to raise the money to buy land on Boars Hill and at Marston, in the Cherwell valley, to safeguard these areas from development. The Trust, still active today, owns 350 acres (140 hectares) of land in and around Oxford, and campaigns to preserve the Green Belt so that the historic city, in its ring of hills, may retain its special setting, free of urban sprawl.

A new look

The architectural face of Oxford changed greatly between the wars. There were some undoubted improvements in the city centre.

creating a strong and obstinately self-contained Welsh community in Cowley, that made its own social life, complete with choirs. The villages close to Oxford – Headington, Marston, Iffley, Wolvercote – also became suburbs of the city.

The industrial expansion of the town caused dismay to many for whom Oxford was Matthew Arnold's "sweet city with her dreaming spires". In 1928, Dr H.A.L. Fisher, Warden

The elegant new Elliston & Cavell store was built in Magdalen Street, and the corner of Broad Street and Cornmarket was dignified by the pillared curve of William Baker's furniture shop. Beaumont Street, with its fine 18th-century facades, suffered little from the inclusion of the Playhouse, a piece of infill in the very best of taste. The New Theatre in George Street, spacious inside and simple outside, was also welcome.

For the university, there was much new building in the Parks Road area. The Radcliffe Science Library filled with dignity the northern corner of South Parks Road. Opposite, an eccentricity was designed by Sir Herbert

LEFT: Godley's Own Oxford Volunteers march past the Emperor's Heads on Broad Street in World War I.
ABOVE: old horsepower outside William Morris's original motorcycle shop.

Baker: Rhodes House, headquarters of the Rhodes Trust and its scholars. This was aptly described by the writer Christopher Hobhouse as "a Cotswold manor house with a circular temple of heroic scale deposited in its forecourt". Where Parks Road joins Broad Street, another corner site accommodated the New Bodleian Library, a curiously uninteresting building above ground, but fascinating below, where the vast book stacks are linked by conveyor belt under the street to the subterranean reaches of the Bodleian proper.

The commercial building of the 1930s shows how prosperous Oxford had become, even during the Depression, thanks to the

ships. By 1939, about half the student population was grant-aided, leading to a profound change of attitude to studying. For the scholarship boy, Oxford was a place reached through luck and hard work, carrying the obligation to strive for the best degree possible.

Yet, despite these changes, public schools still provided the majority of students. The criterion of selection was by no means only intellectual ability. A college had have its quota of sportsmen and gentlemen, irrespective of their academic quality. As Ronald Knox put it: "They don't do much harm, and when they've finished playing here, they can go out like good little boys and govern the Empire."

motor industry. The university, too, was expanding with the advent of science and medicine, much of the expansion due to the patronage of Lord Nuffield. He endowed poorer colleges, created a medical institute, and in 1936 gave the university £1.25 million for medical research. More funding was poured into the physical sciences, and social science came to Oxford for the first time with the foundation in 1937 of Nuffield College.

The new boys

The university was gradually changing its character in the 1930s as an increasing number of undergraduates entered with the aid of scholar-

A WORKING-CLASS VIEW

Oxford was a totally unfamiliar environment for many of the new working-class entrants. A Yorkshire miner who won a scholarship described the contrast in *A Pitman Looks at Oxford*, written in 1933 under the pseudonym of Roger Dataller: "Goodbye, University!… Big Tom Tower bell groaning out its plaint… gang of roaring hearties on the tavern doorstep – handkerchief of blackberries on the slope of Cumnor… old port, biscuits, waiters, butlers – white stone, grey stone, greenstone, cloisters – black and white of proctors – sober gait of 'bulldogs'… Now headstocks, coal ranged in many waggons, flicker of pulleys, ochre of fumes, the clatter of clogs."

But in 1939, Oxford again sent out its young men to fight in another war, at the end of which running the Empire was no longer an option. The Oxford University Air Squadron contributed its quota to the Few who fought the Battle of Britain, among whom was Richard Hilary, author of that great war book *The Last Enemy*.

Medical breakthrough

Oxford made many contributions to the war effort, of which the most dramatic was the discovery of penicillin, which founded the science of antibiotics. Penicillin was described and named in 1929 by Alexander Fleming, but he

Lord Cherwell, Churchill's controversial scientific advisor. He made his home in Oxford, and laid a significant part of the foundations of modern physics at the Clarendon Laboratory.

As Oxford entered another post-war period, the same uneasy mixture of ex-servicemen and women and youngsters straight from school was being shaped through three years in the university's old, inimitable way. It was at this time that the city, having grown to an unwieldy size, began to realise that traffic was a major problem. A planning consultant, Thomas Sharp, was engaged for three years by the City Council to produce a detailed study, which was published in 1948 under the

was not able to make it chemically stable. This was the achievement of Howard Florey and his team, who first used penicillin on a patient in the Radcliffe Infirmary in 1941, the start of a breakthrough in healing of the greatest magnitude. The discovery is commemorated in a formal rose garden between Oxford's Botanic Garden and the High Street, the gift of the American Lasker Foundation in 1953.

Another Oxford contribution to the war was the work of Professor F. A. Lindemann, later

LEFT: the Oxford men, known as "the cabbage patch recruits", who dug air raid shelters during the war.
ABOVE: fish stall in the Covered Market in the 1950s.

title *Oxford Replanned*. Over 40 years on, one marvels at its confident comprehensiveness, and thinks, if only it were as simple as that to manage the growth of a city.

Protecting the Meadow

Sharp's study has deservedly become a classic, but its fame rests largely on one of its proposals, the Meadow Road. Sharp wrote: "In the case of Oxford one piece of surgery is required to release the city from a pressure on its spinal column which will otherwise eventually paralyse it." The spinal column was the admired High Street, then ruined by traffic; the surgery was to create a new east/west relief road, running through Christ Church Meadow to cross the river by a new bridge south of Magdalen Bridge. The patient being a city of such fame, the storm that greeted Sharp's proposal was of international proportions, and rumbled on ill-temperedly for the next 25 years.

After a period of shock, the battle lines were drawn. Christ Church, and behind it the university, refused to consider a Meadow Road. But the idea of a relief road, once mooted, continued to occupy the planners' minds, and bore fruit in another route further south, proposed in the 1960s, and called the Eastwyke Farm Road. This was part of a complex of urban motorways that would have carved up the inner residential areas of the city, and for which approval was actually given in 1969.

At this point it was the turn of Oxford's citizens to protest. A Civic Society was formed, a best-selling booklet called *Let's Live in Oxford* was published, and vigorous opposition was mounted to the motorway scheme at a Public Inquiry. A combination of political factors, lack of money and public protest caused the Eastwyke Farm scheme to be abandoned. A couple of years later, a Labour City Council devised the Balanced Transport Policy, using reduced car-parking, improved public transport and a park-and-ride scheme to contain city-centre traffic.

Attempts to rid Oxford's medieval central streets of ever-growing volumes of traffic culminated in the Oxford Transport Strategy, introduced by the City Council in 1999. This scheme has at last emptied Cornmarket Street of all traffic, even the buses, and drastically reduced car access along the High Street and Broad Street. Is it a success? If you like fresh air and a car-free stroll along Cornmarket, you'll probably say yes. But several traders claim that stopping the flow of cars has impeded the flow of customers. The debate is far from over.

The wreckers move in

Although urban motorways did not bring about the wholesale destruction of housing, the new-buildings-for-old enthusiasm of the 1960s produced what some now see as the tragic destruction of the old Oxford as huge shopping centres and a multi-storey car park

THE BREWING TRADITION THAT DIED

Oxford had a head start when it came to brewing: it was in the middle of malting barley country and had easy access to pure well water found deep beneath the Thames. From the Middle Ages onwards, most of the monasteries and some of the colleges brewed their own beer. Those without brewhouses obtained permission to use the facilities of those that had. One of these, Queen's, was founded with a brewer among the servants, and brewing was carried on until 1939 in a building that still exists in the Fellows' Garden. Changes in taste and a new building accounted for the end of college-produced beer and left a clear field to the professional brewer.

Between 1350 and 1500 no fewer than 10 brewers became Mayor. Among those who took office, John Sprunt, who died in 1419, is commemorated by an engraved brass in St Peter's College Chapel. Unfortunately, for a brewer, it has no head on it.

The last brewery in Oxford, Morrell's, produced its final pint in 1998 after selling up to a housing development company. Brewing had already been going on at its site in St Thomas Street for 200 years before Mark Morrell and his son James set up in business in 1782, producing such classics as Varsity Ale. A chain of local pubs retains the Morrell's name, but the beer itself is bought in.

replaced ancient buildings. In the 1980s, the Clarendon Centre, another shopping centre, was built to link Cornmarket with Queen Street, a sensible idea marred by crude and inappropriate execution.

But conservation policies did gain credence, and more sites were treated with sensitivity. On the corner of Ship Street, for example, a medieval building (now housing Laura Ashley) was restored by Jesus College.

University upheavals

Changes in the university after World War II were no less significant and controversial. With its usual capacity for pulling a rabbit

The result was the establishment of a committee under the chairmanship of Lord Franks, whose report led to far-reaching changes in the university's structure. The achievements of the 1960s were extraordinary in financial and practical terms. The Historic Buildings Appeal raised over £2 million, making it possible for the grime of centuries to be removed from Oxford's stone, and restoration work on a huge scale to be done.

The College Contributions scheme, which required the richer colleges to provide funds for the poorer, as well as generous outside funding, enabled new building work to the value of £11 million to be carried out. Six new

out of the hat, Oxford suddenly produced a sporting star of international magnitude in Dr Roger Bannister (now Sir Roger, and formerly Master of Pembroke College), who used his knowledge of physiology to famously run the first four-minute mile on the Iffley Road track in June 1954.

There was a strong feeling that the university must modernise its administration or find itself forced to do so by outside forces.

LEFT: the age-old tradition of brewing in Oxford.
ABOVE: in 1954 Dr Roger Bannister became the first person to run a mile in less than four minutes – he did it in 3 minutes 59.54 seconds.

colleges were established: St Catherine's for undergraduates on the pattern of the older colleges, and another five for graduates only. The science area burgeoned, with 4,000 undergraduates and graduate students working there.

Surviving the 1960s

Oxford suffered less than many of the newer universities from the student unrest that was a feature of the 1960s. But it did not escape entirely, and its reaction was predictable: a committee on relations with junior members, the Hart Committee, was set up, leading to the creation of a Student Representative Council. Pressure for mixed colleges built up all through that radical decade, and this change was implemented from 1970. Today, all the former men's colleges take male and female undergraduates, and the last remaining all-female college, St Hilda's, voted in 2006 to accept male undergraduates. The ratio of men to women in the university is three to two.

The 1980s saw none of the spectacular spending of the previous two decades. All academic expenditure was restricted by the Conservative government, and Oxford found itself at odds with Margaret Thatcher, despite the fact that the then prime minister was herself an Oxford graduate (Somerville College). An attempt to award her an hon-

scarcely more than half the costs of teaching, housing and maintenance. The annual deficit stands at more than £90 million.

The Development Programme for Oxford which was established in 1988, has raised more than £225 million from philanthropic gifts. This money is being spent on securing academic posts as well as maintaining and expanding the university's infrastructure.

But what of the city? The battle is still on between the conservationists, who insist that at least something of the old city should remain intact, and the pressure for more jobs and housing.

Before 1991, few outsiders had ever heard

orary degree was actually voted down. No such snub was delivered to US President Bill Clinton, however. In 1994, a quarter of a century after he had completed his time at Oxford as a Rhodes Scholar, he was awarded his honorary doctorate with great pomp and ceremony.

Fundraising for a new future

Severe spending restrictions remain in force from the government, and the university, keen to expand into new fields of study, is continuously raising money, both at home and abroad. Colleges rely on donations because the income from fees and lodging charges covers

of the Blackbird Leys estate, barely 3 miles (5 km) along the Cowley Road from Oxford's famously dreaming spires. In that year the estate achieved national notoriety as law and order broke down and the habit of joy-riding became firmly established as a popular pastime in deprived areas of Britain.

The anarchy at Blackbird Leys did not last long, but it did highlight the fact that even Oxford has its fair share of economic and social problems. Money worries, accommo-

ABOVE: a newly designed Mini rolls along the production line at BMW's Cowley plant.
RIGHT: animal rights protesters take to the streets.

dation worries and employment worries are nothing new here – not even among students.

The battle against traffic

Over the past decade Oxford has wrestled with all the problems that beset any historic town in an age of expanding population and escalating traffic. Attempts to discourage cars from entering the city centre were initially met with hostility by both traders and motorists, but seem to have decreased congestion in the historic High.

The total pedestrianisation of Cornmarket after the banning of cars has finally rid the central commercial thoroughfare of the remaining buses and has created a space where buskers and street vendors vie for the attention of shoppers. Few would argue, however, that even a traffic-free Cornmarket offers a truly aesthetic experience, even if its paving and benches were controversially expensive. Elsewhere, high parking fees and a Park & Ride service are meant to deter motorists from clogging up an essentially medieval city.

Development versus conservation

If the City Fathers have had some success in stemming the tide of cars, they have been less able, or willing, to prevent the gradual in-filling of Oxford's green spaces by new building. Population pressure, the booming Thames Valley economy and the rapid expansion of Brookes University have all fuelled demand for new housing and business premises.

Some of the new developments are welcome. New university buildings such as the Said Business School by the railway station

grace formerly run-down areas, while the modern Oxford Business Park, built on what used to be the sprawling industrial site of Cowley's car factory, is a pleasant, if unexceptional, collection of landscaped office accommodation. Where possible, city planners have insisted on the redevelopment of "brown field" areas.

But much of the once-picturesque canalside area of North Oxford and Jericho has been concreted over with bland residential developments. Halls of residence for students have sprouted throughout East Oxford, sometimes on what was previously open land. Residents and conservationists are engaged in almost daily battle with developers. ❑

THE VIVISECTION WARS

The old University has also witnessed bitter conflict, particularly with regard to the issue of vivisection and animal testing in scientific research. Professor Colin Blakemore, an eminent neuroscientist, became a target for animal rights protestors from the late 1990s onwards, who argued that his experiments involved unacceptable cruelty towards laboratory animals.

The controversy intensified with the University's decision to construct a new £18 million research facility in the South Parks Road science area. The planned laboratory was alleged by the Animal Liberation Front to be intended for animal experiments.

The ensuing struggle pitted pro-animal extremists against the University's scientific Establishment, who argued that human animal testing was necessary for clinical advances. After death threats were issued against contractors and University staff were intimidated, the construction of the new facility continued behind screens to protect the identity of the builders.

The passions raised over the new laboratory may not have been shared by most students or citizens of Oxford, but they showed that the city, and particularly its venerable academic institution, had lost none of its ability to raise the big ethical questions of the day.

Decisive Dates

1500BC onwards Bronze Age cattle herders and farmers build large, round grave mounds on Port Meadow. During the Iron Age the landscape is dotted with small, mixed farms.

3rd century AD The Romans establish important potteries in the area.

400 Migrants from Germany and Saxon mercenaries in the Roman army forcibly settle local farms; their descendants live there as peaceable tenant farmers.

730 According to legend, Oxford's first abbey is founded by St Frideswide on the site of present-

day Christ Church. This may have been the core of the original town.

912 The first written reference to Oxford in the *Anglo-Saxon Chronicle* during the reign of King Edward the Elder, son of King Alfred, who fortifies the town to guard the river crossing into Wessex and protect the surrounding countryside against the Danes.

1071 Robert d'Oilly, Oxford's Norman governor, erects a castle to the west of town.

12th century Oxford attracts scholarly clerics from far and wide. Monasteries bring prosperity and stability. The Thames provides power for the mills, and economy is based on cloth and leather as well as the trades spawned by the emerging university.

1129 Osney Abbey built on an island in the west. It becomes one of the largest and most important Augustinian monasteries in England.

c1130 Henry I builds his Palace of Beaumont just outside the north gate, setting the seal on the town's rising importance.

1199 King John grants the town his royal charter, and local government, based on the guilds, is free to develop independently.

1200 By this time an association of scholars has been established in the city.

13th century Friars form the various major orders teaching in Oxford. Their students live and work in academic halls dotted around the city. The first colleges are founded by powerful bishops; they are noted for their exclusivity and wealth and cater only for graduates.

1226–40 The city wall is extended and rebuilt.

1349 The Black Death kills one in three people.

1355 St Scholastica's Day. A pub brawl turns into a massacre of dozens of scholars. This event has dire consequences for the future of the town.

1361 John Wycliffe, Master of Balliol, speaks out against corruption within the church. His teachings resonate throughout Europe.

1379 New College is founded as the first college to accept undergraduates. From now on the balance of learning in the town gradually shifts from the academic halls to the colleges.

1400 Oxford is one of the largest towns in England with a population of some 6,000. There are 1,500 students.

1426 Work begins on the Divinity School.

1478 First book (the Bible) printed in Oxford.

1488 Duke Humphrey's Library opened.

1490s Erasmus and Thomas Moore in Oxford, developing Humanist ideas.

1525 Cardinal Wolsey founds Cardinal College (later to be known as Christ Church) on the site of St Frideswide's Monastery.

1536 The university is brought to the brink of destruction by the Dissolution of the Monasteries, but Henry VIII saves the colleges by adopting them to train the state's most loyal supporters.

1542 Creation of the Diocese of Oxford, with its cathedral at Christ Church.

1555–6 The Protestant Martyrs Latimer and Ridley are burned at the stake in the city ditch (later Broad Street) on 16 October. Six months later, Thomas Cranmer suffers the same fate.

1558–1603 Reign of Elizabeth I. The city is transformed as a new civic pride emerges with increased trade and prosperity. The university expands greatly.

17th century Prosperity is fuelled by the famous glovers and cutlers of Oxford. University buildings begin to dominate the central area.

1602 Duke Humphrey's Library reopened to the public as the Bodleian Library.

1613 Work begins on the Old Schools Quadrangle extension to the Bodleian Library.

1621 The Physic Garden, which was later developed to become the Botanic Garden, is established on the site of the old Jewish cemetery opposite Magdalen Tower.

1642–5 Civil War. Oxford is the royal capital and headquarters of the King's army.

1646 Oxford besieged by General Fairfax and his Parliamentary army. Charles I escapes in disguise and the city surrenders.

1650s A group of mathematicians and scientists, including Christopher Wren and Robert Boyle, meet regularly in Wadham College, before moving to London in 1658 to found the Royal Society.

1664–8 The Sheldonian Theatre, designed by Christopher Wren, is built.

1670s onwards Glove and cutlery industries in decline. The university provides new additions to the already famous Oxford skyline; many existing colleges are radically altered or rebuilt.

1715 Hawksmoor's Clarendon Building completed for the Oxford University Press.

1748 The Radcliffe Camera built according to a design by James Gibbs.

1771 Paving Commission established. Much of old Oxford is destroyed to allow traffic easier access to the city centre.

1790 The Oxford Canal arrives from Coventry bringing cheap coal from the Midlands.

1830 The Oxford University Press moves to its present site on Walton Street. The suburb of Jericho is built to house the Press workers.

1833 John Keble preaches his famous sermon on national apostasy, leading to the foundation of the Oxford Movement.

1844 A branch railway line connects Oxford with Didcot.

1853 University Commission is established to reform the university.

1860 The University Museum opens.

LEFT: Wadham College, as seen by the noted artist Rudolph Ackermann.

RIGHT: new horsepower in the Morris works.

1879 The first two women's colleges, Lady Margaret Hall and Somerville, open.

1913 William Morris establishes his car plant at Cowley. In the 1930s, as Lord Nuffield, he becomes the university's most celebrated benefactor in the fields of medicine and science.

1956 A "green belt" is created around Oxford, putting an end to the haphazard development that surrounded the city.

1960s Plans for a link road across Christ Church Meadow are abolished.

1996 Syrian-born businessman Wafic Said offers the university £20 million for the establishment of the Oxford Business School.

1999 Cornmarket Street is pedestrianised as

part of a controversial new road scheme.

2000 The first Cowley Road Carnival is held.

2003 A 1,000-strong crowd gathers in Cornmarket to protest against the Iraq war.

2004 Dr John Hood, a New Zealander, is the first "outsider" in the university's history to become its vice-chancellor.

2005 Oxford is rated fourth best university (after Harvard, MIT and Cambridge) by 20,000 academics around the world.

2006 An exclusion zone is legally enforced around the site of a new biological research centre to counter violent protests by animal rights campaigners. St Hilda's, Oxford's last women-only college, votes to accept men. ❑

THE ACADEMIC LIFE

Dons and students have always encouraged an image
of effortless superiority. But to what extent is
this assumption of elitism still justified?

The image of Oxford conveyed in countless films and books has given rise to two great myths. The first is the so-called "Brideshead" image, after Evelyn Waugh's 1945 novel *Brideshead Revisited*, which shows beautiful young aristocrats living a life of eternal summer and champagne in ancient ivy-clad colleges. The 1911 novel *Zuleika Dobson* by Max Beerbohm also paints a similar picture.

The second myth is that of pale intellectuals and palaeolithic dons festering in crumbling cathedral-like libraries, their lives devoted to the study of Homer or Hegel.

Both myths are outdated; but try as it might, the university cannot completely break free from its past. The world still regards it as a bastion of punting and privilege.

Fact or fiction?

Certainly, Oxford is very different from any other university in the world, except perhaps Cambridge – once referred to rather preciously in Oxford as "the other place". To differentiate itself, Oxford has its dons, scouts, tutorial system, Union, Boat Race and balls. But the people who inhabit the place are not, in reality, all that different from students elsewhere.

Where once Oxford was the preserve of the upper-crust public school boy, today's reality

PRECEDING PAGES: Christ Church custodians confer.
LEFT: detail from Edward's Halliday's 1937 painting of Worcester's undergraduates – many were soon to die in service during World War II.
RIGHT: the annual Encaenia parade, Radcliffe Square.

is rather more complex — with students coming from a wide range of schools and backgrounds. About 35 percent of applicants are from the independent sector and they have a slightly higher success rate than those from other schools. But the university is striving, with some record of achievement, to attract applicants from a diversity of backgrounds, both by making the selection process fairer and less weighted towards purely academic prowess and by offering a generous system of support for those from less wealthy families.

Women now account for approximately 47 percent of admissions. Mixed colleges were not introduced until the 1970s, and until recently Oxford was very much a male-dominated institution. Now, about 10 percent of professors are women, and about a third of all academic staff are female. The balance has also recently shifted in favour of postgraduate students, and the University is keen to develop research and graduate studies in line with other elite universities around the world.

The myth of Oxford as a book-lined ivory tower is not entirely without foundation, however. Academic concerns are still very much a priority; and, although Oxford no longer enjoys the pre-eminent status it once did, university departments find it relatively easy to attract funding from industry, especially in the sciences. This partly explains the emphasis on postgraduate research. One university fund-raising group, the Development Programme for Oxford, trades on Oxford's elitist image and raised almost £350 million within four years of being set up in 1988. Even so, this is dwarfed by the sums raised by individual colleges in regular appeals to old members.

The academic life

Oxford's academic reputation is challenged only in the UK by Cambridge and by America's Ivy League universities such as Harvard and Princeton. Nonetheless, its teaching is sometimes criticised for being too intense and

ACTING, JOURNALISM AND POLITICS

Talented and/or ambitious students seek to climb quickly to the top of the organisations that control acting, journalism and politics in Oxford. This has been a traditional preparation for the assumption of real power in later life.

The clique-filled world of Oxford drama is presided over by OUDS, the Oxford University Dramatic Society. Many colleges also have their own theatre groups. The standard of productions varies, but the best are very good.

Oxford journalism has long been dominated by the weekly newspaper *Cherwell* (founded in 1920) and the literary magazine *Isis* (founded in 1897). Several national newspaper editors were former Cherwell editors. Even Rupert Murdoch once worked on the paper. The usual stereotypes are that *Cherwell* is frivolous and *Isis* pretentious, but both regularly win national awards and are worth looking at if you can get hold of a copy (they are both distributed in the colleges' lodges).

But the Oxford Union debating society, by turns frivolous and influential, is by far the best-known student institution. Five British Prime Ministers have been officers. The various political clubs are also well-trodden training-grounds for future politicians; the Conservative Association, for example, can point to Margaret Thatcher as one of many ex-presidents who made the big time.

too traditional. The intensity springs from the fact that terms are only eight – or at most nine – weeks long (compared to at least 10 at most other British universities) and students are required to complete a minimum of one essay or problem-sheet a week, and sometimes as many as two or three. And the rigidly traditional nature of many of the courses is quite exceptional – for example, law students are required to study Roman Law, and English students have to study Anglo-Saxon.

However, the university's famous tutorial system means that most courses are quite unstructured. Science students may have compulsory lectures and practicals, but for Arts

the student-tutor relationship, because of small numbers and collegiate life, is unlike other universities. If an undergraduate dislikes his or her tutor (or vice-versa) there can be problems.

Lectures were once solemn occasions, the students rising as the gown-clad don entered the lecture hall. The don then, all too often, mumbled semi-coherently for an hour. The advent of lecture return forms, in which students evaluate the quality of a lecture course, have largely put paid to incompetent lecturing, although the odd don still insists on wearing a gown.

Exams remain solemn – and terrifying. All students taking exams must wear "sub-fusc", a mode of dress descended from 13th-century

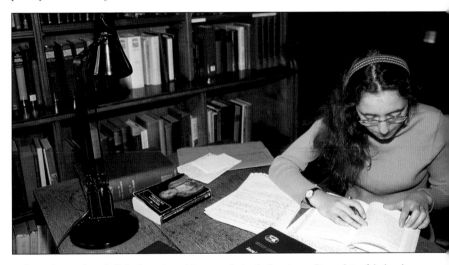

undergraduates there is little formal teaching apart from the one hour a week spent with a tutor. Tutorials used to be mostly one-to-one but are now increasingly attended by two or three students, who are also taught in seminar groups.

The system works brilliantly if the student and tutor are "compatible", but it can backfire badly. The traditional picture of the tutorial – an ancient, book-lined study, an even more ancient don sipping sherry, a timorous student stumbling through his Aristotle – is by now the stuff of nostalgic fiction. But the intensity of

LEFT: stepping out at the Ballroom Dancing Society.
ABOVE: studying at St John's College.

ecclesiastical costume. It consists of dark suit, gown, white tie and mortar-board for men; gown, white blouse and black tie, skirt and stockings for women.

A matter of degree

Students sit a preliminary exam, called Mods or Prelims, in their first year. Finals, which were first set in 1807, are taken in the summer of the third year. Students are awarded a degree, or "Final Honour School", of either a First, 2:1, 2:2 or Third. About 80 percent are awarded a 2:1, which in practice is what most students hope for. This has led to calls for further bands within the 2.1. Despite some moves to introduce dissertations and other course work into the final degree assessment, the system remains heavily weighted towards the dreaded final examination. Unlike other universities, exams are public – set centrally and marked by committees of academics from all colleges. This is very different from systems in which the tutor sets and marks the work submitted by those on his or her course.

Student life

The student's way of life has remained essentially unchanged for hundreds of years. Training for the ministry as an undergraduate's principal objective began to decline in the 19th

THE COST OF LIVING

Most colleges provide their students with accommodation for at least two years, some of it in modern buildings, but much of it in the college itself. Living in an ancient college room is a unique experience – romantic, stimulating and extremely draughty. Most students have to "live out" at some stage or another, usually sharing a house with other students. The average rent in Oxford is high (around £80 a week) and the rising price of college rooms has provoked some normally unmilitant students into staging rent strikes. In the face of pricey and scarce rented rooms, most colleges have also built or bought up accommodation in Oxford.

century, and over the years new subjects have been added so that there are now 18 separate faculties. But all students' lives are still shaped by the fact that they are members of a college – and that is how they think of themselves, rather than as members of a faculty.

The college has always been much more than just a place of residence; lectures and exams are organised by the university, but the colleges are responsible for a student's weekly tutorials and classes. This is perhaps more the case for those studying arts degrees than scientists, who spend more time in laboratories. In addition, the college is the centre of the student's social life. Every college has sports facilities and organised teams in most sports, plus a bar and a Junior Common Room which usually provides newspapers and a TV set.

All the colleges have clubs, some of which are hundreds of years old; these can be musical, cultural and academic in orientation or purely social dining and drinking societies. You can guess which have the most members.

Psychological pressures

As well as the cost of accommodation *(see panel)*, the cost of a student's social life is considerable. One recent survey showed that more than two-thirds of students expected to owe over £3,000 by the time they graduated.

Concerns about the welfare of Oxford students are nothing new. The suicide rate has always been very high, and 43 percent of students claimed to have suffered from bouts of depression or anxiety.

However, the city's bars, pubs, clubs and cinemas do a brisk trade during term-time, and some are almost deserted during the vacations. If anything, Oxford students are notorious for "japes" – many see alcohol as the easiest antidote to essays. Complaints about student indiscipline are as old as the university itself: Proctors were appointed to enforce discipline as early as 1248.

Donnish distinctions

All teaching at Oxford was originally conducted by clergymen, and its academics are still universally known as "dons". Not all dons actually do any teaching. Many students are taught by postgraduate students, or Junior Research Fellows, who are in most cases appointed for a three-year period. The next step up is a Lecturership, a permanent teaching post at a faculty attached to a particular college.

A Lecturer can then become a Reader, with fewer teaching duties and more opportunity to concentrate on his or her own research. Readers may become Professors, who are responsible for overseeing a particular subject area, in which they are said to hold a "Chair". Professors give few or no undergraduate tutorials, while Readers are few and far between.

A comfortable existence

Oxford dons live a fairly comfortable life—although many would deny it. Most receive

there is the "young fogey", too untrendy to appear on TV but too youthful to be accepted as an academic. The "Great and Good don" who has the ear of the Prime Minister is dying out, and in fact many feel the prestige of being a don is beginning to wane.

Recent years have witnessed huge changes in the way that most dons work. Largely gone is the old ethos of ivory tower exclusivity and cloistered college life, to be replaced by the pressures of chasing research grants and meeting exacting academic standards. Faculties now have to prove their worth to government and other funding agencies by producing quantifiable and quality-tested research in the form

housing support from their college (ranging from a free house to a £1,000 income supplement), they have the right to dine at High Table (though few do so regularly), and of course they have long holidays. These, however, are the time when research must be pursued, as term time contains too many other teaching and administrative demands.

There are as many different types of don as there are student. Some never leave the library (the "old fogey"). Others appear regularly on television (the "trendy young don"). Then

of books, articles and papers produced by their members. Presentations must be made to bodies such as the Economic and Social Research Council, which funds postgraduate research programmes and enables academics to pursue their specific areas of interest. This means that dons are expected to publish regularly, take part in the international conference circuit and generally market their academic work in a highly competitive world.

The university currently has 194 Professors, 91 Readers and 954 Lecturers, but many Chairs have lain vacant through lack of funds. Fewer graduates are seeking to become dons and, of those who do, many decide to leave for

LEFT: the traditional image of a student in summer.
ABOVE: the traditional image of a don in his study.

the private sector before they are 30, owing to poor prospects and salaries.

Scouts and porters

Aside from the don, the scout is probably the best-known Oxford figure. Scouts date back to the early 18th century and have traditionally been attached to a particular staircase of a particular college. As late as the 1950s they performed the role of a manservant, waking their students, cleaning their rooms, preparing light meals and running errands for them. Nowadays nearly all scouts are women and act simply as cleaning ladies or waitresses in hall.

The other familiar college figure is the porter, who fills the duties of receptionist and security guard at the entrance to every college. They are involved in college discipline, and a minority are notorious for their obstinacy and rudeness. Each college is headed by what is variously titled the Rector, Master, Principal, President, Warden or Provost, who is the supreme authority within the college, as well as the face the college presents to the outside world.

The Fresher experience

The chaotic first week of their first term is an experience no one forgets. First-year students, or "Freshers", go through a hectic schedule, dominated by two events: Matriculation and Freshers' Fair.

The Matriculation ceremony is a ritual by which students are officially admitted as members of the university, and is conducted by the Vice-Chancellor in the Sheldonian Theatre. Students dress up in sub-fusc and listen to various Latin formulae. Other important first-week ceremonies include registering at the Bodleian Library, at which students have to swear, among other things, not to "kindle flame" in the building.

But the Freshers' Fair is the craziest, most diverse event of the year. The Schools' building on the High Street is invaded by stalls representing all the different university clubs and societies, hoping to sign up Freshers as new members. There are over 200 clubs to choose from, ranging from the sensible (the Strategic Studies Group, the Industrial Society) to the surreal (the Pooh Sticks Club, the Heterosexual Decadence Society).

The end of the week is marked by a series of college "subject parties", at which the second and third-year students in each subject ply their Fresher counterparts with alcohol. If students can survive the first week, they can survive anything Oxford will throw at them.

The social life

Predictably, Oxford students do most of their socialising at pubs and parties. But for a few weeks every summer they indulge in the unashamed opulence of the summer balls.

Admission to the top balls costs the equiv-

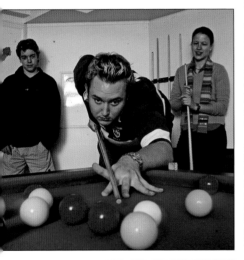

THE SPORTING LIFE

The Boat Race, held in early April between Putney and Mortlake on the River Thames in London, is the focus for Oxford–Cambridge sporting rivalry. It was first held in 1829, since when it has been raced almost every year, with Cambridge enjoying a slight lead of 78–72 by 2006. In 1877 it was a dead-heat.

Oxford–Cambridge matches began with a cricket match in 1827. They are now held in every sport. Two are televised: the Boat Race and the Varsity rugby match, held at Twickenham in December. Training is deadly serious, and players are awarded a "Blue", perhaps as prestigious as a First Class degree.

LEFT: unwinding in the snooker room.
RIGHT: clubs tout for recruits at the Freshers' Fair.

alent of an average week's wages for a double dining ticket, anachronistically priced in guineas (£1.05) rather than pounds. Yet the vast majority of Oxford students go to at least one ball during their time at the university, considering them a harmless excuse for dressing up and having a good time.

The summer is the most active social season, as students go punting on the river, and roam the streets to raise money for charity during Rag Week. But long gone are the extravagances of the 1930s when the "gilded youth" of Britain's great families supposedly squandered fortunes in a day and flitted from lunch party to cocktail party to dinner party.

Private societies

Private dining societies with names like the Disraeli Society and the Russell Club still exist, but today's social scene tends to reflect the wider social mix of today's Oxford. Parties are generally unpretentious and alcoholic – they are also becoming more infrequent as increased academic pressure takes its toll.

However, Oxford is still alive at weekends with groups of students leaving their favourite pubs (the King's Arms, the Turf Tavern, the Bear or the White Horse) and heading for a party, easily recognisable by the alcoholic offerings they carry – today's party invitations invariably command: "Please Bring A Bottle." ❏

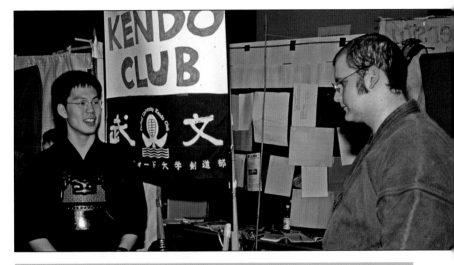

TOWN VERSUS GOWN

The relationship between the university and the city of Oxford has historically been one of hostility and mutual suspicion. In some ways Oxford is two cities, with certain shops and pubs never visited by students because they are "too townie", and others shunned by locals on the grounds that they are "too full of students".

Because of its cheap housing, Cowley is popular with students, but they do not always mix well with the locals. With Cowley Road itself famous for its curry restaurants, the area's population includes many immigrants, plus a large "alternative" community *(see page 60)*.

But there are some institutions whose status doesn't quite fit the Town/Gown stereotype. Principal among these are the numerous secretarial and tutorial colleges, which find it easy to attract both students and teachers because of the proximity of the university. Students at secretarial colleges are universally known to Oxford University students as "seccies" and are often accused (in most cases unfairly) of coming to Oxford more to snare an eligible bachelor than to perfect keyboarding skills.

In the summer, many students make a little extra money by teaching at language schools or giving guided tours to tourists. This is generally considered to be the lowest known form of paid employment.

OXFORD COLLEGES: A WHO'S WHO

Football fans can seem restrained compared to supporters of individual colleges. We cut through the snobbery to assess their strengths and weaknesses

Oxford University consists of 39 colleges and seven permanent private halls (originally religious institutions), each of which is financially independent and self-governing and responsible for the tutoring, feeding and housing of its students. Of the 39 colleges, eight are for graduates only and one (All Souls') is exclusively for Fellows. This chapter profiles the undergraduate colleges and, because of its academic and architectural importance, includes All Souls'. It charts the political persuasions, sporting accolades and other passions of students past and present, and lists architectural and historical highlights and other key characteristics of each college.

For each entry, we cite the number of undergraduates and graduates (eg *300/100*) as well as famous alumni. Frequent reference is made to the Norrington Table, Oxford's unofficial academic ranking system, which classes the colleges according to the annual results in the final-year undergraduate examinations.

ALL SOULS'

Founded: 1437
Number of students: varies,
graduate students only.
Alumni: Isaiah Berlin,
T.E. Lawrence, John Redwood,
William Waldegrave.
All Souls', a research-oriented college for Fellows only, stands on the High Street but can also be reached from Radcliffe Square, from where its spectacular twin towers are best viewed. The Front Quad has remained virtu-

ally unchanged since the college's foundation, as has the chapel, and there is a sundial designed by Christopher Wren, a former All Souls' bursar. To be elected a Fellow of All Souls' is perhaps the highest academic honour in the university – every year the top finalists are invited to sit an examination to apply, and only two are actually elected to fellowship.

BALLIOL

Founded: 1263
Number of students: 422/221
Alumni: H.H. Asquith, Hilaire
Belloc, Graham Greene,
Denis Healey, Edward Heath,
Aldous Huxley, Roy Jenkins, Boris Johnson,
Harold Macmillan, Howard Marks, Chris
Patten, Siegfried Sassoon.
Occupying a huge area between Broad Street and Magdalen Street, Balliol is one of the oldest, biggest, wealthiest, highest-achieving and most prestigious colleges in the university. The college has a strong political tradition, and went through an especially radical phase in the 1960s. Formal Hall, the saying of Grace and the wearing of gowns have all been abolished, and students are even allowed to walk on the college grass – an activity deemed a crime in most colleges. Balliol was also one of the first colleges to begin accepting large numbers of non-public school-educated and overseas students, fostering a refreshingly cosmopolitan atmosphere. There is long-standing rivalry between Balliol and its Broad Street neighbour Trinity.

BRASENOSE

Founded: 1509
Number of students: 362/176
Alumni: John Buchan, David Cameron, Colin Cowdrey, William Golding, Michael Palin, Robert Runcie.

"BNC" tends to be overshadowed by the splendour of the nearby Bodleian Library and Radcliffe Camera, although the attractive Old Quadrangle is noted for its colourful sundial. Historically "middle-of-the-road", Brasenose has a good reputation for sport – mostly rowing – and on the academic side it has a distinguished tradition in Law. It acquired its name from a rather unusual door-knocker ("brazen nose"), which now hangs in the hall.

CHRIST CHURCH

Founded: 1546
Number of students: 426/154
Alumni: W.H. Auden, Lewis Carroll, Alan Clark, Richard Curtis, Anthony Eden, Albert Einstein, William Gladstone, Lord Hailsham, Sir Robert Peel, Auberon Waugh, John Wesley, Sir Christopher Wren.

Originally founded in 1525 by Cardinal Wolsey and re-founded by Henry VIII in 1546, "The House" is Oxford's largest and best-known college as well as being one of the top colleges both academically and in sport. It is the one college *every* tourist visits, despite the entrance charge and the risk of being shouted at by the bowler-hatted "Bulldogs" on duty there. The grandiose architecture is imposing to the point of being intimidating, especially Sir Christopher Wren's Tom Quad, with its famous tower and fountain – and the college even has its own cathedral, picture gallery and meadow. The college architecture may be familiar to some from the *Harry Potter* films.

For many years the cradle of the British aristocracy, Christ Church still produces its fair share of bishops and MPs, though there is a slightly wider social mix at the college today; women were first admitted in 1980.

CORPUS CHRISTI

Founded: 1517
Number of students: 246/115
Alumni: Matthew Arnold, Sir Isaiah Berlin Vikram Seth, William Waldegrave.

Corpus is the smallest undergraduate college but has a main quad that is among the most

HOW THE COLLEGES ARE GOVERNED

All undergraduate colleges have a Governing Body of Fellows in charge of almost every aspect of college life. Some Fellows are more important than others, although key posts, such as Senior Tutor or Dean, are normally filled by one Fellow for two or three years only. The Senior Tutor is concerned with academic achievement, while the Dean has the unenviable task of enforcing discipline. The other top jobs are the Bursar, responsible for finances, and of course the Principal (or Warden, Master, Provost, President, Dean or Rector). The head of house is elected by all the Fellows and is recruited depending on his or her expertise and connections.

The Governing Body meets regularly to discuss the day-to-day running of the college. Some subcommittees, such as those supervising the college gardens or the wine cellar, tend to be more popular than those dealing with investments or building works. Votes are taken on all issues, and there is often a surprising degree of articulate argument.

One of the Governing Body's duties is to sit in judgment on students in trouble. There is a procedure for those who fail exams, involving a further test, with the threat of expulsion if the exam is failed again. The old punishments of "gating" (confinement to college) and "rustication" (sending out of residence for a term or two) are obsolete, as are the arcane rules that made attendance at chapel compulsory or imposed curfews. Nowadays, serious disciplinary matters are more likely to involve vandalism or other forms of anti-social behaviour, and students will be "sent down" (expelled) only for serious misdemeanours.

Undergraduates also have regular meetings, under the auspices of the Junior Common Room (JCR). Motions, some serious and others frivolous, are debated, with budding politicians trying out their oratorical skills.

beautiful in Oxford, its most notable feature being the Pelican Sundial. Academic standards are traditionally high, but the college is also known for its tolerance and friendliness. It is also the home of the annual tortoise races, the slowest spectator sport in the university.

EXETER

Founded: 1314
Number of students: 328/177
Alumni: Martin Amis, Roger Bannister, Alan Bennett, Edward Burne-Jones, Richard Burton, Ned Sherrin, William Morris, Philip Pullman, Will Self, J.R.R. Tolkien.

One of the three Turl Street colleges (along with Jesus and Lincoln), Exeter is an architectural mish-mash of styles, as bits were added on over the centuries. Highlights include the Gothic chapel, with its vast spire, and the tiny garden at the back of the college, with beautiful views over the Bodleian and Radcliffe Camera. Exeter has traditionally been known as an unpretentious, slightly unremarkable, even apathetic college, although feelings have traditionally been strong regarding the college food (dreadful) and the bar (excellent).

HARRIS MANCHESTER

Founded: 1786
Number of students: 108/150
Alumni: James Martineau.

Originally established by English Presbyterians in Manchester in 1786, "HMC" moved to Oxford in 1889 and was given full college status only in 1996, making it the university's newest college. It's also the only one to cater solely for mature students – candidates must be at least 21 to apply, although there is no upper age limit. Architectural highlights include the stained-glass windows by William Morris and Edward Burne-Jones in the chapel.

HERTFORD

Founded: 1740
Number of students: 370/220
Alumni: John Donne, Charles James Fox, Thomas Hobbes, Jonathan Swift, Evelyn Waugh.

A hall for students known as "Hart Hall" was established as long ago as 1282, but Hertford College has had a chequered history and has been plagued by financial problems, which remain to this day. The most remarkable and attractive feature of this close-knit, medium-sized college is the famous Bridge of Sighs (an echo of the one in Venice), which connects its two halves. This attracts hordes of tourists, partly because of its proximity to the Bodleian.

JESUS

Founded: 1571
Number of students: 330/130
Alumni: T.E. Lawrence (of Arabia), Magnus Magnusson, Harold Wilson.

Jesus was founded by Queen Elizabeth I, but much of the money behind the foundation was provided by a Welshman called Hugh Price, and the college retains very strong links with Wales – the college newspaper is entitled *The Sheepshagger*. Architecturally the least interesting of the Turl Street colleges (the other two are Exeter and Lincoln), Jesus has fallen over backwards to keep a low profile over the years – except in 1974, when it became the one of the first of the previously all-male colleges to admit women.

KEBLE

Founded: 1870
Number of students: 422/235
Alumni: Imran Khan, Andreas Whittam-Smith.

Keble was originally founded with the intention of making an Oxford education more accessible to people from different social backgrounds. Links with the Church (John Keble was a leading figure of the Oxford Movement – *see page 92*) ensure that the college retains a strong social conscience. It's a dynamic place, active in sport and politics, with academic achievement being especially strong in the sciences.

Keble's buildings have aroused enormous controversy. The main quad is a neo-Gothic palace of red-and-white chequered bricks, with the appearance of a Victorian mental institution. Other buildings are modern glass-and-steel affairs – the bar often being compared to a space ship. Local rival St John's has a "Demolish Keble Society", the membership requirement of which is to bring along a brick removed from Keble to your first meeting.

LADY MARGARET HALL

Founded: 1878
Number of students: 424/148
Alumni: Benazir Bhutto,
Antonia Fraser, Nigella
Lawson, Ann Widdecombe.
Its out-of-town location (15 minutes on foot from St Giles) and 12 acres (5 hectares) of beautiful grounds make this college idyllic in summer, though it does look like a prison from the front. LMH was the first "academic hall" for women at Oxford – it became a full college only in 1960 and went mixed in 1978. It is known for its general tolerance, though it has been radical enough to stage an anti-pornography protest.

LINCOLN

Founded: 1427
Number of students: 303/240
Alumni: John Le Carré,
Emily Mortimer, Dr Seuss,
John Wesley.
One of the most beautiful sights in Oxford is the view up Turl Street towards All Saints' Church, now the Lincoln College library. The college itself is rather small, but very picturesque. It was originally founded as a "small college" in order to create a friendly, cosy atmosphere – a tradition that is still strongly adhered to. Lincoln enjoys long-standing rivalry with the other Turl Street colleges, Exeter and Jesus.

MAGDALEN

Founded: 1458
Number of students: 389/235
Alumni: Sir John Betjeman,
William Hague, Ian Hislop,
Martha Lane Fox, C.S. Lewis,
Dudley Moore, Desmond Morris, Ivor
Novello, Oscar Wilde, Cardinal Wolsey.
Pronounced "maudlin", Magdalen's academic traditions are as fine as its romantic architecture. Its buildings include the 15th-century tower overlooking Magdalen Bridge from which its acclaimed choir sings on May Morning, Cloister Quad and the Regency New Buildings. The gardens are just as impressive,

with over a mile of riverside walks and a Deer Park. Magdalen probably captures the spirit of Evelyn Waugh's *Brideshead Revisited* more than any other college.

MANSFIELD

Founded: 1886
Number of students: 191/51
Alumni: C.H. Dodd,
Nathaniel Micklem.
Originally a Congregationalist theological college, diminutive Mansfield has the advantage of beautiful and tranquil surroundings in a fairly central location off Holywell Street. The college is historically short of cash and strong in the Arts. In undergraduate life, it contributes more than its fair share to journalism, and its Women's Group has been active. Pool is another college forte.

MERTON

Founded: 1264
Number of students: 309/212
Alumni: Andy Cato (half of
Groove Armada), T.S. Eliot,
Jeremy Isaacs, Kris Kristof-
ferson, Robert Morley, John Wyclif.
Merton has the oldest quad in the university, beautiful gardens and a fine academic pedigree. From the cobblestones of Merton Street to the medieval library in Mob Quad to the old city wall that borders the garden, this college constantly delights the eye. It is noted for extremely high academic standards, its inexpensive but top-notch food, its students' musical talents and for holding the only Winter Ball in Oxford. The college also hosts an annual Arts Festival. During the English Civil War, Henrietta Maria, wife of Charles I, set up house at Merton in what is now the Queen's Room, while her husband was installed at nearby Christ Church.

NEW

Founded: 1379
Number of students: 420/180
Alumni: Kate Beckinsale,
Tony Benn, Gyles Brandreth,
Richard Crossman, John
Fowles, Hugh Gaitskell, John Galsworthy,
Hugh Grant, Dennis Potter, Rick Stein.
New College looks anything but new. In fact,

it's one of the oldest colleges in the university, and many of the buildings, including the front quad, dining hall, chapel and cloisters, have survived from the original foundations and look positively medieval. The college has a kind of austere beauty – certainly it is difficult not to be impressed by its size and sheer solidity. It's a prestigious and well-known college, with well-established links to the Civil Service and to Winchester (it was founded by William of Wykeham). Strong in sport (especially rowing), academia and music, New is currently considered to be one of the main social centres of university life.

ORIEL

Founded: 1326
Number of students: 304/158
Alumni: Beau Brummell,
John Keble, Cardinal New-
man, Sir Walter Raleigh,
Cecil Rhodes, A.J.P Taylor.

Oriel was the last college to remain all-male, admitting women only in 1985. Traditional in more ways than one, it is also known for the right-wing leanings of its students, having the only Junior Common Room that refuses to subscribe to the Oxford University Student Union. It has a strong rowing tradition, with the college having long dominated the river. Oriel is in a lovely location, just off the High Street – the wonderfully picturesque Oriel Square has become one of the most-filmed locations in Oxford.

PEMBROKE

Founded: 1624
Number of students: 416/112
Alumni: Sir Rocco Forte,
Michael Heseltine, Samuel
Johnson, William Fulbright.

Compact, unassuming Pembroke is tucked away behind Carfax and suffers somewhat from being opposite the far more grandiose Christ Church. Academically it's a pretty middle-of-the-road place, and the laid-back atmosphere in college reflects this. Pembroke is anything but apathetic when it comes to sport, however, with both its men's and women's rowing teams consistently close to the top of the university rowing charts. Music is also a strong area in the college.

QUEEN'S

Founded: 1341
Number of students: 304/133
Alumni: Rowan Atkinson,
Edmund Halley, Brian
Walden.

This college is named after Philippa, wife of Edward III, whose chaplain, Robert Eglesfeld, founded it. But the statue above the main gate, overlooking the High Street, is of Queen Caroline, wife of George II, who in the mid-18th century funded the building of its two unusual and impressive baroque quads. The college has links with the north of England and is traditionally a sporting college, being especially strong in rugby (with appropriate beer cellar).

ST ANNE'S

Founded: 1893
Number of students: 437/187
Alumni: Edwina Currie,
Helen Fielding, Zoë Heller,
Penelope Lively, Iris Murdoch,
Libby Purves.

This former women's college, which looks like a 1970s polytechnic, now has equal numbers of men and women. One of Oxford's more "unpretentious" colleges, "Stan's" also does its bit for student drama and journalism. Academic standards have been on the up recently, with the college making the top ten of the Norrington Table three times since 2002.

ST CATHERINE'S

Founded: 1963
Number of students: 447/187
Alumni: J. Paul Getty,
Joseph Heller, Peter
Mandelson, A.A. Milne, Eric
Partridge, Matthew Pinsent,
Jeanette Winterson.

"Catz" is viewed either as an architectural masterpiece or a sprawling modern monstrosity. Designed by Danish architect Arne Jacobsen, even down to the cutlery used by the tutors, and situated out of town by the River Cherwell, it is lovely in summer. It has yet to perform a feat remarkable enough to attract the attention of the rest of the university, but its liberal establishment (for example, it has no chapel – the only Oxford college without one) makes it popular with students.

ST EDMUND HALL

Founded: circa 1278
Number of students: 400/150
Alumni: Sir Robin Day,
Terry Jones, Al Murray.
"Teddy Hall" is a compact college just off the High Street,
with an interesting combination of a delightful 17th-century front quad and several 1970s
tower blocks. It has always been famous for
sport, and its women's rugby team is currently
one of the best in the country. It has an extraordinary library with a tall, book-lined tower –
this is in a converted church and students have
to cross a graveyard to get to it.

ST HILDA'S

Founded: 1893
Number of students: 419/116
Alumnae: Monica Ali, Susan
Blackmore, Wendy Cope, Bar-
bara Pym, Gillian Shepherd.
Just over Magdalen Bridge, St
Hilda's lies on the banks of the River Cherwell, with superb views over Christ Church
Meadows. The last remaining all-women college, it finally decided in 2006 to admit men.
Many felt this would ruin the charm and character and pointed out that "Hildabeasts" were
anything but cloistered and participated
actively in university life. The college's principal, Lady English, argued: "The ability to
consider men as well as women for fellowship
appointments will have immediate benefit by
allowing us to strengthen our science teaching. However, our commitment to supporting
women's careers remains a priority."

ST HUGH'S

Founded: 1886
Number of students: 419/226
Alumni: Kate Adie, Brigid Bro-
phy, Barbara Castle, Theresa
May, Joanna Trollope.
St Hugh's is a close-knit former women's college, founded by Elizabeth Wordsworth, great-
niece of the poet. Mixed since 1986, it is sited
far out in North Oxford, on the extreme edge
of the university area. The college 14-acre (6-
hectare) grounds are said to be quite pleasant,
but the joke goes that no one except St Hugh's
students have actually seen them.

ST JOHN'S

Founded: 1555
Number of students: 397/185
Alumni: Kingsley Amis, Tony
Blair, Robert Graves, A.E.
Housman, Philip Larkin.
It is sometimes said that you
can walk all the way from Oxford to Cambridge on land owned by St John's. It is the
richest Oxford college, and is believed to own
a fair chunk of Switzerland as well as large
tracts of London's West End. The college's
extreme wealth means glorious buildings and
luxurious accommodation for the students
(there are even rumours of Jacuzzis). Only a
modern block – dubbed "a fish tank on stilts"
– lets things down. Situated on St Giles (which
the college owns and under which is report-
edly a highly impressive wine cellar), St John's
has traditionally been the most academically
successful college, consistently topping the
influential Norrington Table.

ST PETER'S

Founded: 1929
Number of students: 390/125
Alumni: Edward Akufo Addo,
Ken Loach, Peter Wright.
"St Pete's" has long been considered a backwater of
Oxford. Situated next to the former Oxford
Prison (now a Malmaison boutique hotel) and
rooted firmly to the bottom of the Norrington
Table, it is mostly noted for the ugliness of its
buildings and the beer-drinking exploits of its
students. Highlights, however, include the
snazzy set of automatic doors at the entrance
to the main quad; these have the notable dis-
tinction of being the only pair of their kind in
an Oxford college.

SOMERVILLE

Founded: 1879
Number of students: 370/102
Alumnae: Indira Gandhi,
Iris Murdoch, Esther
Rantzen, Dorothy L. Sayers,
Margaret Thatcher, Shirley
Williams.
Baroness Thatcher's old college is not overly
proud of its most illustrious graduate – in 1989
a bust of the Supreme Leader had to be taken

off display and stored in a broom cupboard after being repeatedly daubed with graffiti. The college site up the Woodstock Road is grassy and pleasant, and its members are sociable and outward-looking. Long an all-women college, it went mixed in 1994 and now has equal numbers of men and women. Like Trinity, Somerville houses some keen croquet players.

TRINITY

Founded: 1554–5
Number of students: 297/121
Alumni: Anthony Crosland,
Miles Kington, William Pitt
the Elder, Terence Rattigan,
Jeremy Thorpe.

Trinity is essential viewing for visitors. The path leading from the impressive wrought-iron gates on Broad Street through the beautiful college buildings to the spectacular gardens is a pilgrimage for every tourist. Generations of Trinity students have spent their summers playing croquet or just relaxing on the lawn, with the result that, despite its long history, the college has never really distinguished itself academically. It is, however, a great place for a picnic. One issue said to stir the passions of easy-going Trinitarians, however, is the age-old rivalry – mostly friendly – between members of this college and their wealthy Broad Street neighbour Balliol.

UNIVERSITY

Founded: 1249
Number of students: 420/144
Alumni: Clement Attlee, Bill
Clinton, Chelsea Clinton,
Stephen Hawking, Richard
Ingrams, V.S. Naipaul, Percy
Bysshe Shelley, Willie Rushton.

"Univ" is said to have been founded by King Alfred the Great in 812, but this is disputed. What is certain is that "Univ" was the first Oxford college to be founded, and has never ceased to set high standards for its students, whether in the library or on the games field. The college has a strong reputation in the sciences, and its students have always been very active in university life – perhaps in order to escape the architecture of their own college, which has been likened by some to an Alcatraz on the High Street.

WADHAM

Founded: 1610
Number of students: 480/190
Alumni: Sir Thomas
Beecham, Melvyn Bragg,
Michael Checkland, Cecil
Day Lewis, Michael Foot,
Rosamund Pike, Sir Christopher Wren.

Once nicknamed the "People's Republic of Wadham", this college has always been a centre for radical thought. In its early days it was the meeting place for the leading figures of the Scientific Revolution, who went on to form the Royal Society. It was later one of the first colleges to admit women. The Parks Road college has a long tradition of political activism – it is the only college to have its own Student Union rather than a Junior Common Room and remains fiercely left wing. The college buildings are attractive, especially the original front quad, but the notoriously trendy Wadhamites are more likely to be found in the neighbouring King's Arms than in college.

WORCESTER

Founded: 1714
Number of students: 413/185
Alumni: Richard Adams,
Sir Alastair Burnett, Richard
Lovelace, Rupert Murdoch,
Thomas de Quincey, Lord
Sainsbury.

Secluded Worcester is set in 26 acres (10 hectares) of beautiful grounds on the western edge of the university area – something that you might not realise from its forbidding, grim even, entrance on Walton Street. It stands on the site of the former Gloucester Hall, a Benedictine foundation of 1283 that was dissolved during the suppression of the monasteries. The college's unusually spacious front quad isn't really a quad at all – the money ran out after only three sides had been finished.

Worcester is the only Oxford college to possess its own lake – complete with ducks – next to which outdoor drama is held in summer by the college's thriving "Buskins" theatre group. Other highlights include the acclaimed food at Formal Hall and the recently renovated chapel, of which Oscar Wilde wrote: "as a piece of simple decorative and beautiful art it is perfect, and the windows very artistic." ❑

Oxford Brookes University

Although Oxford is synonymous with its medieval university, the city contains another centre of academic excellence: Oxford Brookes University, to be found at the top of Headington Hill. Brookes can claim little of the longevity of its illustrious neighbour, but it has its own claims to fame and a burgeoning student population, estimated at over 18,000 in 2006.

The institution's history involves many a change of name and site. Originally the Oxford School of Art, housed in the Taylor Institution in St Giles, it became the Oxford City Technical School and moved to St Ebbes in 1894. These premises were soon judged inadequate but it took a further 50 years before the land on Headington Hill was acquired. During that time the school spread into different buildings, at one stage being scattered over 19 separate sites.

The modern-day university was named after John Brookes, whose vision was of a single college on a single campus, offering a mix of academic and vocational courses. Under his inspirational stewardship from 1928 to 1956 the college not only found its physical home but also began to develop a high reputation in disciplines such as architecture and catering. Brookes also persuaded well-known academics and experts to lecture at the school.

After its official opening in 1963, the College of Technology (as it was now called) started offering degree-level courses. As part of the nationwide trend towards the creation of a network of polytechnics, it was then renamed Oxford Polytechnic in 1970. With an emphasis on vocational and professional courses, it continued to excel in training architects as well as pioneering work in publishing and hospitality. The Polytechnic's size and range of academic options were further increased with the merger in 1976 with the Lady Spencer Churchill teacher training college in nearby Wheatley. The Oxford School of Nursing also came into the Polytechnic fold in 1988.

RIGHT: an exam room at Oxford Brookes.

Full university status was acquired in 1992. With new funding, Brookes built much-needed student accommodation and took over the 14-acre (5.7-hectare) Headington Hill Hall site, formerly the fiefdom of the disgraced media mogul Robert Maxwell.

Today Brookes attracts an eclectic mix of students from the UK and further afield to a wide and often imaginative range of courses. The modular system allows for a greater choice within academic fields than conventional degree courses, while degrees and post-graduate qualifications in the established subjects of architecture and publishing remain highly sought-after. A mix-

ture of innovation and established academic prowess means that Brookes has on several occasions won the coveted best new university award judged and published by *The Times*.

Brookes is also proud of its sporting and social facilities. A state-of-the-art sports centre rivals anything the old University has to offer, while Brookes rowers are proud to point out that they have more than once beaten their venerable rival on the river. And with its own top-quality restaurant *(see page 209)*, the newer university has some attractions that the older one, for all its heritage, cannot hope to match. ❏

LITERARY OXFORD

**The university has nurtured writers and given them
a place in which to develop their craft, but it has
also made enemies of men and women of letters**

*And that sweet City with her dreaming spires,
She needs not June for beauty's heightening.*
                                    –Matthew Arnold

The waiting list for the single "local author" review slot in the weekly *Oxford Times* must be one of the longest literary queues in the world. Sometimes it seems that almost everyone in Oxford is an author (when they're not working in publishing or a bookshop), and parts of genteel North Oxford must surely echo to the sound of clattering keyboards. Look at the browser in Blackwell's Bookshop surreptitiously turning a book face outwards; he or she is a local author.

Oxford has always been a mecca for writers, partly because of its proximity to the literary heartland of London, partly because of its cultural buzz, but mostly because of the old university. Countless novelists, poets and playwrights have passed through the various colleges, some with more success than others, while a good many others have stayed on to find a day job in academia.

The Athens of England

The university literary connection goes back to medieval times, and in Chaucer's *Canterbury Tales* (c. 1387) we read of the Clerke of Oxenforde, an unworldly and impoverished bookworm – and a prototype for generations of students to come. The Middle Ages witnessed the heyday of the university's religious institutions, and much writing was of a theological or philosophical nature. It was not until Elizabethan times that the city – and university – developed a reputation as a centre of aesthetic excellence. The historian William Camden made a bold claim for Oxford's cultural status in 1586 when he wrote of "Our most noble Athens, the seat of the English Muses."

Muses or not, a succession of eminent writers passed through Oxford from the 16th century onwards. Some, like Shakespeare, were just en route to somewhere else, but others stayed, adopting the almost monastic life that University dons had to endure until the reforms of the 19th century. Robert Burton, author of *The Anatomy of Melancholy* (1621), taught and studied at Christ Church, where he claimed: "I have liv'd a silent, sedentary, solitary, private life, penned up most part in my study."

Nothing could have been further away from the gregarious, excessive and distinctly non-monastic lives led by the sons of the rich as the university became a finishing school for England's social elite during the 18th century. Men of letters did attend the University, but many were scathing about its dons and students. The poet Robert Southey (1774–1843) lambasted his tutors as "a waste of wigs and want of wisdom", while the great historian Edward Gibbon thought the time spent at Magdalen to have been "the most idle and unprofitable of my whole life".

The long-overdue reforms that swept

Oxford eulogised by Wordsworth and, in the 1860s, by Matthew Arnold, a fellow of Oriel College and Professor of Poetry. To Arnold we owe the immortal phrases "city of dreaming spires" (later wittily transformed into "city of perspiring dreams") and "home of lost causes".

Literary associations

Prominent among writers who have loved and celebrated the university were Charles Dodgson, a.k.a. Lewis Carroll and fellow of Christ Church, William Morris of pre-Raphaelite fame, the aesthete John Ruskin and T. E. Lawrence "of Arabia". The first half of the 20th century marked the golden age of Oxford's lit-

through the University from the 1830s were bound up with religious debate but also with new directions in literature. Dons such as Walter Pater at Brasenose and Mark Pattison at Lincoln were inspirational leaders of movements devoted to the development of the intellectual life and the pursuit of "art for art's sake". As Oxford lost both its clerical and aristocratic dominance, the city's literary prestige rose accordingly. The Romantic period saw

LEFT: Matthew Arnold, who coined the phrase "city of dreaming spires".
ABOVE: the 1981 TV adaptation of *Brideshead Revisited* conveyed a sybaritic view of Oxford life.

WRITERS WITH RESERVATIONS

Not all Oxford-educated writers have been enamoured with the place. The most famous rebel to be thrown out was Percy Bysshe Shelley, whose sojourn at University College came to an end in 1811 when he was expelled for publishing a pamphlet in defence of atheism. "Mad Shelley" later complained that "I never met with such unworthy treatment." Another poet to be shown the door (in his case of Magdalen) was John Betjeman, who failed an exam in 1927 and saw his dream of becoming a don evaporate. And poor Samuel Johnson was sent down in 1729 from Pembroke because he couldn't pay his bills (though he maintained a fondness for Oxford).

erary associations, as the city and university featured in classic novels such as Max Beerbohm's *Zuleika Dobson* (1911) and Evelyn Waugh's *Brideshead Revisited* (1945). The terrible death toll of the Great War encouraged a mythic image of pre-war Oxford and the generation of gilded young men who did not return.

Many Oxford writers, such as C.S. Lewis and J.R.R. Tolkien, have chosen not to write about Oxford. Others have written about the place in coded form. Thomas Hardy's *Jude the Obscure* (1896), for instance, is set in "Christminster", a thinly disguised version of Oxford. Increasing numbers, moreover, have set their work beyond the cloistered confines of the uni-

versity and have used the "real" city as the backdrop for their work. This was the case with Hardy, but more recently John Wain, in his trilogy *Where the Rivers Meet*, and writers such as A.S. Byatt and Barbara Trapido have dealt with non-university Oxford.

Women writers

Literary Oxford, like academic Oxford, was long a male monopoly, but now the coveted local author slot is as likely to be occupied by one of the many women writers who live in the city. Pre-eminent among them until her death in 1999 was Iris Murdoch, a philosophy don at St Anne's before becoming an

MURDEROUS INTENT

The city is thankfully not a crime hot spot, but detective novels and murder mysteries abound. Millions of readers have been introduced to Oxford via Colin Dexter's ingenious Inspector Morse novels and John Thaw's popular portrayal of Morse on television kept camera crews busy around the city for years. Morse follows in a line of Oxford sleuths, starting with Dorothy L. Sayers' Harriet Vane in *Gaudy Night* (1935) and including the investigative creations of Michael Innes, Michael Dibdin and Veronica Stallwood. To read these, you might be excused for thinking that every college quadrangle and city street is fraught with murderous danger.

acclaimed novelist. Other women authors with an Oxford University pedigree include Vera Brittain (famous for *Testament of Youth*, 1933), Dorothy L. Sayers, Barbara Pym and Penelope Lively.

Nowadays, Oxford's love affair with the book takes many forms, from a plethora of local reading groups to the prestigious annual Oxford Literary Festival. Authors such as Ian McEwan live in the city, while the university attracts poets of the calibre of Craig Raine, James Fenton and David Constantine. ❏

ABOVE: John Thaw, who played Inspector Morse on television, with the books' author, Colin Dexter.

Lewis Carroll

Alice in Wonderland is a love story. It indirectly expresses Lewis Carroll's feelings for the young daughter of the Dean of Christ Church and reveals his thinly disguised passion for Oxford itself. Growing up brought the first affair quickly to a close – "No thought of me shall find a place/In thy young life's hereafter," he wrote in dedicating *Alice Through the Looking Glass* to her. The other relationship ended only with his death in 1898. In all that time he was scarcely ever away from his beloved Oxford.

Carroll was born Charles Ludwidge Dodgson in Christ Church rectory, Lincolnshire, and entered Oxford's Christ Church at the age of 18 in 1850. He became a lecturer in mathematics and was ordained Deacon. Outside his academic studies he was a keen photographer, developing his own plates in a darkroom he was given permission to build on the roof of his rooms overlooking Tom Quad.

Extremely shy, he was most at ease with children and they became his favourite subjects. His first meeting with the Liddell daughters was in the Deanery garden, where his intention of photographing the Cathedral was diverted by their insisting on getting in the picture.

The friendship with the girls grew, and soon they were posing for his camera in his rooms. Dressed in Chinese costumes or the rags of beggar waifs from the cupboards in his dressing-room, the children began their games of "Let's pretend", and Alice's adventures were about to begin.

During the summer Dodgson took the children on the river, making up stories that lived and died "like summer midges". One expedition, on 4 July 1862, took them upstream to Godstow. The children, as always, pressed their friend for more stories and, when they returned to the Deanery, Alice implored him to write down her adventures. Dodgson began the carefully hand-written book with his own illustrations and gave it to her as a Christmas gift.

RIGHT: Lewis Carroll, afflicted by shyness.

Alice's Adventures were so well thought of that Dodgson agreed to their professional publication, and on the advice of John Ruskin, the artist and social reformer, to have them illustrated by a professional artist. John Tenniel was chosen, and the author's name changed to Lewis Carroll (Lewis from Ludwidge, Carroll from Charles).

A second book, *Through the Looking Glass and What Alice Found There*, was not published until 1871. The relationship had ended with the end of her childhood, and Alice was now 19. She married a Christ Church man and went to live at Lyndhurst.

From the moment Alice clutches the jar

of "orange marmalade" Lewis Carroll starts an intriguing guessing game in identifying Oxford references and characters. Dodgson was currently advertising for sale his brother's orange marmalade. The Cheshire cat is Dinah, Alice's tabby. The Rev. Robinson Duckworth, a friend of Lewis Carroll's, who often went on the picnics, becomes, affectionately, the Duck.

The Dodo is the author himself, and was derived from visits to the new University Museum. The Dormouse's story of three children living at the bottom of a treacle-well leads us to the healing well at Binsey. You've only to push open the door... ❑

ALTERNATIVE OXFORD

For a place many automatically associate with elitism and conservatism, Oxford has a long and honourable history of nonconformism and radicalism

O ver the centuries Oxford's colleges have turned out legions of Establishment figures, from politicians and civil servants to generals and high commissioners. But they have also produced their fair share of dissenters and agitators – political radicals, angry artists and critics of the existing order. From Wyclif's 14th-century attempt to bring the Bible to ordinary people, through Ruskin's vision of labouring undergraduates, to the full-fledged revolutionary rage of Tariq Ali in the 1960s, the university has given us many proponents of social change.

The city, too, has not always been a model of genteel conformism. It has witnessed many a riot and demonstration, a good deal of organised protest and a solid tradition of sheer bloody-mindedness. Oxford people, as opposed to students, have often been at the forefront of movements that have sought to go against the received wisdom of the day

Cowley Road's "cool"

Nowhere is this story of "alternative" Oxford more clearly legible than in the ordinary-seeming suburban thoroughfare known as Cowley Road. This street is simply different from its equivalents north, south and west. It has a reputation for being different, bohemian and, to the young, "cool".

Once a "respectable" white working-class suburb, inhabited in the first part of the 20th century by tradesmen and college "servants", Cowley Road developed into something quite different during the five decades that followed World War II. In the post-war period it was just another suburban street, with corner shops, pubs and a hand-

ful of churches and entertainment venues serving its mostly locally-born population.

Then came the first wave of immigrants, attracting by employment at Cowley's car factory. People from the Caribbean began to settle on and around the road, followed by Pakistanis, Indians and Bangladeshis. As an Asian and West Indian community grew, it generated its own employment, and shops and restaurants began to open. By the 1960s the traditional "greasy spoon" was giving way to the curry house – to the pleasure of residents of all ethnic backgrounds.

Next to arrive were large numbers of students, filling the houses that had once been family homes. They brought with them new and different tastes in food, music and fashion. As the area's property became relatively cheap, young couples bought homes. In those radical decades students found common cause with trade unionists and left-leaning Labour activists, and the street became a heartland of radical politics.

The New Age dawns

As the political fervour of the 1980s waned, Cowley Road remained both radical and different. The new politics of environmentalism quickly involved large numbers of locals, and Oxford's first Green councillors were elected in the area. Anti-war and anti-corporate thinking also spread widely, expressed in demonstrations.

Oxford's premier non-mainstream music venue. Local bands Supergrass and Radiohead sponsored the initiative and have played there along with jazz, reggae, rock and indie performers.

To some respectable citizens of north Oxford Cowley Road may represent too much of a walk on the wild side. There are occasional problems, often related to drugs, and the area is not entirely free of petty crime. But, on the whole, the street's risk reputation is wildly exaggerated.

This triumph of community relations – and celebration of alternative credibility – takes joyous form each June in the Cowley Road Carnival, a day-long street party that sees traffic banished and partying encouraged. ❑

More significantly perhaps, East Oxford's ethnic minorities began to make their presence felt in ways beyond restaurants and shops. Three mosques are now to be found in the area, with a magnificent gold-domed building completed in 2005. Cowley Road's multi-ethnic mix is today self-evident in the street decorations that celebrate Eid, the shops selling the latest Bollywood classics and the activism of individuals and groups within community associations.

Cowley Road's claim to coolness was cemented with the opening in 1995 of the Zodiac,

THE ETHNIC MIX

Look at Cowley Road today and you will see Polish and Middle Eastern restaurants, Russian and Greek delicatessens, "Indian", Italian and Jamaican eating places, a sushi bar, Chinese takeaways, a huge number of Asian-run grocers and (still going strong) Uhuru. Add to this the pubs, tapas bar, kebab and fish and chip shops and occasional surviving old-style café – the Exelsior, unchanged in 50 years – and you have one of the most varied range of eating options imaginable. Then there are the alternative shops and services: Chinese medicine, head massage, Brazilian artefacts, fair trade goods and much more. This ordinary looking suburban street is really very different.

LEFT: graphic murals brighten up the Cowley Road.
ABOVE: the annual Cowley Road Carnival.

ARCHITECTURE

For more than a thousand years, the rich and powerful in Oxford have employed the best architects to create showpiece buildings in which to live, study, work and worship. The result is a three-dimensional catalogue of all that's best in British architecture

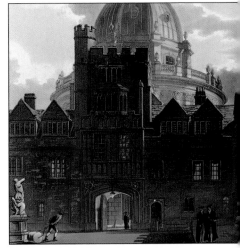

Not much remains of Oxford's earliest architecture, the only surviving Saxon relic being the tower of the church of St Michael at the Northgate, which was built as a lookout tower against the Danes. From the Norman era there is the fine crypt of St Peter in the East, as well as St George's Tower, part of the castle. The abbeys which played such a pivotal role in establishing the city as a centre of learning were almost completely destroyed during the Reformation, although most of the Augustinian priory church built on the site of St Frideswide's priory was saved, and subsequently became Christ Church Cathedral.

Both St Michael's and St George's towers are constructed of the coral rag limestone quarried in the Cumnor hills, a stone so tough it could not be shaped into regular blocks, thus accounting for their rough-cast look. When the great abbeys and early colleges were built, the builders preferred the more manageable Jurassic limestone found in great quantity in Headington and to the west of Oxford. Like some modern polymer, it came out of the ground "soft", and was easily cut and carved but, once in place, it weathered into a tough hard-wearing stone.

College blueprints

Founded by rich and powerful bishops, Oxford's first medieval colleges were a stark contrast to the cramped academic halls in which most students lived and worked. Their creators could afford to construct fine build-

Magpie Lane (**LEFT**) and *Brazen Nose College* (**RIGHT**), two of Rudolph Ackermann's engravings.

ings for the college members. Components included a chapel, a grand dining hall, accommodation set around an intimate quadrangle (much in the style of a medieval cloister or inn) and a library to house the priceless manuscripts. The colleges were private places looking inwards, with few external windows and only one great gateway giving entrance

While we can see the blueprint for some of these features in the surviving Mob Quad and chapel at Merton, it wasn't until the foundation of New College in 1379 that all of them were combined for the first time into a unified whole, with the chapel and hall and library all occupying space within the main quadrangle.

Medieval miracles

Gothic architecture transformed the city. By the early 14th century, the spire of the University Church of St Mary in the High Street soared above the town and, at 62 metres (203 ft), was almost three times as high as St Martin's tower at the old City Church on Carfax. As the colleges grew, they either expanded or were in some cases completely rebuilt. Nevertheless, some fine examples of the medieval stonemason's art remain in Oxford, principally in the chapels. Though not part of a college at the time they were built, both the Latin Chapel and the Lady Chapel in Christ Church Cathedral are fine examples of the Early Eng-

lish style of Gothic architecture. With their pointed lancet windows and clusters of shafts in place of monolithic columns to support the vaulted roof, they are a marked contrast to the rather crude Norman nave.

Merton College Chapel demonstrates the transition that took place in the early 14th century to the Decorated style. With its flowing and curvaceous tracery, the chapel's huge east window is one of the finest examples in England.

As the university grew in stature, it needed more of its own buildings, independent of the colleges. The first major step in this direction was the all-important Divinity School. Completed in 1488, it is a fine example of Perpendicular Gothic, with its intricate fan or lierne vaulting. Further examples of this form of vaulting include the Christ Church choir.

Later overlays

During the reign of Elizabeth I, college and university buildings began to dominate the central area. But the Elizabethan era and the first half of the 17th century also brought enormous changes to the town. Streets were extended and lined with three- and four-storey houses, mainly of timber-framed construction, of which several notable examples remain, including Kemp Hall just off the High Street. Medieval courtyard inns expanded to take up much space in the central streets; parts of such an inn remain in the Golden Cross off Cornmarket and The Mitre on High Street.

The 17th century also saw the emergence of Oxford's very own style of architecture, the Jacobean-Gothic, incorporating a tentative

---

WREN'S ROLE IN OXFORD

When the monarchy was restored in 1660, Oxford was rewarded for its Royalist loyalty by extended patronage and money flowed back for new building projects. The favoured style now was Classical and the University found the ideal architect in its young professor of astronomy, Christopher Wren. The Sheldonian Theatre was his first building. His U-shaped design was based on the antique Theatre of Marcellus in Rome. However, whereas the classical equivalent was safely left open to the elements, Wren had to cover the 22-metre (72-ft) span with a permanent roof and couldn't spoil the audience's view with pillars. His complicated series of trusses taking the strain from

the roof to the outside walls is hidden from spectators by a great painted ceiling but can be seen by visitors who visit the cupola on the roof.

Wren was booked for more architectural work at Trinity and Queen's colleges, though he was also rebuilding the churches lost in the Great Fire of London when he came back to complete his other Oxford landmark, Tom Tower at Christ Church. The great master of the classical style agreed to work in Gothic form to fit in with the existing gatehouse, built in Henry VIII's time. The ogee-shaped dome on the tower and the smaller gate turrets are a masterly touch, harking back to early Tudor architecture.

mixture of Gothic and Classical features and motifs and best exemplified by the magnificent Old Schools Quadrangle. But less than 100 years later, Classical architecture began to alter the Oxford skyline, with fine university buildings being erected in the central area, including Wren's Sheldonian Theatre (1668), Hawksmoor's Clarendon Building (1715) and Gibbs' Radcliffe Camera (1748).

Magnificent though they are, these buildings did not destroy the essentially medieval face of Oxford. Even when they were rebuilt, most colleges remained very conservative. The ancient-looking frontage of University College was completed at the same time as the

Oxford became a bastion of Gothic Revivalism, apparent in Sir George Gilbert Scott's Martyrs' Memorial, completed in 1843, and the impressive chapel of Exeter College, built in 1854–60 by the same architect and almost an exact copy of Sainte Chapelle in Paris. Gothic forms and motifs were also used for secular buildings, the most notable example of which is the University Museum (1855).

The founder of the Oxford Movement, John Keble, is remembered in Keble College, which was founded in 1868. However, William Butterfield's daring design transgressed Oxford's hallowed traditions, for it was built not of stone, but of a byzantine riot

Clarendon Building. Hawksmoor submitted plans for a neoclassical rebuild of All Souls, but these were not accepted; nor were the designs of Sir John Soane for Brasenose, whose medieval High Street facade wasn't completed until the early 20th century.

Gothic revivalism

Oxford and Gothic go naturally together; that was the feeling of the influential Oxford Architectural Society, which from the 1830s tried to influence anyone building in the city.

LEFT: Merton Street retains a medieval feel.
ABOVE: Nicholas Hawksmoor's Clarendon Building.

of red, yellow and blue brick. Oxford had seen nothing like it and, while the undergraduates treated it as a joke, older members of the university were outraged.

Geological harmony

Oxford is home to a profusion of architectural styles, and the fact that, by and large, these appear to hang together so harmoniously is largely down to the local limestone, of which most of the older buildings are constructed (*see page 69*). Nowhere is the harmonising power of the Oxford stone more evident than in Radcliffe Square, whose buildings were all built at different times but nevertheless combine to form one of the most magnificent architectural ensembles in Europe. And if you cross the High Street, the facade of Brasenose College (19th–20th centuries), the spire of St Mary's (14th-century) and the portal of St Mary's (16th-century baroque) all appear to be part of the same intricate scheme.

Stained glass

There are many fine examples of stained glass in Oxford, much of it, including the magnificent east window of Merton Chapel, the handiwork of local medieval craftsmen. But foreign artists, too, played their part, the most prolific being the German Abraham von Linge, who arrived in the city in 1629. His exquisite craftsmanship and intense colours can be admired in the chapel of The Queen's College, as well as at Lincoln.

Later contributions came from William Morris and Edward Burne-Jones, who met while studying at Exeter College in the 1850s and were influenced by the ideas of John Ruskin and the Pre-Raphaelites. Exeter College chapel houses one of their tapestries of the Adoration of the Magi, but it was in stained glass that they left their most notable mark on Oxford, particularly in the chapels and choir of Christ Church.

MODERN CONTROVERSIES

Throughout the 20th century, controversy regularly courted new building plans, from the "Cotswold domestic" style of Nuffield College to what was seen as the totally alien International Style of Arne Jacobsen's St Catherine's College. Worcester College's Colditz-style watchtowers overlooking Hythe Bridge Street and the city council's nautical-theme Ice Rink apparently moored by the Thames in Oxpens both seemed out of place and, in the 21st century, the dull box that is the Said Business School and the exotic luxury of the Islamic Studies centre in Marston Road have both had their vociferous detractors.

Atmospheric streets

In the end, though, more than the details of great buildings, it's the overall effect of the city that most visitors remember. There are places where one can escape the 21st century and recapture the past. New College Lane has hardly changed since 1400, cobbled Merton Street maintains a quiet medieval air and Holywell Street, built in the early 17th century to rehouse those displaced by the building of the Bodleian, seems almost untouched. The lack of traffic in these streets helps. Walk down any of them at daybreak or dusk and the magic multiplies. ❏

ABOVE: detail in Magdalen College Chapel.

Gargoyles

It's worth carrying binoculars in order to appreciate the intricacies of some of the countless carved heads that gaze down on passers-by from Oxford's ancient buildings. The carvings, whose expressions vary from joy to disgust, are a reminder of the university's medieval origins, yet many are quite modern, their faces inspired not by the piety of a Christian saint but by the lugubrious expression of some contemporary don or even the managing director of the firm that created the stone sculptures.

Although today's faces are purely ornamental, their original purpose was rigorously functional. Rainwater, channelled into them from roofs, was ejected through their mouths. This projected the water away from a building, stopping it running down the exterior walls, discolouring and decaying them. It was this "gargling" function that gave them the name gargoyles – probably after the French *gargouille* (throat). Carvings which don't have this purpose are more properly termed grotesques.

Vices and virtues

Animal-shaped waterspouts can be traced back to the ancient Egyptians and Etruscans, and the gargoyles which decorated Europe's Gothic cathedrals from the 12th century constituted a medieval bestiary.

Gradually, human heads joined those of the beasts and their creators' sense of

mischief gave them an individuality that painters of the day seldom conveyed. Because facial subtleties could not easily be seen from ground level, there was a tendency to exaggerate features to the point of caricature.

The allegorical meaning of many gargoyles is a source of endless debate. Some obviously portray vices and virtues, from lust to temperance, reminding the citizenry of the ever-present evils that tempt most mortals. But the majority of gargoyles may have been designed simply to entertain. Today's taste for horror movies and Tolkein's hobbits may once have been satisfied by the imagination that turned decorative waterspouts into works of art.

Wear and tear

Some original 13th-century carvings, such as those in Merton College's chapel and Christ Church Cathedral, have been preserved. But wind, rain and modern pollution are the enemies of outdoor carvings. The so-called Emperors' Heads in front of the Sheldonian Theatre, for example, were replaced in 1868 and then again between 1970 and 1972. The heads adorning New College are all modern.

Happily for the safety of the stone carvers, replacement grotesques are created not *in situ* but in their yards and studios. The large blocks of which the heads form part are then hoisted into position on a building. As is true of so many areas of knowledge, medieval stone-carving skills are kept alive in Oxford. ❑

PLACES

A detailed guide to the city, with the
principal sites clearly cross-referenced
by number to the maps

What, precisely, gives Oxford its special appeal? In 1856 the American writer Nathaniel Hawthorne, in his *English Note-Books*, put forward an interesting theory: "The quality of the stone has a great deal to do with the apparent antiquity. It is a stone found in the neighbourhood of Oxford, and very soon begins to crumble and decay superficially, when exposed to the weather; so that 20 years do the work of a 100, so far as appearances go. If you strike one of the old walls with a stick, a portion of it comes powdering down. The effect of this decay is very picturesque."

Despite the subsequent destructive emissions of the internal combustion engine, Oxford's walls have yet to fall down. But the city retains its allure, seldom better expressed than by another 19th-century American writer, Henry James: "I walked along, thro' the lovely Christ Church meadow, by the river side and back through the town. It was a perfect evening and in the interminable British twilight the beauty of the whole place came forth with magical power. There are no words for these colleges. As I stood last evening within the precincts of mighty Magdalen, gazed at its great serene tower and uncapped my throbbing brow in the wild dimness of its courts, I thought that the heart of me would crack with the fulness of satisfied desire."

The setting is equally magical. Oxford is not a large town and you don't need to climb far up one of the dreaming spires in order to spy the green countryside which encircles it. Beyond the town centre traffic-jams and the undistinguished suburbs beckon the Cotswolds, their showpiece villages appearing to grow out of the earth, so perfect is their relationship with the landscape. For some, Stratford-upon-Avon will be a place of essential pilgrimage. For others, the sleepy Thames-side towns will hold more attractions.

Oxford provides a convenient base for exploring this rich part of England – that is, if you can drag yourself away from the dreaming spires. As Nathaniel Hawthorne put it: "The world, surely, has not another place like Oxford; it is a despair to see such a place and ever to leave it." ❏

PRECEDING PAGES: the classic "dreaming spires"; graduation day at Queen's College.
LEFT: the Radcliffe Camera and its surroundings from the air.

Central Oxford

UNIVERSITY PARKS

SPORTS GROUND

GREAT MEADOW

Cherwell

0 — 200 m
0 — 200 yds

niversity Science Area

Pitt Rivers Museum of Ethnology

University Museum

Radcliffe Science Library

Linacre College

Psychology & Zoology Faculties

South Parks Road

Hinshelwood Rd

Sibthorp Rd

E. Abraham Rd

South Parks Road

Mansfield Road

St. Cross Road

Holywell Mill Stream

Holywell Manor

Library & Law Facility

Manor Road

Manor Place

St Cross

St Catherine's College

Rhodes House

Mansfield College

New College School

BALLIOL COLLEGE SPORTS GROUND

Parks Road

Savile Road

Wadham College

Harris Manchester College

School of Geography

Jowett Walk

ity ege

New Bodleian Library

The King's Arms

Holywell Music Room

Holywell Street

ackwell's Century ttages

Broad Street

Clarendon Building

Sheldonian Theatre

Hertford College

Bridge of Sighs

New Hertford College

Holywell Buildings

City Wall

Site of William Morris' Garage

MAGDALEN GROVE

DEER PARK

Longwall Street

Bodleian Library

College Lane

New College

Exeter College

Divinity School

Brasenose Lane

Brasenose College

Radcliffe

Radcliffe Camera Square

All Souls' College

Queens

St Peter in the East (Library)

Queen's College

Lincoln College

ered rket

All Saints'

High Street

King Edward St

Rhodes Building

University Church of St Mary the Virgin

University College

Queens Lane

St Edmund Hall

High Street

New Buildings

Magdalen College

OUP Bookshop

eum ford Boat St

Bear Lane

Orie Sq

Magpie Lane

Logic Lane

Examination Schools

Eastgate Hotel

Alfred St

Oriel College

Kybald St

Merton Street

Rose Lane

Magdalen Water

Magdalen Bridge

Headington

hrist Church College

Tom Quad

Corpus Christi College

Merton College

Deadman's Walk

James Sadler Plaque

BOTANIC GARDEN

Victoria Fountain

St Clement's St

The Plain

Cowley Rd

Cowley

Palace e's p

Bate Collection of Musical Instruments

Christ Church Cathedral

Merton Grove

MERTON FIELD

St Hilda's College

Cowley Place

Itffley Road

Floyds Row

Police Station

Broad Walk

MAGDALEN COLLEGE SCHOOL CRICKET GROUND

Boat House

Magdalen College School

CHRIST CHURCH MEADOW

Iffley

THE HUB OF THE UNIVERSITY

One area of town can be described as the heart of the university. Lying between the High Street and Broad Street, it includes the Bodleian Library, the Sheldonian Theatre and the Radcliffe Camera

A precious and rather feeble Oxford joke is sometimes told about the American tourist who stops an undergraduate in the High Street and asks to be directed to the university. At this point, those in the know are supposed to chuckle over their port for – "as every educated person is aware" – Oxford does not have a central university campus. Like Cambridge, these two ancient universities differ from others in Britain in that they constitute a federation of independent colleges.

Yet, if our American tourist had stopped a helpful student instead of a prig, he would have been directed down Broad Street to the heart of Oxford, where an impressive group of buildings might loosely be termed "the University" – in the sense that they provide central facilities for all college members.

The Emperors' Heads

Walking east down **Broad Street**, the eye is drawn to the curious set of railings that separate "the town" from the realm of ceremony and scholarship. Towering above the railings is a series of 13 outsize stone busts, the **Emperors' Heads**, or Bearded Ones ❶. They follow the curve of the apsidal end of the Sheldonian Theatre, and were put up in 1669, the year the theatre was completed.

Armless busts like these have been used to surmount gateposts since antiquity, and are called "terms", from the Latin terminus, a boundary, or "herms" if they represent Hermes, the messenger of the gods. Nobody knows what these splendid giants represent. Max Beerbohm, in his 1911 Oxford-based novel *Zuleika Dobson*, wrote that "they are, by American visitors, frequently mistaken for the Twelve Apostles" – having yet another dig at the poor, untutored tourist from

Map on page 84

LEFT: doorway to the Divinity School.
BELOW: outside the Sheldonian Theatre.

The Sheldonian Theatre.

the New World. He also calls them "the faceless Caesars", and perhaps from that developed the current nickname, the Emperors.

Faceless they were until recently; the original terms were replaced in 1868 but with such poor-quality stone that time and the weather soon reduced their features to what John Betjeman called "illustrations in a medical textbook on skin diseases". In 1970, and despite Henry Moore's objection that the eroded heads had their own awesome power, the Oxford sculptor Michael Black was commissioned to carve new heads. After completing the work in 1972, and following exhaustive research into the form of the original heads, Michael Black added his own theory, that the 13 represent the history of fashions in beards.

The Sheldonian Theatre

In any event, the Sheldonian terms make an impressive approach to the

buildings beyond, starting with the **Sheldonian Theatre ②** (open Mon–Sat 10am–12.30pm, 2–3.30pm, entrance fee; closed on Saturday afternoon on performance days and for university events). The theatre was commissioned by Gilbert Sheldon, Chancellor (or honorary head) of the university, in 1662. Sheldon chose as his architect, the young Christopher Wren, who was then 30. Wren had been appointed Professor of Astronomy the previous year and was regarded as one of the most brilliant mathematicians of his day. He had not yet, however, designed any buildings, and the Sheldonian Theatre was the first commission to launch his architectural career.

It is fashionable among art historians to describe the theatre as the work of a young amateur, but most of us would give this exuberant building, with its rich, honey-gold coloured stone, far higher praise. It was also revolutionary in

The Hub of The University

its time, for Wren rejected the popular Gothic-Jacobean style and chose instead to follow classical antecedents.

Wren modelled the Sheldonian on the antique open-air Theatre of Marcellus, in Rome. The English weather made it necessary to give it a roof, however, so Wren devised an ingenious timber structure (since replaced) that dispensed with pillars and allowed all 2,000 spectators an uninterrupted view of the proceedings. In place of the open sky, Robert Streeter was commissioned, in 1669, to paint the ceiling with a depiction of the *Triumph of Religion, Arts and Science over Envy, Hate and Malice*.

The Sheldonian was built for university ceremonials, rather than for stage drama, and is still used for this purpose, as well as for concerts and lectures. Here successful students receive their degrees and, at the "Encaenia" ceremony in June, scarlet-gowned dons meet to honour the university founders and bestow honorary degrees upon the worthy and famous (*see also pages 126–7*).

At other times of the year the theatre is open to the public and is well worth visiting for the original woodwork of the Chancellor's throne and the two Orators' pulpits – but most of all for the fine views over the heart of Oxford from the rooftop cupola.

The Clarendon Building

On the other side of the Sheldonian is the **Clarendon Building**, created to provide the first permanent home for Oxford University Press. Originally, the Press occupied odd rooms in the Sheldonian Theatre, an inconvenient arrangement.

Between 1702 and 1704 the Press published the Earl of Clarendon's account of the English Civil War, and this three-volume *History of the Great Rebellion* proved to be a bestseller. Despite the fact that some of the profits were embezzled by the university Vice-Chancellor, sales of Clarendon's work were sufficient to provide the Press with a new home next door.

The Clarendon, a rather severe classical building, was designed by

Map on page 84

The Clarendon Building.

BELOW: the degree ceremony moved in 1669 from St Mary's into the Sheldonian.

Nicholas Hawksmoor, Christopher Wren's brilliant pupil, and completed in 1715. The Earl of Clarendon himself occupies a niche on the west wall, where he gesticulates proudly at the building he paid for. Around the roofline are gracious figures, by James Thornhill, of the nine Muses (1717); seven are cast in lead but two are fibre-glass replicas, made in 1974 to replace the originals that had blown down.

The Press moved out of the Clarendon Building in 1830 and the space vacated by the compositors and printers is now filled by part of the Bodleian Library's vast collection of books.

The Bodleian Library

To the south of the Sheldonian lies the **Bodleian Library** ❸ (guided tours included in Divinity School tour, see below; entrance fee), which is entered through a small opening into Old Schools Quadrangle. Before admiring this beautiful courtyard in too much detail, first journey back in time by entering the doors behind the 17th-century bronze

statue by Le Sueur of the Earl of Pembroke (a university chancellor) and proceeding through the vestibule into the much older **Divinity School** ❹ (guided tours only of the Divinity School, Convocation House and Duke Humphrey's Library Mar–end Oct, Mon–Fri 10.30 and 11.30am, 2 and 3pm; Sat 10.30 and 11.30am).

Regarded by many as the finest interior in Oxford, work began on this central school of theology in 1426, following an appeal for funds by the university. As it was the most important of all faculties, Divinity required a suitable space, but money kept running out and the room took almost 60 years to complete.

Its crowning glory is the lierne vaulted ceiling, which was added in 1478, after the university received a gift from Thomas Kemp, the Bishop of London. Completed by local mason William Orchard, the ceiling is adorned with sculpted figures and 455 bosses carved with biblical subjects, real and mythical beasts, and the coats of arms of university benefactors.

Candidates for degrees of Bache-

As a copyright library, the Bodleian is obliged to accept a copy of every book and journal published in the UK. The result is that space for books is rapidly running out, despite the more than 80 miles (130 km) of shelving that have been installed just a few feet beneath the surface of Radcliffe Square.

BELOW:
tour in progress in the Divinity School.

Thomas Bodley

Thomas Bodley (1545–1613) spent his youth in Geneva, since as part of a Protestant family he was liable to religious persecution under the reign of Mary I. When Elizabeth I came to the throne, he returned to England, where, after studying at Oxford, he became a diplomat and was briefly an MP. On his return to Oxford as a fellow of Merton College, the now knighted Sir Thomas Bodley resolved in 1598 to take action to restore Duke Humphrey's Library, wrecked during the reign of Edward VI. He established a collection of 2,000 books, some captured during the 1596 plundering of Cadiz by the Earl of Essex, and the new library opened in 1602. In 1604 it was named the Bodleian.

lor and Doctor of Divinity were not the only people to demonstrate their dialectical skill under this glorious ceiling. It was here that the Oxford Martyrs – Latimer, Ridley and Cranmer – were cross-examined by the Papal Commissioner in 1554, then condemned as Protestant heretics.

Now it is empty, except for an iron-bound chest, with its elaborate lock mechanism, that once belonged to Thomas Bodley, the library's founder. The chest is used to collect donations towards a £10 million appeal for vital restoration work that will eventually allow books back on display in a temperature- and humidity-controlled environment. In the meantime, there is a small display of exhibits, ranging from early copies of Chaucer's *Canterbury Tales* to Victorian playbills, in the School of Natural Philosophy, on the south side of Old Schools Quad.

Duke Humphrey's Library

In around 1440, a substantial collection of manuscripts was donated to the university by Humphrey, Duke of Gloucester, the younger brother of

Henry V. The walls of the Divinity School were built up to create a second storey for **Duke Humphrey's Library** (*see opposite page for guided tours*). The library, with its magnificent beamed ceiling, was first opened to readers in 1488, but was defunct by 1550, largely as a result of neglect and the emergence of book printing (which rendered manuscripts redundant), but also due to the depredations of the King's Commissioners after the dissolution.

It was while he was a student at Magdalen College that Thomas Bodley became aware of this sad state of affairs and resolved to take action (*see panel on opposite page*). The library he founded in 1602 was soon extended with an "Arts End" and, around 1650, by the "Selden End", named after John Selden, who gave 8,000 volumes to the library. Both the "Ends" have beautiful panelled and painted ceilings.

Today visitors can see original leather-bound books dating from the 17th century, some of them turned spine inwards so that chaining them to the shelves (a common practice)

Map on page 84

The Earl of Pembroke's statue in the Old Schools Quadrangle.

BELOW: the ceiling of Duke Humphrey's Library.

BELOW: splendid surroundings for the Bodleian's books.

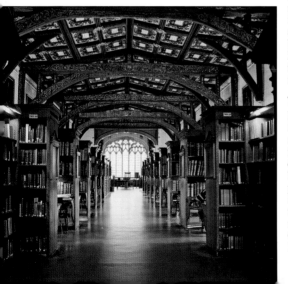

would cause less damage. Sometimes visitors are also shown the top floor of the library, with its painted frieze of 200 famous men, executed in around 1620 and only rediscovered in the 1960s.

Old Schools Quadrangle

In 1610, an agreement was made whereby the library would receive a copy of every single book registered at Stationers' Hall. Soon Bodley's collection had grown so large that a major extension was required, hence the **Old Schools Quadrangle ❺**. This magnificent piece of architecture is designed in Jacobean-Gothic style (a style that characterises many Oxford buildings of the early 17th century). The quadrangle has a wonderful serenity, and despite being built much higher than college quads it is still light and airy.

The complex was designed to provide lecture rooms on the lower floors, and library space above. Above the ground-floor doorways, painted in letters of gold, are the names of the original schools, or faculties, of the university. Note that the

Divinity School facade, covered in panel tracery, is considerably more ornate than the rest of Old Schools Quad – appropriately enough, as Divinity, or Theology, was the principal subject at Oxford until well into the 19th century and the subject for which all other studies were merely a preparation.

Three sides of the quad are regular in composition. James I was on the throne when the building was completed in 1624, and the monarch sits in a niche between allegorical figures representing Fame and the University, in the gate-tower at the east end. This splendidly carved work is called the **Tower of the Five Orders** because it is ornamented with columns and capitals of each of the five orders of classical architecture – Doric, Tuscan, Ionic, Corinthian and Composite – in ascending order.

You will find many more heads (binoculars are essential to appreciate them fully) carved in stone all around the battlement line of Old Schools Quad – grotesques and demons, angels and men, all convincingly medieval in appearance but, in fact, the inspired work of masons who restored these buildings in the 1950s. At ground-floor level as you pass through the passageway between the Schools of Music and Natural Philosophy, look for the portraits of two recent librarians, carved into the stone.

The Radcliffe Camera

Emerging to the south of the Old Schools Quadrangle, the splendid sight of **Radcliffe Camera ❻** rising from a perfect green lawn meets the eye. "Camera" simply means chamber, and John Radcliffe was the physician who, despite his renowned ill temper, made a huge fortune by treating the wealthy – including the monarch, William III. Radcliffe Camera was built after his death in 1714 to house a library devoted to the sciences – just one of the Oxford projects that was funded from his estate.

The gracious round form of the Camera was suggested by Nicholas Hawksmoor, but it was another great 18th-century architect, James Gibbs, who was asked to produce the detailed designs.

The building was completed in 1748 and absorbed as a reading room of the Bodleian in 1860. The Radcliffe Camera was just part of a grand 18th-century scheme to open up this part of the city as a public square, to replace the existing jumble of medieval houses.

All Souls' College

Hawksmoor did, eventually, get his fair share of Oxford commissions, including the great North Quad of **All Souls' College ❼** (open Mon–Fri 2–4pm; tel: 01865 279379; parties of more than six need permission from the Bursar; free), to the left (east) of Radcliffe Camera.

This college, founded in 1438, is unique: it does not admit graduate or undergraduate students. Instead, it retains the medieval tradition of restricting membership to "fellows". There are several means of entry: distinguished scholars from all over the world may be elected as visiting fellows, while others sit a highly competitive examination. The system is, in theory, designed to provide facilities for the brightest and best minds to pursue their research, but it has not always been so, and in the 16th century fellowships were bought and sold, and the college was notorious for the drunkenness and corruption of its members.

A century or so later, the winds of reform swept through the college and, as if in a symbolic break with the past, the medieval cloister was cleared away, and new accommodation planned. Then, in 1710, before the work began, Christopher Codrington, a fellow and Governor of the Leeward Islands, died, leaving much of his sugar wealth to the college, as well as a large collection of books. Thus the building plans were changed, and Hawksmoor designed the grand library block and the imposing twin towers of the east side of the North Quad.

Map on page 84

The Radcliffe Camera.

BELOW:
All Souls' College, open to Fellows only.

TIP

The Codrington Library is strictly a reference library. Researchers wishing to use material from the Early and Special Collections must apply in writing at least a week in advance. Forms may be downloaded from www.all-souls.ox.ac.uk/library/

RIGHT:
Brasenose College.

The **Codrington Library** (viewing times same as All Souls' College) is an ingenious piece of work; outside it is all Gothic, while the interior is fully classical – even the windows are Venetian within but with lancets and tracery on the outside. The sundial on the library wall, moved from the chapel, is renowned for its accuracy; Christopher Wren is reputed to be the designer.

The chapel is essentially 15th-century, with its original hammerbeam roof carved with gilded angels and misericords, which include depictions of a mermaid and a man playing the bagpipes. The floor-to-ceiling reredos is a *tour de force*, although the statues are all replacements, installed in 1870, for those smashed by Puritan iconoclasts. The surviving 15th-century niches were once brightly painted and even now a few have traces of the original pigment.

Brasenose College

At the opposite (west) side of the square is **Brasenose College** ❽ (open daily 10–11.30am, 2–4.30pm; tel: 01865 277830; entrance fee for groups only). Passing through the entrance, you reach the Old Quad with its Tudor buildings, completed shortly after the foundation; the third storey, with its fine dormer windows, was added in the early 17th century. The sundial on the right-hand side was painted in 1719.

The dining hall, on the left side, is usually open, so that the original brazen nose *(see panel below)* can be viewed. First mentioned in a document of 1279, the Romanesque feline head and ring could have been made as early as the 12th century.

A passageway in the southeastern corner leads into Chapel Quad, with its delightful library, carved with a frieze of exuberant swags, and lit below by pairs of oval windows. This work dates to the mid-17th century and is surprisingly innovative for its date, foreshadowing the 18th century's Baroque style.

The chapel is of the same date and mixes Gothic with classical motifs. The unusual fan-vaulted and painted roof is made of plaster. In the antechapel is a bronze plaque with a Greek inscription celebrating Walter

How Brasenose got its name

The college is named after the "brazen nose", a bronze door knocker that once hung on the gates of Brasenose Hall. Anyone fleeing from the law could claim sanctuary within the Hall if they could get their hands firmly round the ring of the knocker.

Perhaps because of the protective powers of the brazen nose, a group of students stole the ring in the 1330s and took it with them to Stamford where they intended to establish a rival university. Edward II refused to sanction the breakaway institution, but while some students settled in Cambridge, others returned to Oxford and the brazen nose got left behind. Here it remained, serving as a door knocker, until Brasenose House in Stamford came on the market in 1890. Even then, the college had to buy the whole house to secure the return of the symbolic piece of bronze – now hung behind the High Table in the dining hall.

Meanwhile, a new knocker was commissioned for Brasenose, on the occasion of its official foundation as a college, as distinct from the pre-existing academic hall, in 1509. Shaped like a human head, this is now fixed at the apex of the main gate of the college.

Pater (died 1894), the writer and aesthete. He is portrayed at the centre of a tree whose other branches bear portrait medallions of Plato, Dante, Leonardo da Vinci and Michaelangelo. The implication that Pater deserved to stand alongside these great artists reminds us that his precious and overblown style was once deemed the epitome of fine writing.

As you turn to leave the college, you realise what a splendid view the students and fellows enjoy, being so close to Radcliffe Square. The huge dome of the Radcliffe Camera looms above the entrance tower and the spire of St Mary's church to the right.

St Mary the Virgin

Returning to Radcliffe Square, the huge University Church of **St Mary the Virgin ❾** fronts on to the High Street. In its grandeur it rivals many cathedrals and can be regarded as the original hub of the university, for it was here in the 13th century that the first university meetings and ceremonies were held, and all the administrative documents kept.

Before entering via its north door, you'll see the sign to the Vaults & Garden **Coffee House**. There can be few cafés with such a history, for it occupies the space of the former Convocation House, an annex built in 1320 specifically to house the university governing body, which continued to meet here until 1534 when the administration moved to Convocation House at the Divinity School.

A library was installed above it, but this was later replaced by Duke Humphrey's Library. The café serves wholesome soups, sandwiches and cakes, and the garden, sheltered by shrubs, is delightful in summer.

Now, instead of disputatious students sharpening their wits in learned debate, the church is often full of visitors queuing to climb the 188-ft (62-metre) spire-topped **Tower**, which dates to the late 13th and early 14th centuries (open daily 9am–5pm; July–Sept 9am–7pm; entrance fee). You need to be fit: there are 127 steps and the last few form a narrow spiral staircase.

The gangway at the base of the spire offers a magnificent view, revealing not only the layout of the

Map on page 84

St Mary the Virgin.

LEFT: Brasenose's Old Quad with sundial.
BELOW: the nave of St Mary the Virgin.

Map on page 84

A gargoyle on St Mary's Church.

BELOW:
picknickers at St Mary
the Virgin church.

city and many of the colleges, but just how much green space there is in the heart of Oxford.

The rest of the church was rebuilt in Perpendicular style in the early 16th century and is really rather dull, except for the eccentric south porch at the High Street side, added in 1637 and designed by Nicholas Stone. Fat barley-sugar columns support the curvaceous pediment and angels surround the central niche containing a statue of the Virgin and Child. Perhaps the Virgin's rather startled look is a legacy of the English Civil War, for her head was shot off by a soldier in 1642 – but replaced 20 years later.

Inside the church, the pillar opposite the pulpit in the north side of the nave has been cut away; this was done to build a platform for the final trial of Thomas Cranmer, Archbishop of Canterbury, in 1556. His fellow martyrs, Nicholas Ridley, Bishop of London, and Hugh Latimer, Bishop of Worcester, had both been executed at the stake the previous year for their support of the Protestant Reformation. Cranmer, however, was given leave to appeal against his sentence, and signed several statements recanting his earlier beliefs.

Burnt at the stake

This was not sufficient for his accusers, the Pope's commissioners and the zealous supporters of the Catholic Queen Mary. Cranmer was brought to St Mary's to make a public statement of his errors; but he refused to do so, and instead retracted his former recantations. Like Ridley and Latimer before him, having been dragged from St Mary's Church he was burned at the stake in Broad Street (he was imprisoned first at Bocardo Prison, by the church of St Michael at the North Gate, and brought to St Mary's for the final verdict).

Return along Catte Street, looking back to admire Radcliffe Square. The view is at its most splendid from opposite the Bridge of Sighs (*see page 139*). The gateway to the Old Schools Quadrangle, the dome of the Radcliffe Camera and the spire of St Mary's create one of the finest urban panoramas in Europe. ❏

The Oxford Movement

In 1833 John Keble preached a famous sermon in St Mary Le Virgin, leading to the foundation of the Oxford Movement. John Henry Newman, then Vicar of St Mary's and a leading supporter of the Movement, brought down a storm of indignation for his increasingly pro-Catholic views; his sillier supporters affected an ascetic appearance, fasted on toast and water and smoked Spanish (Catholic) cigars – while some colleges altered the times of compulsory chapel services to keep students away from Newman's sermons. In the end, he resigned, became a Catholic and ended up a Cardinal. To this day Oxford remains a centre of High Church Anglo-Catholicism.

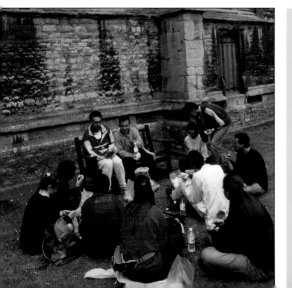

They Studied Here

Oxford has been a centre of teaching since the 12th century, and part of the fun of exploring the city lies in knowing that so many of the world's most illustrious people have walked the same streets.

Tony Blair

Prime Ministers

Two dozen British prime ministers have been educated at Oxford. In recent times they have included Clement Attlee, Sir Anthony Eden, Harold Macmillan, Sir Alec Douglas-Home, Harold Wilson, Edward Heath, Margaret Thatcher and Tony Blair.

Writers

John Ruskin (1819–1900), who was at Christ Church until 1836, became a renowned art critic and author. The poet Percy Bysshe Shelley (1792–1822) was sent down from Oxford for his pamphlet *The Necessity of Atheism*. Other literary luminaries include the lexicographer Dr Samuel Johnson (Pembroke 1728); Oscar Wilde (Magdalen 1874); Robert Browning (1812–89), who attended Balliol; and Lewis Carroll (Charles Dodgson), a mathematical don at Christ Church and author of *Alice in Wonderland*. More recent names include J.R.R. Tolkien,

W.H. Auden, Robert Graves, Graham Greene, Evelyn Waugh and T.S. Eliot.

Philosophers

These include Thomas Hobbes (Magdalen Hall, 1603), who published *The Leviathan* in 1651; John Locke (Christ Church, c. 1654) and Jeremy Bentham (Queen's, 1760).

Scientists

Roger Bacon first studied arts at Oxford in 1231, then devoted himself to experimental science, especially alchemy and optics. Founder of English philosophy, he became a Franciscan friar in 1257. Robert Boyle (in Oxford 1654–68) with Robert Hooke (1635–1708) laid the foundation for chemistry and physics. The Astronomer Royal, Edmund Halley, (1656–1742) was at Queen's, 1673. He was the first to predict the return of a comet and his meteorological observations led to his publication of the first map of the winds of the globe (1686).

The Oxford scientists Howard Walter Florey and E.B. Chain shared the Nobel Prize with Alexander Fleming for the clinical development of penicillin. The most widely used antibiotic today, cephalosporin, was discovered in 1955 by Edward Abraham, working in a University laboratory.

Oscar Wilde

Men of Religion

The poet John Donne (1572–1631), later Dean of St Paul's Cathedral, attended Hart Hall. John Wesley (1703–91), the founder of Methodism, was at Christ Church. John Henry Newman (1801–90), best remembered for his *Apologia pro Vita Sua*, tracing the development of his religious thought, graduated from Trinity in 1816.

Indira Gandhi

Women Graduates

Well-known women graduates are mostly writers or politicians: Dorothy Sayers (Somerville, 1920), Indira Gandhi, Dame Iris Murdoch (both Somerville, 1938), and Benazir Bhutto (Lady Margaret Hall, 1973).

Musicians

Famous musicians from Christ Church are Sir William Walton and Sir Adrian Boult. Sir Thomas Beecham was at Wadham.

Young Students

Some precocious students just couldn't wait to attend Oxford. The historian Edward Gibbon (Magdalen) matriculated at 14 after staying up only a year and the philosopher Jeremy Bentham (Queen's) when he was only 12. Ruth Lawrence, born in 1971, came up to Oxford when she was nine and matriculated with First-Class Honours in mathematics at 12. ❏

THE HIGH

High Street, known as "The High", has a grace and
elegance unmatched elsewhere in the city,
inspiring Nikolaus Pevsner to describe it as
"one of the world's greatest streets"

High Street is different from other streets in central Oxford in that it is curved. This is because the layout of the original Saxon town was out of alignment with the crossing point of the River Cherwell to the east, at the site of Magdalen Bridge. So beyond the original east gate (where St Mary the Virgin Church now stands) the road, then nothing more than a track, began a gentle curve down to the river. Over the centuries, not only colleges but also inns and shops were built, resulting in the charming street we see today.

History in the making

The High Street has always been busy, with local and long-distance traffic. In the 18th and 19th centuries, the coach-and-four to London departed with ever-increasing rapidity from coaching inns such as the Angel and the Mitre. Since the car arrived, there have been attempts to limit the numbers of vehicles, including a radical (but abandoned) scheme to construct a link road from St Ebbe's across Christ Church Meadow. In 1999, the most radical shake-up to Oxford's transport scheme in decades closed the western end of the High to Longwall Street to all traffic except delivery vans and buses.

The Carfax end is the commercial end, mostly taken up by shops and the facade of the Covered Market (*see page 123*). But there are interesting details worth examining. Starting on the south side, at No. 137, is Savory's fragrant pipe and tobacco shop, in a medieval building that was once the Fox Inn. Also take a look at the sign above the silversmiths at **No. 131**, a white dog with a giant watch in its mouth. Just here a small alley, one of many that delineated the original medieval plots along this part of the street, leads

Map
on page
96

LEFT:
the High Street, not far
from the countryside.
BELOW:
detail from J.M.W.
Turner's portrait of
High Street.

down to the Chequers Inn, a tavern dating from the 15th century with many interesting features. The next alley along is signposted to the Chiang Mai Kitchen, a Thai restaurant housed in the beautiful **Kemp Hall** . Built by an Oxford alderman in 1637, this is a fine example of the numerous timber-framed houses that sprang up all over Oxford during the great rebuilding of the city in the 16th and 17th centuries. The timber door with its projecting canopy is original, as are many of the windows; the interior is also very well preserved.

Kemp Hall.

Back on the High Street, the next building of interest is **No. 126**. With its elegantly curved windows and fine proportions, this is the best preserved example of a 17th-century facade in Oxford. But the building itself actually dates back a lot further, for it is known to have been owned by a bell founder before being taken over by St Frideswide's Abbey in 1350. This is the story of many of the buildings along the High Street – medieval in origin but given new facades later.

The Mitre

Cross the road at the traffic lights to arrive at the **Mitre** ❷, now housing a restaurant and tearoom but once a popular student inn. It was built in about 1600 over a 13th-century vault, which sadly can no longer be visited. Nevertheless, the Mitre remains full of history, enlivened by anecdotes of ale-supping clergy.

The German clergyman Pastor Moritz relates in his *Travels in England* (1795) that he was taken there by a companion and found it full of convivial parsons debating whether or not a passage in the *Book of Judges* ("wine cheereth God and man") meant literally that God was a wine tippler. A sign in the lobby recalls the Mitre's role as a coaching inn.

The Mitre stands on the corner of Turl Street (*see page 134*), and on

The High

Map on page 96

the opposite corner stands the former **All Saints' Church ❸**, now used as a library by Lincoln College. The splendid tower was rebuilt after the original tower collapsed in 1700, partly to the designs of Nicholas Hawksmoor. Beyond this is the High Street frontage to Brasenose College (*see page 90*), which, despite looking positively medieval, was built only in the latter part of the 19th and early 20th centuries.

On the south side is a fine run of buildings with 18th-century facades. The Regency bow-fronted shop window of Hall Bros, University Tailors is used to display silk-lined academic gowns and clothing embroidered with multi-coloured college crests. **No. 117/118** has a fine Art-Nouveau shop window, while next door at No. 116 are the premises of the **Oxford University Press Bookshop ❹** (open Mon–Sat 9am–6pm), which sells only the books that the Press publishes. Further down, beyond King Edward Street, **Nos. 106** and **107** (The University of Oxford Shop and A-Plan Insurance) are particularly interesting. Together they were originally **Tackley's Inn**, built in 1320 and subsequently rented out for use as an academic hall. A-Plan may allow you through to the back of their premises to see the 16th-century roof structure of the hall as well as a large medieval window. The cellar is regarded as the best medieval cellar in Oxford.

The Rhodes Building

On the other side of Oriel Street, opposite the University Church of St Mary the Virgin (*see page 91*), is the **Rhodes Building ❺** of Oriel College, built in 1910 from funds bequeathed by Cecil Rhodes, the South African statesman who made a fortune in Southern Africa after completing his education at Oriel and ultimately gave his name to Rhodesia (now Zimbabwe). Rhodes also endowed Rhodes Scholarships at Oxford, one of the most notable beneficiaries being Bill Clinton.

Continue along the south side, cross Magpie Lane past the former Barclays Bank buildings, now the Old Bank Hotel and Quod restaurant. Opposite is All Souls' College

Cecil Rhodes gazes down from a building named after him.

BELOW: the Rhodes Building.

(*see page 89*). Dating from the 14th century, this is the oldest surviving part of the college, though it was refaced in the 19th century. A line of grotesque sculptures runs beneath the parapet.

University College

Still on the south side, we now come to the long frontage of **University College ➏** (closed except by special arrangement). The claim that "Univ" was founded by King Alfred was invented by medieval lawyers, but it did not stop the college celebrating its millennium in 1874. Even without this fiction, Univ is respectably ancient: William of Durham, who had fled from Paris after a row between the kings of France and England, left funds for its foundation in 1249, and on this basis it can claim to be the oldest college. None of the original buildings remain, however, the college having been rebuilt from substantial benefactions in the 17th century in the now familiar Oxford Jacobean-Gothic style.

The range facing the High is in two parts, firstly the **Front Quad**

One of those quaint old University College traditions involved the rugby team invading the enclosure housing Percy Bysshe Shelley's naked statue and painting the poet's penis blue. This was not thought to have any political significance.

RIGHT:
Shelley's Monument in University College.

(with main entrance), completed in the 1670s, and beyond the **Radcliffe Quad**, almost an exact copy completed 40 years later. The gate towers contain, respectively, the statues of Queen Anne (which replaced a statue of King Alfred in 1700) and Queen Mary. On the inner face of the front quad is a statue of James II, wearing a toga, one of only two statues in England of this unpopular Catholic king. It was erected in 1676 by the then Master, Obadiah Walker, who supported the monarch's religious views.

Shelley's Monument

Before reaching the main range, you may have noticed a small dome peeping above the wall. This covers the **memorial to Percy Bysshe Shelley**. Shelley spent less than six months as an undergraduate at Univ, having been expelled in 1811 for his joint authorship of a pamphlet on *The Necessity of Atheism*. Some 80 years later, in 1894, Lady Shelley presented the monument to the college. Designed by Edward Onslow Ford, it was intended for the poet's

Transport on The High

Oxford's High Street was once described by the eminent architectural historian Nikolaus Pevsner as "one of the world's greatest streets". It has, however, had a protracted battle with traffic since the advent of the motor car.

Pictures from the 19th century depict a broad, elegant and largely empty thoroughfare, but archive photos from the 1950s onwards show traffic jams. The street has always been an important artery. In the age of horse-drawn transport, the High was the site of several important coaching inns, notably the Mitre, the Eastgate and the long-disappeared Angel Inn. But cars and buses brought pollution and congestion, and several schemes, including a tram system, were proposed to counter the motor car.

The 1999 Oxford Transport Strategy finally banned private cars from the High for large parts of the day, allowing buses, taxis and, of course, bicycles to continue to use the street. Local traders complained loudly that the ban had a negative impact on their business, but the City Council insisted that a traffic-free High Street (and Cornmarket) would attract more rather than fewer shoppers.

PERCY BYSSHE SHELLEY.
BORN AUG 4. 1792.
DIED JULY 8. 1822.

grave, in the English Cemetery in Rome, but was found to be too large. The life-sized sculpture of the naked, drowned poet (he perished off Livorno in 1822), supported by winged lions and the Muse of Poetry, is shockingly pathetic. It can be reached via a passageway in the northwest corner of the Front Quad.

Another attraction of the college is the **Chapel**. Although refurbished by Sir George Gilbert Scott in 1862, it still retains its original, finely detailed stained glass, designed by the German artist Abraham von Linge, his last known work and full of exotic details. The ante-chapel contains fine monuments by Flaxman, including that of Sir William Jones (died 1794), judge in the Calcutta High Court, who is shown compiling his digest of Hindu law.

On the north side of the High, directly opposite the gatehouse of University College's front quad, stands a lone **sycamore tree** , whose presence endows the High Street with a rural flavour. As the only landmark that can be seen from both ends, it has long been regarded

as Oxford's most significant tree and has even been described as one of the most important trees in Europe.

Queen's College

To the right of the tree runs the beautiful baroque facade of **Queen's College** ❽ (access only with an official guided tour booked at the Oxford Information Centre; tel: 01865 726871; entrance fee). Facade is perhaps the wrong term, for the High Street front is no more than a screen, with a handsome domed gatehouse, containing a statue of Queen Caroline. All this work was once attributed to Nicholas Hawksmoor, but is now thought to be by the local Oxford mason William Townesend, and was completed around 1735.

Queen Caroline occupies pride of place because she donated substantial funds to the 18th-century rebuilding of the college, which swept away all the original buildings. The college is, however, named after Queen Philippa, wife of Edward III, whose chaplain, Robert of Eglesfield, founded it in 1340. Queen's still marks the memory of its founder

Map on page 96

Queen Caroline under her dome in the Queen's College.

BELOW:
University College.

Frank Cooper's marmalade remains a breakfast favourite.

BELOW:
Queen's College.

with an ancient ceremony whereby dinner guests are presented with a needle and thread – the French for which (*aiguilles et fils*) is a pun on Eglesfeld's name. The more famous Boar's Head Feast, celebrated in December, commemorates a Queen's student who is said to have killed a wild boar by thrusting a copy of Aristotle's works down its throat.

As one passes through the centre of the Front Quad, the north range ahead has the hall on the left and the chapel on the right. The latter, consecrated in 1719, reused the colourful stained-glass windows from the old chapel, designed by Abraham van Linge in 1636, and is notable for the bold and exotic foliage framing the biblical scenes.

Beyond lies the Back Quad, with its splendid library of 1696 on the left, lit by a great expanse of glass, through which the stucco frieze and ornate bookcases may just be glimpsed. A narrow passage to the left of the library passes between high walls into a tiny rose garden known, for reasons now forgotten, as "the Nun's Garden".

Food, glorious food

Opposite Queen's, connecting the High with Merton Street, is **Logic Lane**, so called because there used to be a school of logicians at the High Street end. Cross Logic Lane and continue along the south side of the High. **No. 84**, with its elegant windows and Corinthian columns, was once the grocery shop belonging to Frank Cooper. It was here, in 1874, that Cooper began selling jars of surplus marmalade produced by his wife, Sarah Jane, from an old family recipe on her kitchen range. It proved so popular that a factory had to be constructed on Park End Street. Although the firm sold out and moved in 1974, the marmalade is still manufactured under the original label.

The premises now house the **Grand Café ❾**, a friendly, Edwardian-style café, with high ceiling, marble, mosaics and chandeliers.

Next door, at **No. 83**, are offices of the Oxford Bus Company, worth mentioning only on account of the delightful Venetian window on the first floor.

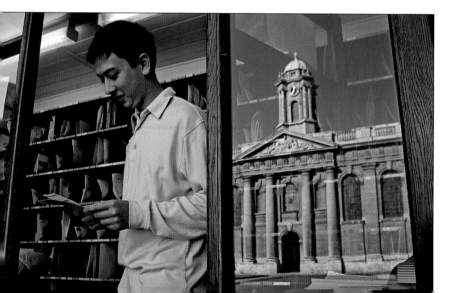

The Examination Schools

Next comes the massive block of the **Examination Schools** , built on the site of the Angel, one of Oxford's most important coaching inns (in 1831 it was operating 11 daily coach services to London and 13 others to all parts of the country). Introduced only in the late 18th century, the first written examinations were held in the Divinity School, before moving to the various rooms of the Old Schools Quadrangle. But by the second half of the 19th century a new, purpose-built edifice was required. This was built in 1882 to replace the Old Schools, now inadequate to accommodate all the students attending lectures and sitting examinations.

The building was designed by T. G. Jackson in neo-Jacobean style with classical and Gothic elements, and the result, especially the High Street facade, has sometimes been described as heavy-handed – designed, perhaps, to intimidate the hapless exam candidates. Students can be seen entering and leaving the building in the main exam month of June, all dressed in "sub-fusc" garb without which they are not allowed to sit their exam. The end of the examination ordeal can be a messy affair as students celebrate with champagne, flour bombs and streamers.

The High Street facade of the Examination Schools building is impressive, but the most beautiful side of the building, with its fine courtyard, overlooks **Merton Street** around the corner. On the same corner stands the **Eastgate Hotel** . It was at this point, in the middle of the street, that the east gate through the medieval town wall stood until its demolition at the hands of the Paving Commission in 1772.

There has been an inn on this site since 1605, but the present hotel was built in 1899 in the style of a 17th-century town house.

Opposite, at No. 48, is a shoe shop which was once the bicycle repair shop of William Morris. Continue as far as the Longwall Street traffic lights, where you cross the road and proceed towards Magdalen College, whose famous tower dominates the eastern end of the High Street.

Map on page 96

The Eastgate Hotel once served as a major coaching inn.

BELOW:
Examination Schools, the students' least favourite building.

Magdalen College

Magdalen College ⑫ (pronounced *maudlin*) (open daily 2–5pm; tel: 01865 276000; entrance fee) was founded in 1458 by William Waynflete, Bishop of Winchester and Lord Chancellor of England under King Henry VI. It was on the site of the Hospital of St John the Baptist, some of whose buildings still survive as part of the college's High Street range. Built outside the city walls, Magdalen had lots of space in which to expand, and its grounds encompass large areas of meadow, bounded in the east by the River Cherwell.

Completed in 1505, the **Bell Tower** is famous for the Latin grace sung from the top by the choristers every May Morning. The tradition probably dates back to the tower's inauguration in 1505. Nobody is certain whether it has continued in unbroken succession since that date, but the ceremony was in full swing in the 18th century, when spectators were pelted with eggs by undergraduates from the tower. Today, when the Magdalen College School choristers sing from the top of the tower at 6am on 1 May, the ceremony initiates a morning of revelries: bells ring out, Morris men dance, and students take their lovers off by punt for champagne breakfasts along the banks of the River Cherwell.

During the Civil War, the tower was used as a vantage post by the Royalist forces who had established themselves in the city after the Battle of Edgehill in 1642. But while Magdalen, along with the rest of the university, lent its full support to Charles I, it did not support the unpopular James II, who tried to make the college a Catholic seminary. In 1687 James briefly had his own man (Bishop Parker) installed as college president and had Mass, run by Jesuits, set up in the chapel.

With the advance of the Protestant William of Orange, however, James promptly did a U-turn and had the original Fellows reinstated on 25 October 1688, an event still celebrated in Magdalen as Restoration Day. But it was too late for the unfortunate king, who soon lost his crown and spent the rest of his life in exile in France.

Magdalen's crest.

BELOW:
Magdalen College
and its Bell Tower.

Enter the college via the porter's lodge on High Street and take the diagonal path across **St John's Quadrangle**. To the right, you enter the low **Muniment Tower** of 1485, which shelters the west doorway to the **Chapel**, carved with figures of St John, Edward VI, Mary Magdalene, St Swithun and William of Waynflete. Originally built in 1480, the chapel was completely redesigned in the early 19th century. But with its stone vaulting and ornamental screens, it is still worth seeing, especially by candlelight at choral evensong. The ante-chapel contains some medieval stalls with carved misericords, a good selection of monuments, including that of the founder's father, Richard Patten (died 1450), and – the most interesting feature – sepia stained-glass windows.

The passageway leads through to the delightful **Cloister Quadrangle**, the 15th-century core of the college. With its vaulted passage, the quad still looks very ancient, though the north and east wings had to be rebuilt in the early 19th century after attempts were made to have the

Cloisters cleared to make way for the New Buildings (*see below*). The allegorical figures on the buttresses, called "hieroglyphicals", were added in 1508. One is free to speculate what they represent, for nobody really knows – though in the 1670s, Dr William Reeks produced a 60-page treatise arguing that they symbolised the virtues (sobriety and temperance) and vices (gluttony, lust and pride) of academic life.

The grotesques of the cloister walls include more dark, mysterious subjects, and several that are explicitly erotic – surprisingly, since most are the work of Victorian carvers.

New Buildings

A narrow passageway in the north range of the cloister debouches into a vast expanse of green lawns, with the stately colonnaded **New Buildings** straight ahead. Completed in 1733, this was intended to be part of a huge neoclassical quadrangle. Fortunately, the money ran out and only one range was ever built.

Opposite the New Buildings turn along the path to the left, where the

Map on page 96

Sepia stained-glass window in the chapel.

BELOW:
choristers walk past Magdalen on their way to the May morning celebrations.

massive **plane tree**, planted in 1801, is a direct descendant of a hybrid that was developed by Jacob Bobart in the Botanic Garden (*see page 116*). It is worth following this path a short way in order to look back, southwards, over the fine jumble of towers, pinnacles and Cotswold-tiled roofs of the college – Oxford's dreaming spires in miniature.

Magdalen Grove

To the north, beyond the fence, is **Magdalen Grove**, winter home of the college herd of fallow deer. The grove once looked considerably more leafy than it does at present. Massive elm trees, planted in around 1689, unfortunately succumbed to disease and were felled in 1978. The deer have been here since the early 18th century, when they were introduced to supply the college with venison. Even today surplus animals are occasionally culled and served up in the hall.

In the other direction, through the wrought-iron gates, is a bridge over a branch of the Cherwell River. Here, if you watch on a sunny day, you are quite likely to see brown trout, or even larger fish, such as perch or pike, basking in the clear, warm waters below, ready to dart back into the shadows created by the overhanging chestnut tree branches beyond if they are disturbed.

Addison's Walk

Across the bridge the narrow path turns left to follow a raised bank beside the Cherwell, with Long Meadow, summer grazing home for the Magdalen deer, to the right. The raised causeway, almost completely enclosed by a tunnel of tree foliage, was partly created out of the remains of Civil War defensive embankments. It is known as **Addison's Walk** ❸, after Joseph Addison (1672–1719), poet and *Spectator* essayist, whose rooms in Magdalen College overlooked these meadows.

The walk was not laid out in its present form, nor named after Addison, until the 19th century, but the name is appropriate since Addison was a pioneer of naturalistic landscape design, arguing in his *Spectator* essays that the works of nature

Joseph Addison, who gave his name to a walkway.

RIGHT: Magdalen Grove's deer.

Oscar Wilde at Oxford

Perhaps Magdalen College's most flamboyant old boy was Oscar Fingal O'Flahertie Wills Wilde, who was a student here between 1874 and 1878, causing controversy in almost everything he did. Already armed with a degree from Dublin, Wilde was a brilliant and precocious Classics scholar who effortlessly won a double First as well as the prestigious Newdigate Prize for poetry.

The future playwright relished his time at Oxford, likening it to Athens, where "the realities of sordid life were kept at a distance". At first, he was a keen sportsman, but gradually he adopted a more mannered, aesthetic posture, pretending to be lazy but secretly working hard throughout the night. Legend has it that he provocatively asked for extra paper after only one hour of a three-hour finals exam and then walked out half an hour before the end – only to be awarded the highest marks in the entire year.

But it was Oxford, too, that contributed to his downfall, as he met Lord Alfred Douglas ("Bosie") on a visit to the city. Their openly homosexual relationship led to his imprisonment in Reading Jail and his eventual exile and early death in Paris in 1900.

Map on page 96

are often superior to the artificial creations of man.

Ironically, the verdant beauty of the walk was almost changed for ever by one of Addison's later followers. Humphry Repton proposed, in 1801, to dam the Cherwell and create an artificial lake out of the meadows. We must be thankful that the plan was not executed, for the meadows are now famous for a far more beautiful sight than a blank sheet of water: in late April, or early May, the grass is filled with the graceful nodding flower heads of purple and white snake's head fritillaries, one of the largest colonies of these rare wild flowers in Britain. Almost picked to extinction in the 19th century, the Magdalen fritillaries have been carefully protected since 1908.

Fellows' Garden

At the northern end of Addison's Walk, there are views across to the modern buildings of St Catherine's College (not accessible from this point). The path turns to the right and, at the eastern angle, a bridge over the Cherwell provides access to Magdalen's **Fellows' Garden**. This delightfully secluded area demonstrates just how much space the college has at its disposal. It is particularly delightful in spring when the ornamental trees are in flower and the grass is covered in daffodils and anemones. To complete the circuit, return to the bridge and turn left, following the riverbank to Magdalen Bridge and right to return to the college grounds.

Go back to the entrance via the cloisters and then the **Chaplain's Quadrangle**. To the left the Bell Tower soars heavenwards and to its right is the oldest bit of the college, which was part of the 13th-century hospital incorporated into the High Street range.

Passing from the Chaplain's Quadrangle into St John's Quadrangle, you'll notice on the left wall an outside **pulpit**, from where a service is conducted once a year on the Feast of St John the Baptist (24 June), a tradition that dates back to the earliest days of the college.

Exit Magdalen, and on the oppo-

The fallow deer grazing around Addison's Walk are part of a careful management programme, introduced to the meadows to keep down the buttercups that threatened to crowd out the vulnerable fritillaries.

BELOW: Addison's Walk.

Map on page 96

Victoria Fountain on the Plain.

BELOW: punts by Magdalen Bridge.

site side of the street you'll see the main entrance to the Botanic Garden (*see page 116*).

Continue along the High to **Magdalen Bridge**. The first bridge to cross the Cherwell at this point was a timber construction built in 1004. It was replaced by a stone-built structure in the 16th century, but this was demolished during the Civil War in the 1640s and replaced with a drawbridge. Today's bridge dates from 1772. It has since been widened a couple of times to cope with the ever-increasing volume of traffic.

Victoria Fountain

At the other side is the triangular junction known as **The Plain** ⓮. This busy junction marks the divergence of St Clement's, Cowley and Iffley roads, fanning out to the suburbs of Oxford. Isolated in the island in the centre stands the **Victoria Fountain**, which was originally used as a drinking trough for horses. It was unfortunately constructed two years too late to commemorate Queen Victoria's Diamond Jubilee in 1897. Until its destruction at the

hands of the Paving Commission in 1772, the church of St Clements had stood on this site.

Off to the right, in Cowley Place, is the **Magdalen College School**, originally founded in 1480 but relocated to this new site in 1894.

St Hilda's

A bit further down is **St Hilda's College** ⓯ (open daily 2–5pm; tel: 01865 276884; free), founded in 1893 but occupying a fine 18th-century house with fine views of the Cherwell and Christ Church Meadow.

St Hilda's, Oxford's last all-woman college, voted in 2006 to admit men. Its founder was the formidable principal of Cheltenham Ladies' College, Dorothea Beale, and she named the new institution after the 7th-century Abbess of Whitby, who had been the first great educator of women in England.

Miss Beale stated, in documents relating to the aims of the college, that "I want none to go for the sake of a pleasant life", and the strict chaperonage system, along with measures such as iron grilles fitted on the hall windows, were all designed to prevent encounters between ladies at the college and members of the opposite sex.

A contemporary wit penned a few immortal lines of protest on behalf of Miss Beale's charges: *Miss Buss and Miss Beale/Cupid's darts do not feel./How different from us/Miss Beale and Miss Buss.*

St Hilda's was given an exciting new dimension in 1995 when the purpose-built Jacqueline du Pré Music Building opened after a successful £1 million appeal in memory of the late cellist. Now one of Oxford's premier music venues, the complex hosts a wide variety of events and is famed for its state-of-the-art acoustics.

Walk across Magdalen Bridge for a superb view of the High Street. ❏

RESTAURANTS, PUBS & CAFÉS

Restaurants

Chiang Mai Kitchen
130a High Street. Tel 01865
202233. Open: daily. ££
www.chiangmaikitchen.co.uk
Stylish and authentic
Thai cuisine served in a
beautifully preserved
Tudor building. Extensive
vegetarian options are
on offer, and the staff
are extremely helpful.

Café Zouk
135 High Street. tel 01865
251600. Open: daily. ££
www.cafezouk.co.uk
A cut above the usual
Tandoori place, this cen-
trally located and taste-
fully decorated place
aims to recreate the
spicy flavours of the
Mughal dynasty.

Quod Restaurant & Bar
92-94 High Street. Tel
01865 202505. Open: daily.
££
www.quod.co.uk
A very popular and
bustling brasserie-style
establishment, with an
emphasis on Italian
cooking. The atmos-
phere, enhanced by eye-
catching paintings from
young artists, is relaxed
and is considered pleas-
antly fashionable.

The Rose
51 High Street. Tel 01865
244429. Open: daily. £

RIGHT: the Mitre's facade
is better than its food.

A restaurant/tea room
serving good traditional
English food, ranging
from cooked breakfasts
to delicious afternoon
teas. The restaurant
closes at 6pm.

Pubs & Bars

The Mitre (17–18 High
Street) has an impres-
sive historic facade and
spacious panelled inte-
rior, and is a good place
for an early evening
drink. Its formulaic
Beefeater menu, how-
ever, is unexceptional.
Across the High, **The
Chequers** (131a High
Street) is a well-main-
tained 15th-century
building hidden down an
alleyway. Popular with a
non-student clientele, it

has a pleasant courtyard
area. **The Wheatsheaf**
(129a High Street) is
also invisible from the
High and is reached
down Wheatsheaf Yard.
It has a fairly predictable
menu and is best known
for its Tuesday evening
jazz sessions. **Merton's
Bar and Brasserie** (73
High Street) has devel-
oped an excellent reputa-
tion for its cocktails,
although prices are on
the high side. It stays
open until 2am (except
Sundays) after many
other pubs have closed.

Cafés

The **Grand Café** (84 High
Street) is housed in the
old marmalade factory
and exudes a rather

faded Edwardian charm.
Good-value breakfasts,
light meals and after-
noon teas are all avail-
able, as are cocktails.
The **Queen's Lane Cof-
fee House** (40 High
Street) is a veritable
Oxford institution, dating
back to 1654. After a
welcome refurbishment
it serves good snacks,
light lunches and cream
teas to a mostly student
clientele.

PRICE CATEGORIES

Prices for three-course
dinner per person with a
half-bottle of house wine:
£ = under £20
££ = £20–£30
£££ = £30–£45
££££ = more than £45

A THIRST FOR KNOWLEDGE

Oxford is a city of learning, of course, but also a city of drinking, with a huge variety of pubs ranging from medieval inns to modern theme bars

There are pubs to suit all tastes in Oxford. Pubs for students, of course, but also establishments that cater for other inhabitants of the city. George Street is now almost entirely comprised of places for eating and drinking, many of them catering for a young, non-student clientele, and the street is animated – to say the least – on Friday and Saturday evenings.

But there are also plenty of more traditional and sedate pubs. Some of their names reveal their historic connection with a particular trade or profession: the Bookbinders Arms in Jericho (publishing), the Waterman's Arms on Osney Island (canal haulage), the Bullnose Morris in Cowley (named after the first vehicle produced by William Morris, founder of the motor-car industry in Oxford).

Each suburb or inner-city neighbourhood has its local, complete with loyal regulars, but there are some pubs that have strong associations with the famous, and sometimes the infamous, some of whose drinking habits were as pronounced as their literary or artistic talents.

William Shakespeare, so tradition has it, used to stop off at the Crown Tavern in Cornmarket on his way from London to Stratford-upon-Avon. Naturally, many other writers have followed his example.

ABOVE: The Turf Tavern is difficult down a warren of narrow lanes nea College, but is worth seeking out. T hard-drinking Welsh poet Dylan Th used to quench his thirst here.

LEFT: The legendary Welsh actor R Burton often came to perform at O Playhouse, and was nicknamed "B Burton" for none too subtle reason

BELOW: The "Inklings", a group of literary cronies including C.S. Lewi and J.R. Tolkien, used to meet in t back bar of the Eagle and Child, an unspoiled pub on St Giles.

LEFT: The historian Anthony Wood recounted in 1690 how one Fellow of All Souls' died at the Mitre after immoderate drinking.

A GHASTLY, GHOSTLY INN

The Mitre Inn on the High Street has been a pub in continual use since 1310. It has always had strong religious connections and in the 17th century was a hotbed of Catholicism, when secret Masses were held on the premises. This affront to Protestantism led to a riot in 1688 as mobs smashed every window and went in search of other Catholics.

One of the worst chapters in the city's long history of religious intolerance occurred here during Henry VIII's Dissolution of the Monasteries. A secret tunnel then linked the Mitre with buildings across the High Street and it seems that Henry's soldiers drove a group of monks underground and then bricked up both ends of the tunnel. According to local lore, the monks' screams can sometimes still be heard in the dead of night.

RIGHT: C.S. Lewis, the celebrated creator of the Narnia novels, used to meet J.R.R. Tolkien, author of *The Lord of the Rings*, for drinks at the Eastgate Hotel on High Street.

E: The Bookbinders Arms is a friendly n Jericho that has associations with ctor Morse. Fans of the fictional tive can visit it on a Morse guided tour, chronicles Morse's pub crawls.

: The late novelist Kingsley father of Martin, was a mporary of the poet Philip n at St John's College. He a jazz fanatic while at d and a regular at the s Arms in Broad Street.

BELOW: Inspector Morse, the fictional detective created by Oxford-based writer Colin Dexter (centre), loved Oxford pubs. The Trout and the Eagle & Child have appeared in the TV series starring the late John Thaw (left).

SOUTH OF THE HIGH

You can visit an old tavern and some venerable colleges, including Merton, on the way to the Botanic Garden, one of Europe's finest and Britain's oldest

This route starts at Carfax and heads east, but soon forsakes the High Street for more evocative back streets. Merton College is especially important, as many of its features provided the model for later college foundations.

From Carfax, cross over to the south side of the High Street and proceed east as far as Alfred Street. Turn right to arrive at the **Bear ❶**, one of Oxford's oldest pubs (there has been a pub on its site since 1242), and full of genuine charm. Enclosed in its tiny, panelled rooms, with their smoke-kippered ceilings, are over 7,000 ties displayed in cabinets on the walls and rafters – from the Cheltenham College Mind Games Society to the East of Suez Golfing Club. There is excellent pub food, and in summer you can eat outside in the adjoining yard.

Oriel and Christ Church

Walk east along Bear Lane to arrive in Oriel Square, with its 18th-century houses. At the southwest corner is the Canterbury Gate of Christ Church (*see page 151*). **Oriel College ❷** (closed to the public), founded in 1324, originally occupied a house called La Oriole, because of its prominent upper bay window (medieval Latin: *oratoriolum*).

Nothing medieval survives now,

but Oriel does have a splendidly ostentatious Front Quadrangle, built from 1620 to 1642 in the Jacobean-Gothic style. This form of architecture is peculiar to Oxford and combines beautifully shaped gables with traceried windows of medieval appearance. Dominating the quad is the staircase entrance to the hall, with its open strapwork cresting, and its inscription *Regnante Carolo* making a bold statement of Royalist support for Charles I. In the niches above are statues of Charles I and

Map
on page
112

LEFT:
Corpus Christi College.
BELOW:
students at Oriel.

Students at Corpus Christi College.

Edward II (Oriel's founder, Adam de Brome, was one of Edward's civil servants) as well as a matronly Virgin and Child.

Adjacent to the Canterbury Gate, at the beginning of cobbled Merton Street, is the entrance to **Corpus Christi College** ❸ (open daily 2pm–5pm; tel: 01865 276700; free). Founded in 1512 by Richard Foxe, Bishop of Winchester, this small college has always been somewhat radical. In 1963, the college took the radical step of allowing women to dine as guests in hall: they were not finally admitted as students, however, until 1979.

The intimate Front Quad of the college contains a famous **sundial** of 1581, topped by the emblem of the college, a pelican wounding her breast to feed her young, a symbol of Christ's sacrifice. The plinth below is inscribed with a perpetual calendar from 1606. A passageway on the left leads to the chapel, with its colourful Arts and Crafts window depicting St Christopher, designed by Henry Payne in 1931.

Visitors should not leave without also seeing the small college **garden** behind the Fellows Building. Dominated by a magnificent copper beech, the garden provides a fine view of Christ Church Meadow, with the Fellows Garden of Christ Church in the foreground. The view from the raised platform at the back is even better, and you can see down into the secretive Deanery Garden of Christ Church, where Lewis Carroll first got to know young Alice Liddell (*see page 65*).

Along to Merton

Beyond Corpus Christi is the tower of Merton College Chapel. Founded in 1264 by Walter de Merton, Lord Chancellor of England, **Merton College** ❹ (open Mon–Fri 2–4pm, Sat–Sun 10am–4pm; tel: 01865 276310; free) claims to be the oldest college in Oxford. Two other colleges dispute this primacy: University College, on the spurious grounds that it was established by Alfred the Great, and Balliol, which was certainly in existence as a community of scholars by 1263 but was not formally endowed until 1282 (*see page 131*). It is generally accepted, however, that the statutes of Merton served as the model for all the other colleges of Oxford and Cambridge. Like other early colleges, Merton was an exclusive institution with a privileged minority of mostly graduate Fellows.

Merton Chapel, parallel to Merton Street, dates to 1290. The massive gargoyles that leer from the battlements are another example of brilliant modern masonry – put up in the 1960s to replace the eroded stumps of the originals.

The statues of Walter de Merton and Henry III in the **gate-tower** are also recent, but the mysterious woodland scene carved above the arch is 15th century. It probably depicts St John the Baptist in the wilderness – but it is a wilderness populated by numerous rabbits and bears, while the fruit-filled trees are crowded with a chorus of nesting birds. In the foreground, Walter de Merton kneels before the *Book of Seven Seals* from the Revelation of St John while a lamb and a unicorn, representing Christ, look on.

Pass through the entrance into the Front Quad, which lacks the calm regularity of some others in the city. With buildings dating from the 13th to 19th centuries, it is typical of the piecemeal development of the early colleges. Straight ahead is the Hall, the first building on the site to be completed, but virtually rebuilt in 1794 and again in 1874 when Gilbert Scott added the fine roof. The original 13th-century door, with its ornate scrollwork, has survived.

To the left of the Quad is the **Fitzjames Arch**, built by the Warden (head of the college) Robert Fitzjames in 1497. He had a horoscope cast in order to find the most propitious date on which to begin building, and his astrological interests are reflected in the signs of the zodiac carved in the vault of this arch. It

Map on page 112

Walter de Merton (c1200–1277), a lawyer by training, made his money from property. His aim in establishing Merton College was to extend the educational benefits which the friars had established for themselves in universities. Such was his influence at court that he ran the country as Regent for two years after Henry III died in 1272 until his son, Edward I, returned from the Crusades.

BELOW:
Merton in winter.

leads through to the 17th-century **Fellows' Quadrangle**.

Merton has some special features that provided models for later foundations. Principal among these is the **Mob Quad**, reached by going through the arch to the right of the Hall and turning right. Enclosed by 14th-century buildings, this is the oldest quad in Oxford. The origin of the name is not known, but members of Merton like to think that the characteristic form of the Oxford and Cambridge enclosed quadrangle owes its origin to this group of buildings.

Its form is probably based on that of a medieval inn. The north and east ranges (for accommodation) were completed first, in 1311, followed by the south and west ranges, built to house, on the first floor, the **Library**, the most perfect example of a medieval library in England (guided tours with the verger for a maximum of five people are available Mon–Fri 2–4pm; entrance fee).

The entrance is in the southwest corner of the Mob Quad, where the ancient oak door is believed to have been taken from Beaumont Palace, the Royal Palace of Henry I that once stood on Beaumont Street (*see page 160*). The library itself is up a flight of stone steps. Though its medieval structure remains intact, substantial alterations were carried out subsequent to its completion in 1379. The wooden ceiling, for example, is Tudor, while the panelling and plasterwork date from the late 16th and early 17th centuries. The library still has an original 14th-century reading stall, with chains to protect the valuable manuscripts from theft.

The west wing is adjoined by the **Max Beerbohm Room**, full of drawings by the famous caricaturist (1872–1956), who studied at Merton and wrote *Zuleika Dobson* (1912), a satire on Oxford undergraduate life.

To the north of Mob Quad is Merton's splendid 13th-century **Chapel**. Again, the plan of the chapel, consisting of an ante-chapel, screen and choir, set the pattern for all the other colleges – although this form evolved by accident: Walter de Merton intended a massive building, with an extensive nave, that was never built, probably because of lack

Stained-glass window in Merton Chapel.

RIGHT:
Merton's gatehouse.

Anyone for Real Tennis?

In Merton Street, opposite Merton College's porter's lodge, stands one of England's 25 Real Tennis courts. Real Tennis has been played on this site since the late 16th century, and the present court dates from the late 18th century. The word Real is probably derived from Royal, but now mainly emphasises the sport's difference from more conventional lawn tennis. Its roots go back to medieval monastery life, when monks would play a sort of handball.

Known in French as the Jeu de Paume (literally "the palm game"), the sport evolved into a more intricate affair involving rackets, a net and a complicated set of rules. What differentiates Real Tennis from the better-known lawn variety is that it must be played inside. Players deliberately use the walls for particular shots, as in squash, while at the same time hitting the ball over a net. The ball is solid rather than pneumatic, made of tightly-bound tape, and is rather like a soft cricket ball. Rackets are asymmetrical and heavier than those that are used for lawn tennis.

Visitors are welcome between 9am and 6pm on weekdays (tel: 01865 244212; entrance fee).

of funds and space. Even so, the choir alone is huge and lofty. The magnificent east window, with seven lancets, meeting to form a wheel with 12 spokes at the apex, is one of the finest in Europe.

Nearly all the windows retain original late 13th-century glass, representing apostles and saints in gorgeous colours. The choir screen is made up of pieces salvaged from one designed by Christopher Wren, sadly broken up in 1851. Of the many monuments to Fellows and benefactors, the finest is to Thomas Bodley (died 1613) on the west wall; the founder of the Bodleian Library is surrounded by allegorical figures representing the arts and sciences.

As one re-emerges into cobbled Merton Street, there is a good view of Magdalen College tower to the east. On the left is **Logic Lane**, leading through to the High Street.

Recommended walks

Exit Merton and retrace your steps to the left as far as the wrought-iron gateway (open daily until 7pm) leading along the attractive **Merton Grove** between Merton and Corpus Christi. A turnstile at the end provides access to the broad expanse of Christ Church Meadow. Immediately on the left is **Deadman's Walk**, following the old city wall to the east. It was along this path that funerals once processed to the old Jewish cemetery, now the Botanic Garden. It's possible to turn left here, but for better views continue south, past Christ Church Fellows' Garden, to the **Broad Walk**. To the right is the enormous neo-Gothic Christ Church, from where the delightful tree-lined **New Walk** provides a detour past Christ Church Meadow to the Thames and the College Boathouses. The main route goes left along Broad Walk, a wide avenue once planted with elm trees. The stump of one giant remains, but old age and Dutch elm disease killed them off in 1976; plane trees have been planted in their place.

When you get to Rose Lane, turn back a little along Deadman's Walk. In a wall on the right, a **plaque ❺** commemorates James Sadler, who was born in 1753 (*see page 142*), as

Map on page 112

Logic Lane, a former bridleway known as Horseman Lane, acquired its new name in the 17th century when a school of logicians established itself there. Gates at each end of the lane are kept locked between dusk and dawn.

BELOW: Mob Quad.

Map
on page
112

TIP

The gardens can look
bleak in winter, but the
massive glasshouses
(open daily 10am–
4pm) provide an
instant change of
climate as well as the
sight of luxuriant palms
and lotuses, ferns and
alpines, and a number
of carnivorous plants.
A stroll along the
Cherwell here is
delightful, the river
crowded with people in
punts in the summer.

BELOW:
the Botanic Garden.

the "first English aeronaut who in a
fire ballon made a successful ascent
from near this place on 4 October
1784 to land near Woodeaton".

The Botanic Garden

On the right is the side entrance to
the **Botanic Garden ❻** (open daily
9am–5pm, 4.30pm in winter; tel:
01865 276920; entrance fee), incorporating the fine archway paid for by
the founder, the Earl of Danby,
which contains his statue as well as
that of Charles II in the niche to the
right and Charles I to the left.

At around 5 acres (2 hectares), the
Garden is small but packed with
interest. It was founded in 1621 by
Henry Danvers, Earl of Danby, and
is the oldest physic garden in Britain.
The first head gardener was a retired
German soldier and publican called
Jacob Bobart, but he knew how to
create a good growing environment.
He ordered 4,000 loads of "mucke
and donge" to be spread on the original 3-acre (1.2-hectare) site to raise
it above the Cherwell floodwaters,
and built the 14-ft (4.3-metre) wall
that still encloses the garden.

The fourth side is enclosed by laboratory buildings and the massive
stone triumphal arch designed by
Nicholas Stone as the main entrance
in 1632 (the statues of Charles I,
Charles II and the Earl of Danby
were added later).

Within this sheltered, well-
drained and fertilised plot, Bobart
laid out a series of rectangular beds,
each one devoted to one of the principal plant families. This arrangement, designed to serve the scientific
objectives of the garden, has survived, although the regularity is soft-
ened by many fine specimen trees.

At the far end of the central path,
on the right, is a huge yew tree, sole
survivor of an avenue of yews
planted in 1650 by Bobart. Beyond,
the triangular New Garden, enclosed
in 1944, contains a lily pond, bog
garden and two rockeries for lime-
loving plants. Another part of this
garden is planted with roses illustrating the development of hybrid vari-
eties in the 19th and 20th centuries.

From the central pond, the **view**
through the arch to Magdalen Tower
is magnificent. ❑

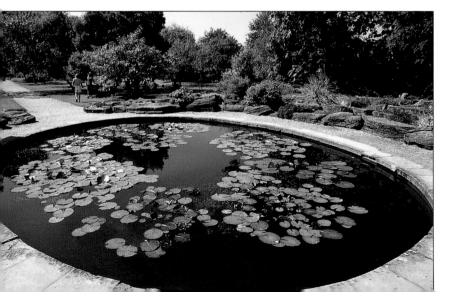

Elusive Gardens

Few cities in the world contain, within so few square miles, so many gardens and open spaces. There are two explanations. First, the colleges jealously guard their individual gardens and refuse to build on them; second, the rivers Cherwell and Isis almost encircle the city and have provided along their banks a ring of flood meadows which also form an effective barrier to building.

In contrast to the Botanic Garden and University Parks, it is not always possible to see the colleges and their gardens. However, most colleges do have set opening times. Further restrictions are usually only applied during exam times, and occasionally during vacations.

The gardens are run almost as eccentrically as the university itself. In each college a Fellow or group of Fellows directs the college gardeners. Traditionally each Fellow had some particular enthusiasm.

For example, the "Keeper of the Groves" at St John's, who favoured rhododendrons and their allies which sulk in Oxford's alkaline soil, had a huge pit dug, lined with concrete blocks and then filled with peaty soil to keep these plants happy. A Fellow of Wadham has a liking for rare Chinese trees. The garden committee at Christ Church, under the influence of one member, banned yellow flowers. The gardener at All Souls' once found himself planting a particular plant in one bed under the direction of one committee member, then having to replant it elsewhere at the whim of another, and so on...

Picking gardeners

The gardeners are a mixed bunch. Some come from other parts of Britain, lured by the variety, the supposed prestige, and the general ambience of the city. Others are hoping to escape to a world where their distracted dreams will rarely be interrupted. But a new drive for efficiency is encouraging many colleges to get rid of their aged retainers in favour of contract gardeners who drive from college to college – smart and tidy, perhaps, but without the personal touch.

The gardens of St John's, the richest college, are probably the grandest. The path twists and turns between carefully tended shrubs and groves of trees, providing a wonderful blend of the formal and the natural.

Another fine garden is at New College. It has probably the longest old-fashioned herbaceous border, and is dominated by the Mount, an avenue of clipped trees and elaborate parterres of box. The gardens of Worcester College have a willow-fringed lake, their beauty endorsed by Lewis Carroll in *Alice's Adventures in Wonderland*.

One feature that does unite the colleges is the lawn. There are basically two types: those you can walk on and those displaying the ubiquitous command KEEP OFF THE GRASS. It is on the informal lawns that the outdoor life of the college takes place: tea in the afternoon, Greek tragedies on summer evenings, croquet, bowls and frisbee-throwing. Essays are attempted, discarded and made into paper darts skimming over the grass. After the exams, elegantly attired students stroll across them on their way to summer balls. ❑

RIGHT: the gardens of St John's College.

CORNMARKET AND CARFAX

This is the bustling commercial heart of modern Oxford, with a trading history dating back to Saxon times. Old coaching inns and the Covered Market are echoes of the past, and St Michael-at-the-Northgate is the city's oldest surviving building

After the beauty of the High Street, Cornmarket, Oxford's main shopping street, may come as something as an aesthetic anti-climax. Its timber-framed or stone medieval buildings were almost entirely demolished and replaced by commercial and office accommodation in the late 19th and 20th centuries in a process that the aesthete William Morris described as "the fury of the thriving shop". Several inns and traditional grocers gave way to larger department stores, creating today's shopping hub.

The street's mostly modern architecture and youth-oriented retailing may still not appeal to the city's many conservationists, but it is normally busy with shoppers and at weekends is the focal point for many of Oxford's younger citizens. While most of Cornmarket's shops and cafés are branches of predictable high street chains, it is worth straying a few yards from the main thoroughfare to explore some truly original outlets. The street's remaining historical buildings and landmarks are also worth exploring.

Carfax

The busy crossroads at the southern end is known as **Carfax**, after the Norman *Quatre Vois* (four ways). This is the ancient heart of Saxon

Oxford, where the four roads from north, south, east and west met. The prime attraction is **Carfax Tower ❶**, all that remains of the 13th-century St Martin's Church which was pulled down as part of a road widening scheme in 1896 and was itself built on the site of an earlier, late-Saxon church. The east side of the tower, which can be climbed for fine views of the city (open late Mar–late Oct 10am–5.30pm, Nov–early Mar 10am–3.30pm; entrance fee) is embellished with quarterboys which

Map on page 120

LEFT: the Carfax quarterboys.
BELOW: the view from Carfax Tower.

Traditional sales technique at Carfax.

strike the bell every 15 minutes (replicas of those taken from the original church), as well as the original church clock. Note above the gateway to the right of the tower the sculpture of St Martin giving his cloak to a beggar. Beggars were long a feature of Carfax.

As well as beggars, Carfax was historically a place of trading. As early as the 11th century the crossroads was crammed with market stalls, offering all manner of goods, and over the next seven centuries the district remained a noisy and no doubt smelly jumble of stalls, with fish, meat and vegetables on offer. It

was only in 1774 that the creation of an official market rid Carfax of its commercial clutter.

Also on Carfax stood the Swindlestock Tavern, where, on St Scholastica's Day (10 February) 1355, an argument between scholars and the landlord developed into a riot, resulting in the deaths of many scholars. The site of the tavern is indicated by a plaque in the wall of the Abbey Bank.

It takes an effort of the imagination to picture Carfax in 1610 when a large and elaborate stone conduit was built in the middle of the crossroads in order to distribute the water

Cornmarket, Carfax and Around Broad Street

0   100 m
0   100 yds

Ashmolean Museum

St Giles'

Taylor Institute

St John's College

Garden Quad

Randolph Hotel

Martyrs' Memorial ❾ ❶

Balliol College

Chapel

Trinity College ⓮

Cumberbatch Quad

New Bodleian Library

The King's Arms

Holywell Street

History Faculty Library

Magdalen Street

Garden Quad

Chapel

Front Quad

17th Century Cottages ⓯

Blackwell's ⓰

Broad Street

Hertford College

Friars' Entry

St Mary Magdalen ❿

Broad Street

Emperors' Heads

Clarendon Building

Bridge of Sighs

Apollo Theatre

Oxford Information Centre ⓫ ⓬

The Oxford Story

Oxfam Shop

Museum of the History of Science (Old Ashmolean Museum) ⓱

Sheldonian Theatre

Bodleian Library

George Street

Cornmarket Street

St Michael's Street

St Michael-at-the-Northgate ❻

Exeter College

Chapel ⓳

Convocation House

Divinity School

Old Schools Quadrangle

Cattle Street

Ship Street

Chapel

Turl Street

former Ship Inn ❺

Jesus College ⓲

Brasenose Lane

Radcliffe

Oxford Union Society ❽

Front Quad

Lincoln College ⓴

Brasenose College

Radcliffe Camera

Radcliffe Square

Frewin Hall

Frewin Court

Market Street

Chapel Quad

Chapel

Chapel

Clarendon Centre

Covered Market ❼

University Church of St Mary the Virgin

Shoe Lane

Golden Cross Yard ❹

Crown Inn ❸

Painted Room ❷

All Saints' (Library)

Oxford University Press Bookshop

The Mitre

High Street

King Edward Street

Rhodes Building

Oriel Street

Carfax Tower ❶

High Street

Alfred St

N

that was piped from springs on distant Hinksey Hill into the centre of the city. In a revealing example of the Town and Gown divisions of the day, the water pouring from one part of the conduit was for the use of the colleges, while the townspeople had to make do with a separate supply.

The structure, featuring "a wealth of images" and "exquisite carving", also apparently boasted a carved ox's penis, from which water – or on special occasions – wine could flow. The conduit was pulled down in 1789 in a road-widening project.

On rare occasions, perhaps early Sunday morning, you can stand beneath Carfax Tower and enjoy an uninterrupted view of the beautiful High Street, or look down St Aldate's to the great pepper-pot tower of Christ Church (*see page 154*).

Cornmarket

Cornmarket, which runs from Carfax to the former North Gate and St Michael's Church, is nowadays mostly lined with unexceptional retailers and refreshment venues, but in its day it was a vibrant mix of independent traders and bustling inns. It is estimated that in the 16th century one-third of all establishments on the street were pubs and inns. As its name implies, the street was once also a locale for the buying and selling of corn, and in 1536 an open-sided building with pillars was erected to shelter the grain from bad weather. The corn-market was demolished in the course of the Civil War, when the occupying Royalist troops melted down the lead roof in order to manufacture bullets.

Shakespeare's godson, William Davenant (himself a playwright), was christened in St Michael's Church in 1606, and Shakespeare is known to have stayed regularly with Davenant's father, landlord of the Crown Tavern. This building, just across the street from Carfax Tower (No. 3 Cornmarket), was changed almost beyond recognition in 1744 when Cornmarket was widened and the tavern, then renamed the Bull Inn, had its frontage removed. Further "improvements" in the 1920s, led to the discovery by E.W. Attwood, a gentleman's outfitter, of

Map on page 120

TIP

Preoccupied window shoppers should take special care at either end of Cornmarket. It's all too easy for the unwary to step out into the path of an oncoming bus.

BELOW:
view of Ship Street from Cornmarket.

16th-century wall paintings, concealed behind oak panelling.

The so-called **Painted Room ②** is thought to have been a guest's bedroom, owned by one John Tatleton of the Bull Inn, and features a design of flowers in barbed quatrefoils on a terracotta background. The room is now part of a private office but the design can be viewed by appointment through the Oxford Preservation Trust (tel: 01865-242918).

The Crown Inn

Another historic inn stands across the road at No. 59a, hidden behind unpromising modern shop frontages. The **Crown Inn ③** (not to be confused with the long-disappeared Crown Tavern) dates back to the 11th century and by 1490 was known as Drapery Hall, then the King's Head and by 1625 the Crown Inn. The establishment's heyday was the 18th century when it developed into an important coaching inn. The pub that still survives was then probably the stables and outhouses of a much grander building, the site of which is now, ironically, occupied by

McDonald's. Inside, it retains a somewhat Elizabethan atmosphere, although claims that Shakespeare was a regular are wide of the mark.

The third of Cornmarket's historic inn sights is **Golden Cross Yard ④**, an enclosed courtyard surrounded by timber-framed ranges dating from the 16th to 19th centuries. The buildings were meticulously restored in 1987 to create a stylish precinct. The courtyard was originally formed in the Middle Ages for the Cross Inn; indeed, an inn may have existed on this site as early as 1193. In the 16th century the inn was used by travelling companies of players and it is said that Shakespeare stayed there on occasion. The bishops Latimer and Ridley were cross-examined here in 1555 while imprisoned at the nearby Bocardo. The first floor of the Pizza Express occupies the former bedroom accommodation of the inn and contains the major fragments of two painted rooms, the Crown Chamber and the Prince's Chamber.

The Ship Inn

Continue walking down Cornmarket until you get to the corner of Ship Street. Here is the former **Ship Inn ⑤**, one of Oxford's finest timber-framed buildings. Originally built in 1389 as the New Inn, it was recently restored by Jesus College to its 18th-century appearance, and is now occupied by Nokia and a shoe shop.

Oxford's oldest building

At the other side of Ship Street stands the **tower** of the church of **St Michael-at-the-Northgate ⑥**. Built as a look-out against the Danes, this sturdy tower (open Apr–Oct 10am–5pm, Nov–Mar 10am–4pm; entrance fee) is Oxford's oldest surviving building and dates to around 1050, exhibiting characteristic late Saxon features.

The tower was built up against the north gate of the city walls, part of

Coaching inns grew up to service the needs of the stage-coach, which forged a vital transport link between the town and London in the 1660s. Initially the journey took two days but by 1669 the "Flying Coach" had reduced this to one day, leaving the Mitre Inn in Oxford at 6am and, barring accidents, reaching London at 7pm.

BELOW: the Saxon tower of St-Michael-at-the-Northgate.

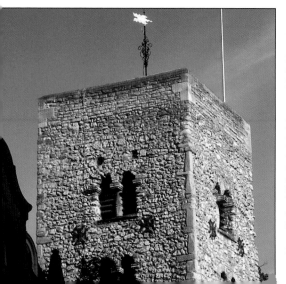

the fortifications of Edward the Elder's original Saxon town. The gate (dismantled by the Paving Commission in the late 18th century) was enlarged in 1293 to create a prison known as the Bocardo. Scholars debate whether Bocardo simply means "boggard", a privy, or whether it derives from the medieval logician's term for a syllogism, implying a difficult trap from which to escape.

The Oxford Martyrs Cranmer, Latimer and Ridley were all imprisoned here before being taken outside the city wall in 1555 to be executed (*see page 92*). Their cell door is in the tower.

St Michael's Church was substantially restored after a fire in 1953 but some fine 15th-century glass has survived, including a window showing Christ crucified on a lily flower (symbolising purity). The medallions in the window above the altar are the oldest examples of stained glass in Oxford, dating from 1290. The font is late 14th century. The treasury in the tower is used to display a beautiful silver chalice of 1562, a lustful sheela-na-gig (a late 11th-century erotic stone carving) and a charter of 1612 bearing the great seal of King James I. In the cellar of an adjacent building a shop specialises in fair-trade produce from around the world.

Map on page 120

The Covered Market

Only a minute down Market Street from the chain-store culture of Cornmarket is the cornucopian **Covered Market** where no quarter is given to the sensibilities of vegetarians, who will find haunches of meat, plump turkeys and blood-dripping game of every kind, hung in great quantities outside the butchers' stalls in true Edwardian style. This is particularly the case around Christmas, when the market becomes a spectacular tribute to gastronomic excess.

The market was originally built in 1774 as part of the Paving Commission scheme to rid Oxford of its untidy and often foul-smelling street markets. Fish and meat sellers, later to be joined by butter and fruit retailers, were brought into one place under the supervision of a beadle.

The present structure dates largely

Busking on Cornmarket.

BELOW: the Covered Market at Christmas.

Map
on page
120

*Turl Street epitomises
the architecture of
old Oxford.*

from the 1890s when the market was rebuilt and roofed over. It retains its turn-of-the-century atmosphere, and it is possible to buy a great range of locally produced "poor man's meats" – haggis, brawns, faggots, raised pies, black puddings and Oxford sausages – not to mention fresh fruit and fish, cheeses and rich pastries. There's also a high-class delicatessen and a pasta shop, as well as cake shops and tea shops all vying for custom alongside smart boutiques and florists. The market wouldn't be the same without its traditional "greasy spoon" café, but there also several more upmarket eateries. This is also the place for practical everyday services such as a cobbler and a shop specialising in pet supplies. The market is open from 8.30am to 5.30pm Mon–Sat.

Side streets

A couple of alleys and side streets take you away from the bustle of Cornmarket into a quieter sort of urban environment. Ship Street, between St Michael's Church and the former Ship Inn, steers the visitor towards the gentler atmosphere of Turl Street and has a couple of pleasant cafés. Opposite, St Michael's Street is a peaceful lane that leads to New Inn Hall Street and contains some attractive shops as well as the popular Nosebag café and the Three Goats' Heads pub.

Here is the main entrance to the red-brick Gothic premises of the **Oxford Union Society ❽** (closed to the public), built in 1857 as a permanent home for the debating club founded in 1823. Harold Macmillan, Britain's prime minister from 1957 until 1963 and later Chancellor of the University, called it "an unrivalled training ground for debates in the Parliamentary style". The list of past Union Society presidents reads like a *Who's Who* of the political and journalistic world *(see opposite page)*. ❑

Pubs

The **Crown Inn** (59A Cornmarket) is a rare reminder of what the street might once have looked like. Tucked away behind modern buildings, the Elizabethan-era pub, with a good-value menu, is a quiet and civilised place for lunch or an early evening drink.

The **Three Goats' Heads** (3A St Michael's Street) is a surprisingly ornate confection of wood and plasterwork, serving an impressive range of beers and less impressive food to a largely youthful clientele. An excellent place to escape the shopping frenzy of Cornmarket.

Cafes

Situated directly under Carfax Tower, **Sofi 2** is an offspring of the successful French-owned Sofi de France in the Covered Market. It has the same successful formula of good sandwiches, panini and pastries together with excellent coffee.

Georgina's, in the Covered Market, caters to a youthful health-conscious crowd, serving organic and mostly vegetarian food and delicious cakes in a cosy upstairs retreat that tends to fill up quickly at lunchtime.

Brown's Café, also in the Covered Market, is the polar opposite in terms of style and nutrition. If you want a classic cholesterol-loaded breakfast or lunchtime fry-up, this is the place, with its unreconstructed post-war ambiance. Once there were three such greasy-spoon establishments in the market; this is the last.

The **News Café** (1 Ship Street), as its name implies, aims to keep its visitors up to date with the news as well as refreshed. Newspapers and a plethora of TV sets should satisfy the most avid news junkie, while the menu, ranging from big breakfasts to pasta and salads, is top-quality.

Across Cornmarket, the **Nosebag** (6–8 St Michael's Street) is a long-standing student favourite, housed in a beautiful 15th-century building. It has an unashamedly 1970s feel, with the emphasis on quiches, salads and irresistible cakes.

More or less next door, **Meltz** (8 St Michael's Street) is a trendy sandwich bar, offering panini and cappuccinos to Oxford's gilded youth.

The Oxford Union

Again and again in its history, the young speakers who catch the president's eye have gone on to catch the eye of the country, even the eye of the world," wrote political journalist David Walter in his book *The Oxford Union*. It's a fair claim: the Oxford Union Society, founded in 1823, is the most famous student-run body in Britain, possibly in the world, and seven of its officers have become prime ministers.

Like most such student organisations, the Oxford Union runs discos and jazz evenings and operates a cheap bar. But what sets it apart are its weekly showpiece debates. Modelled on Westminster's parliamentary procedure, these constitute a top-notch political training ground. They give students a chance not only to hear leading public figures defend their views but also to hone their own debating skills in preparation for the anticipated day when they themselves will be leading public figures.

Richard Nixon and Jimmy Carter have both spoken here. British cabinet ministers regularly make the 50-mile (80-km) trek from London. Preachers, playwrights and popular comedians have all pitted their wits against the difficult acoustics and an unusually discerning and frequently rowdy audience. Even Hitler was given false hope in 1935 when the Oxford Union carried the controversial motion that "This House would not fight for King and Country". (Oddly, he failed to appreciate that what people say they would do in certain circumstances often bears little relation to their actual behaviour.)

The Union's training for the rough and tumble of real politics is ruthlessly practical. To become president of the Union a student must clamber up the proverbial greasy pole by winning various elections, perhaps becoming initially a committee member and later secretary, treasurer or librarian. Just to make things a bit more interesting, the Society's celebrated Rule 33 forbids a candidate from informing anyone, except "close personal friends", that he or she is running for office.

This awkward handicap spurs candidates to find ingenious ways of circumventing the rule. They are thus liable to buy drinks for total strangers, casually letting slip in the conversation the fact that they just might be standing for election this term. This practice, known as "hacking", is scorned by the non-political students.

Once elected, the president assumes significant responsibilities. Four speakers have to be found for each of the eight debates held every term, and the Union, which has a staff of 30 and a turnover of around £500,000 a year, has to be managed efficiently and profitably.

It is no small task. In the mid-1980s, the Union's fine Victorian buildings, including a library with pre-Raphaelite murals, were in serious disrepair and bankruptcy seemed a possibility. But sponsorship of debates and events and a Japanese bank donation of £1 million helped towards restoration. The resulting new-found vitality boosted university membership to 7,000 and there are now around 65,000 members worldwide. Dues are £176 for lifetime membership – not bad value. ❑

RIGHT: in 1978 former US President Richard Nixon guested at an Oxford Union debate.

TOWN AND GOWN THROUGH THE YEAR

The rhythms of university life have little impact on the city – but once a year, on a May morning, an event to mark the coming of summer is shared

With its three-term calendar and time-honoured diary of events and ceremonies, the university has an annual rhythm all of its own.

Each term witnesses the ritualistic conferring of degrees on successful students, the various gatherings of gowned academic notables and the occasional feast days celebrated by individual colleges.

For rowing enthusiasts, highlights of the year are the inter-college races known as Torpids (seventh week of Hilary Term) and Eights Week (fifth week of Trinity Term).

Events in the town

The city has its own annual fun events: the Lord Mayor's Parade over the Easter weekend, and St Giles' Fair in early September.

A more recent innovation is the City Council's series of Fun in the Parks days, with fairs, music and multicultural activities around the city. They usually take place on Bank Holidays in spring and summer and are well attended by the non-student population.

ABOVE: May Day is an excuse for revellers of every description to stay up all night and continue the festivities into the next day.

LEFT: Degree ceremonies bring a splash of colour to the city. Led by the university's Chancellor, dignitaries who are to be awarded degrees proceed with all the pomp and ceremony they can muster, dressed in academic regalia.

ABOVE: Encaenia is the university's most colourful academic ceremony. Each June visiting dignitaries from politics and the arts are presented with honorary degrees.

RIGHT: The 18th-century St Giles' Fair was a toy and craft fair, but today the two-day event offers hair-raising rollercoaster rides, garish rides and sticky candyfloss.

YOU *SHALL* GO TO THE BALL

Most colleges hold a lavish party at least every other year at the end of Trinity Term. Officially known as "Commemoration Balls", these extravagant events celebrate the end of exams and the prospect of a lengthy summer vacation.

The dress code for undergraduates and their guests is traditional and rigorously enforced: dinner jackets and black bow ties for men, ball gowns for women. Tickets are very expensive (£100 plus for a double), and the richer colleges compete as to who can organise the most luxurious food and the best entertainment. Big-name bands often appear, paid for by the inflated ticket prices, while champagne and good food are *de rigueur*.

Understandably, security is tight, as gate-crashers attempt to scale college walls to join in the fun. Those with stamina carry on until dawn, when champagne breakfast is served, and some even set off on punting expeditions.

While undoubtedly enjoyed by those involved, college balls do not find favour with all Oxford residents, some of whom object to the noise and the ostentatious extravagance of the students.

LEFT: Eights Week, lasting four days in late May, has been around since 1815 and allows rival college rowing teams (eights) to compete against one another. It is around this time, before students depart for the long summer break, that the university lets its hair down with May Balls and parties.

RIGHT: Oxford's most notable celebration takes place early on 1 May, when crowds from all walks of life assemble on Magdalen Bridge for the traditional ceremony of May Morning. This begins at 6am, when choristers from Magdalen College School sing an invocation to summer from Magdalen College Tower. The school was set up around 1478 by William Waynflete, Bishop of Winchester, founder of Magdalen College itself.

AROUND BROAD STREET

This area combines peaceful college quads with the bustle of shopping streets and some of Oxford's favourite tourist attractions

The route begins at the southern end of broad St Giles', at the neo-Gothic **Martyrs' Memorial** . Erected by public subscription, to the designs of Sir George Gilbert Scott from 1841 to 1843, it contains statues of the martyrs Latimer, Ridley and Cranmer, and an inscription stating that they died for maintaining sacred truths "against the errors of the Church of Rome".

The Oxford Martyrs were burned at the stake in the town's north ditch, now Broad Street, just around the corner, where a cross in the road opposite Balliol College marks the site of their execution. Latimer and Ridley went to the stake first, in 1555. Latimer offered the following words of comfort to his desperate colleague before both were consumed by the flames: "Be of good comfort, Master Ridley, and play the man. We shall this day light such a candle, by God's grace, in England, as I trust shall never be put out."

Charles I's church

Immediately to the south of the Martyrs' Memorial the road splits into two and the **Church of St Mary Magdalen** ❿ occupies the island in the middle. Usually locked, this church is a centre of Anglo-Catholicism, and the congregation remains loyal to the memory of

Charles I, celebrating the Feast of King Charles the Martyr on 30 January. The north aisle, funded out of money left over from the building of the Martyrs' Memorial, is an interesting early example of Gothic Revival architecture, and was designed by Gilbert Scott in 1842. Scott was a keen supporter of the Oxford Society for the Study of Gothic Architecture, founded in 1839, whose members believed that this medieval style was morally better than the pagan classical.

Map on page 120

LEFT: the Martyrs' Memorial.
BELOW: Balliol College.

BELOW: the Oxford Story invites you to ride through history on a medieval desk.

Broad Street

Broad Street is aptly named, though it was originally known as Horse-mongers Street after a horse fair held here from 1235. Narrow at each end and wide in the middle, it has a feeling of spaciousness, emphasised by the grounds of Trinity College on the north side, which are separated from the street by a wrought-iron gate. The far end is dominated by the Sheldonian Theatre and Clarendon Building and much of the south side is distinctive for its colourful facades above some interesting shops including **Oxfam** (Oxford Committee for Famine Relief), the first permanent shop to be opened by the charity in 1948 *(see panel below)*.

The Oxford Story

Here, too, is **The Oxford Story** ⑪ (open Apr–Oct daily 9.30am– 5pm; July and Aug 9am–6.30pm; Nov– Mar 10am–4pm; entrance fee), a museum primarily devoted to the history of the university. After a brief introduction in a "common room", visitors are propelled through the ages on a motorised medieval desk,

experiencing the sights, sounds and smells of this 800-year-old institution (children's and foreign-language commentaries are available).

Close to the Oxford Story, at 15-16 Broad Street, is the **Oxford Information Centre** ⑫ (open 9.30am–5pm Monday-Saturday, 10am-4pm Sundays). The centre offers advice on accommodation, events and special attractions and is one of the best places to find a qualified guide for tours of the University.

Balliol College

At the other side of the street is **Balliol College** ⑬ (open daily 2–5pm; tel: 277777; entrance fee), a college that has produced a greater number of eminent men – in particular statesmen and politicians – than any other. These include Lord Jenkins of Hillhead, and prime ministers Harold Macmillan and Edward Heath.

The liberal traditions and academic strengths of the college in its heyday were due to the reforming measures of Benjamin Jowett (Master 1870–93), who believed that his students should not merely be filled

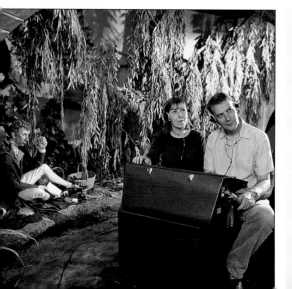

Oxfam

The Oxfam shop in Broad Street was the UK's first permanent charity shop. Today the Oxford-based aid agency has a network of more than 800 retail outlets, an annual income of over £90 million and a staff of 1,300 (plus 30,000 volunteers) in the UK. It works in 70 countries and lobbies for an end to unfair trade and the debt crisis in the Third World.

The Oxfam story began in 1942 when the Allies blockaded Greece, then occupied by the Nazis. As Greeks began to die of hunger and disease for lack of food and medicines, the Oxford Committee for Famine Relief was established to send supplies. A week of fund-raising netted £12,700.

with facts but educated for life. His self-proclaimed mission was to "innoculate England with Balliol" – which he sought to do by encouraging his charges to devote their lives to public service. But Jowett wasn't the first Balliol Master to espouse progressive ideas: back in 1361 the religious reformer John Wyclif spoke out against corruption and worldliness within the established church. His teachings resonated throughout Europe.

Jowett also supervised the near-total rebuilding of the college and, sadly, it is difficult to find much of merit in the result. William Morris, who watched the demolition of the medieval Balliol buildings with dismay, later founded the Society for the Protection of Ancient Buildings with the avowed aim of seeking means to repair and protect old buildings rather than replacing them.

The Fellows of Balliol, however, thought the buildings too decayed to be rescued. They had stood for a long time; Balliol claims to be the oldest Oxford college (also a claim of University College and Merton)

Map on page 120

on the grounds that John Balliol founded it in 1263, as penance for insulting the Bishop of Durham; the statutes, drawn up under the patronage of Balliol's widow, Dervorguilla, date to 1282.

The college was never very wealthy, however, until some ancient estates in Northumberland were discovered to be a rich source of coal. Three major Victorian architects were employed in the rebuilding that resulted – Salvin, Butterfield and Waterhouse – yet all produced second-rate work.

The Front Quad, entered from Broad Street, contains the former hall, now the library, and one of the few surviving pre-Victorian buildings, last remodelled in the 18th century. The chapel, Butterfield's work of 1856–57, was once lavishly decorated with Gothic furnishings – too ornate for the taste of Balliol dons who had them removed in 1937. The silver-gilt altar frontal commemorates college members who died in World War I.

The chapel exterior, partly clad in ivy and Virginia creeper, is built in

Balliol College Hall.

BELOW: May Morning celebrations at Balliol.

alternating bands of buff and red stone and is best appreciated from the Garden Quad. Here things begin to improve slightly: a group of trees and rose beds softens the appearance of the ill-harmonised buildings, and the steep flight of stone steps up to the porch of the dining hall – the work of Waterhouse, 1876 – makes a dramatic statement.

Trinity College

Adjacent to Balliol is **Trinity College** ⓲ (open daily 10.30am–noon, 2–5pm; tel: 01865 279900; entrance fee). Unlike in most other Oxford colleges, the Front Quad is not closed off, and its tree-filled lawn almost invites visitors to enter, which they do through a small entrance between the wrought-iron gates and a row of humble **17th-century cottages** ⓳, which were rebuilt in 1969.

A path leads northwards across the lawn to Durham Quad, so called because it occupies the site of the original Durham College, founded in 1286 by the monks of Durham Abbey. When the monasteries were

dissolved by Henry VIII, the property was purchased by Sir Thomas Pope, a wealthy Treasury civil servant, and he re-founded the college in 1555.

Durham Quad is fronted by the elegant Baroque chapel – so much like Wren's City of London churches that the design has been attributed to him, although any college records that could prove or disprove this theory are missing. Certainly the chapel, which attracts the highest eulogies from architectural historians, was the first in Oxford to break away from the Gothic style. Completed in 1694, the tower is carved with fruit and flowers, and the pinnacles consist of allegorical figures representing Theology, Medicine, Geometry and Astronomy.

Inside, the panelling, stalls and screen, carved with figures of the Evangelists, are principally of juniper wood, with walnut veneer. The beautiful reredos, all cherubs and foliage, is certainly good enough to be the work of the great 17th-century master of wood carving Grinling Gibbons. The centrepiece of the

Map
on page
120

plaster ceiling is painted with an Ascension by the Huguenot artist Pierre Berchet.

A passageway on the north side of Durham Quad leads through to the peaceful Garden Quad. Here the north range, of 1668, is known to be Wren's work, but 19th-century alterations have obscured his design beyond recognition.

Four handsome lead urns form a prelude to the college garden, to the right, entered through a wrought-iron gateway, made as a World War II memorial. The expansive gardens stretch all the way to Parks Road, creating a fine vista that is closed at the far end by 18th-century wrought-iron railings.

The heart of publishing

Blackwell's ⓰ (open Mon–Sat 9am–6pm, Tues 9.30am–6pm, Sun 11am–5pm), on Broad Street, was opened in 1879 by Benjamin Henry Blackwell. The original shop was tiny, and even today the initial impression is of an average-sized provincial bookshop. Downstairs, however, is the underground **Nor-**rington Room**, an enormous space stacked with shelves devoted to truly every topic under the sun. The pre-eminence of Blackwell's in Oxford is reflected not only here in its flag-ship shop, but in other premises in the city, including the Music Shop at 23 Broad Street and the Art Shop, just across the street. (*See profile of Blackwell's, page 137.*)

Old Ashmolean Museum

Before leaving Broad Street, go back to the Emperors' Heads (*see page 83*). Just to the right is the **Old Ashmolean Museum**, built between 1678 and 1683 to house the "cabinet of natural curiosities" inherited by Elias Ashmole from the Tradescants. Designed, perhaps, by Thomas Wood, it picks up motifs and ideas from Wren's building alongside, and is equally ornate.

The contents of the museum were transferred to the newly built Ashmolean in Beaumont Street in the late 19th century and the building now houses the **Museum of the History of Science** ⓱ (open noon–4pm Tues–Sat, 2–5pm Sun; free), a com-

Blackwell's was founded in 1879.

BELOW: exhibits at the Museum of the History of Science.

*Bringing home
the baguettes.*

prehensive collection of early instruments. The museum may seem daunting, with its cases packed with complex astrolabes, quadrants and armillary spheres, but there is much to enjoy, even for non-scientists.

The ground floor has a collection of very early photographs, dating from the experimental period of the 1840s; they include one of John Ruskin's views of Venice, used as reference material by the artist for his own hand-drawn illustrations for his pioneering work on Renaissance architecture, *The Stones of Venice*. There are also some novelties among the exhibits: George III's ornate silver microscope and an extraordinarily elaborate machine turning handwriting into minuscule engravings,which can be seen only under a microscope.

In the former chemistry laboratory in the basement, a blackboard covered with Einstein's neatly chalked theorems is carefully preserved, a memento of his first Oxford lecture on the Theory of Relativity, given on 16 May 1931. It is partnered by an assortment of gruesome medical and dental instruments, early radios, gramophones and phonographs, and a display on the war-time work of Oxford scientists racing against time to prepare penicillin for large-scale production, using improvised materials such as milk churns and tin baths.

Turl Street

Between Blackwell's Art Shop and a lingerie emporium on Broad Street, **Turl Street** marks a boundary of sorts between Town and Gown, for most of the colleges lie to the east and the shops and markets to the west. The street is thought to be named after a pedestrian turnstile or twirling gate that stood in the city wall at the Broad Street end. Looking south, you can see how the street gradually narrows to its original medieval width.

Jesus College

Down Turl Street, on the right, is **Jesus College** ⑱ (open daily 2–4.30pm; tel: 01865 279700; free). It is said that college porters hate being on duty on Christmas Day because of the constant stream of telephone calls from pranksters ringing to ask "Is that Jesus?" – to which, if the answer is yes, the caller responds by singing "Happy Birthday to you".

Jesus is also known as the Welsh college because it was founded, in 1571, by Brecon-born Hugh Price, and took many of its students from the grammar schools of Wales until 1882. T. E. Lawrence ("Lawrence of Arabia") was one of the non-Welsh alumni, admitted in 1907, although he resided only a term in college and spent most of his time studying medieval military architecture in a summer house built for him by his parents in the garden of their North Oxford home (2 Polstead Road). There is a bust of Lawrence in Jesus College Chapel.

The chapel itself, consecrated in

Map on page 120

1621, contains a High Victorian altar reredos so out of keeping with the surviving 17th-century woodwork that it is usually curtained off from view. In the same north range of the first quad, the Principal's Lodging has a delicate shell hood of 1700 over the doorway.

Exeter College

Exeter College ⓲ (open daily 2–5pm; tel: 01865 279600; free), opposite Jesus, was founded in 1314 by the Bishop of Exeter, Walter de Stapledon. Much of the college now looks Victorian, due to rebuilding, and the first quadrangle is dominated by the over-large chapel. This was built from 1854 to 1860 to the design of Sir George Gilbert Scott, and the resemblance to a miniature French cathedral is no accident – Scott borrowed freely from the Sainte Chapelle in Paris.

The interior is bathed in the rich colours of stained glass, even on a dull day, and the sense of opulence is enhanced by the mosaic work of the apse. On the right of the altar, the large tapestry of the *Adoration of the Magi* was made in 1890 by the firm founded by William Morris, and designed by Burne-Jones. The two artists met in 1853 as fellow students at Exeter College, and their shared interest in the ideas of Ruskin and the pre-Raphaelites led them to devote their lives to the revival of medieval arts and crafts.

Another Exeter man was J. R. R. Tolkien, author of *The Lord of the Rings*, who much enjoyed the magnificent chestnut trees of the Fellows' Garden, beyond and to the rear of the front quad.

The vast tree, "Bishop Heber's chestnut", seems as ancient as the college itself, and members of the Exeter boat club watch its growth in spring with interest. It is said that if the foliage of the branches, arching over the garden wall, succeed in touching Brasenose College opposite, Exeter will beat its neighbour in the Bumping Races.

The magnificent **view** from the top of the garden wall (accessible by stone steps and a walkway) provides a fresh perspective of Radcliffe Square (*see page 92*).

Stained-glass window in Exeter Chapel.

LEFT:
Exeter College's front quad.

Tolkien's Turning-Point

John Ronald Ruel Tolkien was born in 1892 in Bloemfontein, South Africa, but was brought up in Birmingham, England. Both his father and mother died when he was young, and he and his brother came under the care of a stern aunt and a local parish priest.

A natural linguist, Tolkien had studied Greek and Latin and was interested in lesser-known languages such as Finnish even before he went to Exeter College in 1911. There he specialised in Old English and also developed his childhood habit of inventing private languages. After World War I, a spell working on the *Oxford English Dictionary* and a teaching job at Leeds, Tolkien returned to Oxford as Professor of Anglo-Saxon. A turning-point came when he met the young writer C.S. Lewis, who encouraged him to publish what he had thought was unpublishable: *The Hobbit* (1937). The huge success of this book was followed in 1954 by *The Lord of the Rings* trilogy.

But such was Tolkien's following and so insistent were his fans, especially in the psychedelic days of the 1960s, that he was forced to escape Oxford for the anonymity of Bournemouth. He eventually returned to rooms in Merton College, where he died in 1973.

Map
on page
120

Lincoln's library.

Lincoln College

Lincoln ⓴ (open Mon–Sat 2–5pm, Sun 11am–5pm; tel: 01865 279800; free) is the last of the colleges fronting on to Turl Street. It was founded in 1427 by the Bishop of Lincoln, Richard Fleming, but he died four years later, leaving the college with little income and few endowments. Because it remained relatively poor, many of the original 15th-century buildings escaped "improvement", and much of the charm of the Front Quad is its unspoiled character.

The Chapel Quad, to the south, was added in the 17th century. The chapel exterior (1629) is conservatively built in the Perpendicular style of the previous century, but the fine carved woodwork inside is much more typical of its age. Richly coloured stained glass shows prophets, apostles and biblical scenes.

One of the ironies of Lincoln College is that, founded during an age of heresy specifically to train priests in orthodox church teachings, it nevertheless elected John Wesley to a fellowship in 1726. Members of the Holy Club – nicknamed "the Bible moths" and "Methodists" because of their regular and methodical devotions – used to meet in his college rooms, in Chapel Quadrangle. Another room in the Front Quad, erroneously thought to have been Wesley's, was restored as a memorial by American Methodists in 1925.

Brasenose Lane, shaded by the chestnuts of Exeter, has a leafy, rural feel and the cobbled gulley down the middle marks the line of the original open sewer. Undergraduates use the lane as an unofficial cycle path.

The lane ends on Radcliffe Square with the Radcliffe Camera and Brasenose College (*see page 90*). Opposite Brasenose Lane, Market Street leads westwards to arrive at the north entrance of the Covered Market (*see page 123*).   ❑

Restaurant

Restaurant du Liban
1 Broad Street. Tel 01865 242494. Open daily. Extremely good-value Lebanese food is on offer in the rather unlikely setting of a spacious premises above Boswells' department store. The Liban serves all the national staples-from hummus and kebabs to spicy sausage and fetta-filled pastries, with a good wine list and very generous portions. Belly dancing may or may not be an added attraction. Budget under £20 per person for a three-course meal.

Cafes

The Campus Buttery (11 Broad St) is housed in what used to be the legendary second-hand Thornton's Bookshop and offers above-average sandwiches and snacks as well as delicious teas.

Similar fare is to be found at **Morton's** (22 Broad Street), one of a local chain of sandwich shops. This café has a pleasant upstairs room in its 18th-century premises, where you can look out on to Balliol College. It is worth remembering that there are very attractive cafés and snack bars in

Blackwell's, **Waterstone's**, on the corner of Broad Street and Cornmarket, and nearby **Borders**. All provide a comfortable place to enjoy a coffee and sandwich while browsing on the written word.

The **QI** café-bar (16 Turl Street) is another cerebral place of refreshment, part of a beautifully restored Georgian townhouse complex that includes a bookshop and members-only basement bar. The café is open to non-members up until 6pm and serves good food all day.

The White Horse (52 Broad Street) is squeezed between two Blackwells' buildings in a much-restored 16th-century building. The pub is small, intimate and friendly, with a very good lunchtime menu. Several real ales are available, and Inspector Morse enthusiasts will recognise the front bar from the popular TV series.

The Turl Bar (Turl Street) is actually connected to the Mitre on the High, but operates as a separate venue. Catering to a rather youthful crowd, it has a decent menu and an outdoor courtyard, but it has lost some of its former appeal.

Blackwell's

Blackwell's is one of the most famous bookshops in the world. It first opened in October 1879 and is situated at the end of Broad Street, in one of the most beautiful parts of the city, surrounded by Trinity, Balliol, Exeter, Hertford and Wadham colleges and opposite Wren's Sheldonian Theatre.

Benjamin Henry Blackwell's shop was just 12 ft (3.6 metres) square and was criticised by many for its situation – furthest from the city centre and with two well-established bookshops opposite. Frederick Macmillan, proprietor of the publishing house of Macmillan and forebear of Harold Macmillan, who was prime minister and Chancellor of Oxford University, said: "Well, Mr Blackwell, we shall be pleased to open an account with you but I fear you have chosen the wrong side of the street to be successful."

This pessimism was soon disproved. Blackwell's devotion to books – he characterised bookselling as "the infinite capacity for taking pains" – quickly became legendary. Professors, dons and undergraduates hastened to his door. The shop was originally so small that, when more than three customers came in, the apprentice had to be sent outside.

Right from the start the tradition was established that customers should be allowed to browse among the books, undisturbed by the staff. The custom has continued until the present day.

Naturally enough, famous literary figures have always been among the customers and the shop itself has been the subject of many writings. In *Summoned by Bells*, John Betjeman wrote: *I wandered into Blackwell's, where my bill / Was so enormous that it wasn't paid / Till ten years later, from the small estate / My father left.*

Other well-known literary customers have included Hilaire Belloc, A.E. Houseman, Oscar Wilde, George Bernard Shaw and Lewis Carroll.

Blackwell's gradually expanded in order to meet the steadily increasing business and took over more space behind the shop. After World War II some departments were moved to nearby premises. The most notable part of the expansion was the development of a vast underground room, the Norrington Room, opened in 1966, and named after the president of Trinity College, under which it extended.

Still a family firm, Blackwell's is also a publisher in its own right. Benjamin Henry Blackwell began publishing poetry in the 1880s, and this was continued by his son, Basil, publishing early works by many writers who subsequently became famous, among them Tolkien and Robert Graves.

From these small beginnings, two major publishing companies have grown: Blackwell Publishers, which specialises in humanities, and Blackwell Scientific Publications, which concentrates on scientific and medical titles. Sir Basil Blackwell, known to all as "the Gaffer", was awarded a knighthood in 1956 for his services to bookselling.

Today, Blackwell's has three bookshops in town, as well as one at Oxford Brookes University and another in the academic centre of the John Radcliffe Infirmary. ❑

RIGHT: one of the busy branches today.

AROUND NEW COLLEGE

Span the entire history of Oxford by taking in
the site of a pagan well, a Norman crypt,
the medieval town walls and the
birthplace of Morris Motors

On the east of Catte Street, linking the two halves of **Hertford College** (pronounced *hartford*) ❶ (open daily 10am–5pm; tel: 01865 279400; free), is the ornate aerial corridor known as the Bridge of Sighs, after the famous Ponte dei Sospiri in Venice. Although it is now a much-photographed landmark, the bridge's erection was strongly opposed when it was built by Sir Thomas Jackson in 1913–14. The other buildings of the college are Jackson's design, too, put up after 1887 and remarkably varied in their use of Italian, French and English Renaissance motifs.

Hertford is a college that only just survived to see the 21st century. The original Hart Hall, named after Elias de Hertford, dates from the late 13th century. For centuries it was embroiled in disputes with its predatory neighbour, Magdalen Hall, which wanted room to expand, and took every opportunity to take control of the impoverished Hart Hall. Magdalen achieved its objective in 1813 – only to be destroyed itself by a fire in 1820. It was then decided to refound the college, calling it Hertford and combining the properties of Magdalen and Hart Halls with funds donated by the banker Thomas Charles Baring in 1874.

The principal buildings, with their

neo-Palladian details, lie on the south side of New College Lane. Traditional English cream teas can be enjoyed in the historic Dining Hall (daily except Monday 2.30–4.30pm).

The Bridge of Sighs

The site on the north side, linked by the **Bridge of Sighs** ❷, was acquired in 1898 and is interrupted on the Broad Street frontage by the History Faculty Library, originally built as the Indian Institute by Basil Champ-

Map
on page
140

LEFT:
the Bridge of Sighs.
BELOW: the lawn
at Hertford College.

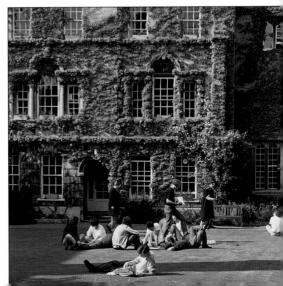

neys, beginning in 1883. Hindu deities and tiger heads carved in stone on the facade, and the elephant weather vane, mark its original use.

Ghostly lane

Pass under the Bridge of Sighs and into the dark, narrow and traffic-free **New College Lane**. This lane is the result of the replanning of the northeast quarter of town in the late 14th century, when many early medieval dwellings were replaced by residential colleges. The original street pattern was obliterated, leaving New College Lane to wind its way be-

Part of the old city wall at New College.

tween the high walls of the college.

Immediately on the left, a narrow opening between two houses, St Helen's Passage (formerly Hell Passage), leads through to the **Turf Tavern** (*see page 145*).

Further along on the left, a plaque on a house wall indicates the home of astronomer **Edmund Halley** (1656–1742). Having calculated the orbit of the comet that now bears his name, and carried out many scientific investigations, Halley was appointed Savilan professor at Oxford in 1703. He built an observatory at his home, still visible on the roof.

New College

The lane turns sharp right, between the cloister walls of New College on the left and the New College warden's barn on the right. Round another bend and straight ahead stands the gate-tower of **New College** ❸ (this entrance open Easter–Oct daily 11am–5pm; in winter use Holywell Street, open daily 2–4pm; tel: 01865 279555; entrance fee in summer). The narrow gate-tower, with statues of the Virgin, an angel and the founder, William of Wykeham, belies the spaciousness and grandeur of what lies beyond.

Wykeham, Bishop of Winchester, founded the college in 1379, having acquired land in the northeast corner of the city wall, which, according to contemporary accounts, was "full of filth, desolate and unoccupied". Building work proceeded speedily – in part because Wykeham was a very wealthy man.

The range of buildings surrounding the Great Quadrangle was largely completed by the time of Wykeham's death in 1404. What is more, most of it has survived intact, although a third storey was added to the accommodation range in 1674.

On the left of the gate-tower is the spacious chapel, a fine example of Perpendicular architecture. A dramatic stone figure of Lazarus, struggling to break free of his funeral bonds, dominates the ante-chapel and was carved by Sir Jacob Epstein in 1951. It stands beneath a controversial window designed by Sir Joshua Reynolds and painted by Thomas Jervais between 1778 and 1785 (the two artists appear as shepherds in the Nativity scene).

Sir Horace Walpole called it "washy" and Lord Torrington described the figures of the Virtues as "half-dressed languishing harlots". As models, Reynolds used society beauties of the day, including Mrs Sheridan, wife of the playwright; she appears as the Virgin.

There is no glass in the east end of the chapel; instead, a great 19th-century stone reredos rises from floor to ceiling, filled with life-sized statues of apostles, saints and martyrs. The hammerbeam roof is also Victo-

Map on page 140

During the Civil War of 1642–49, New College Lane was the assembly point for a Royalist force preparing to ride out from the city and confront the Parliamentarians. Ghost experts maintain that their psychic energy lives on in those high walls. This and other spooky places are included on Ghost Tours (details from Oxford Information Centre, tel: 01865-726871).

BELOW:
New College Gardens.

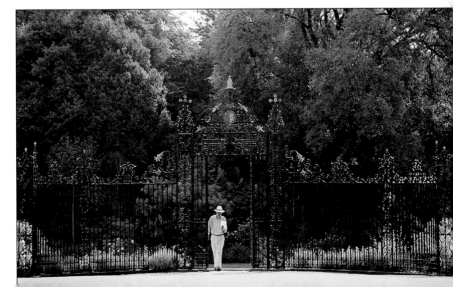

rian, by Sir George Gilbert Scott, as is the stone sedilia (group of three seats) to the left of the altar; one is used to display the founder's gilt and enamelled episcopal staff.

Scott also designed the woodwork of the choir stalls, but incorporated original armrests and 38 misericords that provide a glimpse of 14th-century life, with bishops preaching, acrobats tumbling and monsters with multiple heads.

On the left, as you emerge from the chapel, is the cloister, dominated by a vast and ancient holm oak tree, that evokes medieval Oxford with its original 14th-century waggon roof and atmosphere of tranquillity.

At the northeast corner of the Great Quad is the **Muniment Tower**, again with statues of the Virgin and Wykeham. The steep staircase within leads to the hall, lined with 16th-century linenfold panelling under Scott's 1877 roof. The wall above the high table is hung with portraits of benefactors and Wardens (heads of college).

An archway in the Great Quad east range leads through to the Garden Quad, lined with 17th-century

neo-Palladian buildings and separated from the gardens beyond by a curvaceous wrought-iron screen – a replica of the original designed by Thomas Robinson in 1711.

The gardens contain a substantial stretch of Oxford's medieval town wall, dating from 1226 when the original timber defensive walls of the town were rebuilt. The college was made responsible for maintaining it under the terms of the original land purchase; as a result it is one of England's best-preserved examples of a town wall.

The tree-covered Mound, in the northeastern angle of the wall, looks like a Norman castle motte but was created in the 16th century as a prospect from which to view the gardens.

Saxon church

Exit the college via the New College Lane gatehouse, and turn left under the archway and round another bend into **Queen's Lane**. Traffic-free, the walk along Queen's Lane is enlivened by Michael Groser's series of corbels on the New College buildings to the left, carved in the 1960s

One of the yews in St Peter in the East's churchyard was planted to commemorate James Sadler, the "first English aeronaut", whose inaugural balloon flight took off from Christ Church Meadow on 4 October 1784.

BELOW: New College.

William Spooner

William Spooner (1844–1930), elected as Warden of New College in 1903, is famed for his habit of transposing the initial letters of words to create "Spoonerisms". Many of these lapses – known to academics as methatesis – are thought to be apocryphal, made up subsequently to nurture the myth. There is no evidence, for example, that he once proposed a toast to "our queer Dean". It is also said that he expelled one undergraduate with the words "Sir, you have tasted two whole worms, you have hissed my mystery lectures and you were found fighting a liar in the quad: you will leave at once by the town drain."

with harvest mice, beetles, frogs, lizards and other zoological subjects.

Beyond the sharp right-hand bend in the lane is the church of **St Peter in the East ❹**, whose 11th-century tower is one of the oldest in Oxford. Originally dating from Saxon times, the present church is now the library of neighbouring St Edmund Hall, but visitors can gain access to the cavernous 11th-century **crypt**, one of the finest in Oxford, by asking for the key at St Edmund's porter's lodge.

During the war local residents used the crypt as an air-raid shelter, though Oxford was never actually bombed. A torch is useful for those who want to study the details: the capitals are carved with dragon-like beasts. In summer in the churchyard, St Edmund Hall students study beneath the yews.

St Edmund Hall

Noted for its small, flower-filled quads, **St Edmund Hall ❺** (open daily dawn until dusk; tel: 01865 279000; free), achieved independent status as late as 1957. Before that, it

Map on page 140

had been controlled by Queen's College, next door. It is, however, the only surviving example in Oxford of the medieval halls that pre-dated the foundation of the colleges. By tradition, it dates to the 1190s, when St Edmund of Abingdon taught here, and therefore has every right to be considered Oxford's oldest educational establishment.

Everything about St Edmund Hall is built on a diminutive scale, including the chapel, on the east side of the Front Quad. Note that the pillars supporting the 1682 door pediment are carved to resemble a stack of leather-bound books. Fans of pre-Raphaelite artists William Morris and Edward Burne-Jones should check with the lodge for permission to see some of their stained-glass work in the chapel, together with original cartoon drawings. There is also a bold modern altar painting of *Christ at Emmaeus* (1958) by Ceri Richards.

Morris Oxford's birthplace

The narrow confines of Queen's Lane finish as it emerges on to the High Street. Immediately on the

St Edmund Hall.

BELOW: the quad of St Edmund Hall.

Church of St Cross.

right is Queen's College (*see page 99*), while on the corner on the left you can rest your legs at Queen's Lane Coffee House.

Turn left here and continue for a short stretch along the High towards the traffic lights at Longwall Street. At No. 48 is a shoe shop, once the bicycle repair shop of William Morris, where the famous mechanic began his career.

To follow Morris's career further, turn left again into **Longwall Street**. Just around the first corner on the left is the building that housed the **garage ❻** in which Morris built the prototype of the "bullnose" Morris Oxford in 1912, a project that was to launch him on the road to fame and fortune and launch Oxford into the industrial era. Though the garage was converted to residential accommodation in 1981, there is an information window with further details on the career of Morris, later Lord Nuffield (*see pages 28–30*).

Church of St Cross

Adjacent is Holywell Street, but first continue north along the main road to the **Church of St Cross ❼** on the right. The present church was founded in the 11th century on the site of an ancient chapel of St Peter in the East, which was established beside a pagan Saxon holy well (hence "Holywell"), and became an important place of pilgrimage.

The only surviving Norman part of the church is the chancel, but the 13th-century tower has a fascinating feature, namely the **sundial clock**. The grave of Kenneth Grahame, author of *Wind in the Willows*, is in the churchyard. The key to the church is available from the porter of the neighbouring Holywell Manor; sadly, the ancient holy well is no longer there.

St Catherine's College

Opposite the church are the huge brick cubes of the **Law Library** (1964), while a turn right into Manor Road brings you to a classic example of 1960s architecture, **St Catherine's College ❽** (closed to the public), designed by Danish architect Arne Jacobsen and completed in 1964.

While modern architects rave over its pioneering "functional" style, most find the plain yellow-brick buildings dull. However, the landscaping, also planned by Jacobsen, is now mature and does much to compensate – especially the long vista between the Cherwell and the water gardens, backed by the splendid trees of Magdalen College meadows.

Linacre College

On the corner of South Parks Road is another "new" college, **Linacre** (ask at the porter's lodge to visit; tel: 01865 271650). It was founded in 1962 for students studying for higher degrees, notably graduates of universities other than Oxford. Thomas Linacre (1460–1524) was an Oxford medical scientist and classicist whose multidisciplinary approach the college seeks to emulate.

Back towards the centre, **Holywell Street** is one of Oxford's quietest and most charming streets, closed to traffic and lined with pastel-painted, timber-framed houses and Cotswold-stone vernacular; most are now student lodgings. New College's imposing Holywell Buildings, with the college's main entrance are also here, on the left.

Music and mead

On the other side of the street is the **Holywell Music Room** ❾ (tickets from the Playhouse box office; tel: 01865 305305), opened in 1748 and reputedly the world's oldest surviving concert hall. Restored in 1959–60, it can seat 250 and has acoustics that do particular justice to solo recitals and chamber concerts.

In Holywell Street, too, you can see how effectively the town wall marked the limits of the city, for, apart from the 17th- and 18th-century houses of Holywell Street itself, everything to the north belongs to another age, part of the 19th-century expansion of the city.

Near the western end of Holywell Street, on the left, is **Bath Place**, a narrow, cobbled alley with many right-angled bends, leading past ramshackle houses – former slums but now picturesque leaning cottages backing up against the town wall. Follow it through to the rambling **Turf Tavern** ❿. Recently renovated, the Turf is a splendid, low-beamed English tavern. Its foundations date to the 13th century, though most of the present building is 16th century. At the back is an attractive beer garden, and along the alleyway is another terraced area, tucked up against the exterior wall of New College cloisters.

Another venerable Oxford watering hole is at the end of Holywell Street on the right: **The King's Arms** ⓫ is a pub much frequented by students when exams are over. ❏

Map on page 140

Turf Tavern.

Restaurants

Edamame
15 Holywell Street. Tel 01865 246916. L Tues-Sun, D Thurs-Sat. £
In the rather unlikely setting of pastel-painted medieval Holywell Street, Edamame takes the diner (or, more likely, luncher) into an entirely different cultural eating experience. The atmosphere is authentically Japanese, as is the food, which tends to be limited in choice but of high quality. Canteen-style service and reasonable prices means long queues at lunchtime, but at weekend evenings there is more time and space to enjoy sushi and such Japanese delicacies as squid pieces in soy and ginger.

Holywell's Bar and Brasserie
38 Holywell Street. Tel 01865 203536. Open daily. ££
www.holywells.net
The former Blackwell's music bookshop has been imaginatively reconfigured to house this stylish brasserie, where the centrepiece is the original light well complete with pomegranate tree. Amidst the discreet lighting and understated decor you'll find a wide-ranging, mostly French-influenced menu with plenty of vegetarian options as well as good fish and British classics such as steak and ale pie.

Price indicators for three-course meal with half-bottle of wine:
£ = under £20
££ = £20–£30

Cafés and Pubs

Catering to the area's student population, the **Alternative Tuck Shop** (24 Holywell Street) serves up some of central Oxford's best sandwiches as well as pies and pastries. Queues can be long at the peak lunchtime period.

The **Turf Tavern** (Bath Place) is an Oxford legend. Atmospheric gardens, surrounded by medieval buildings and city walls, and a snug interior are the setting for good food and a wide range of drinks, including (in winter) hot rum punch.

The **King's Arms** (40 Holywell Street) is also practically part of the university. Its solid Georgian exterior has long been a landmark, promising good beer, an extensive menu and a busy atmosphere spread over several attractive bars.

CHRIST CHURCH AND BEYOND

Here can be found the origins of the city, the only
college with a cathedral, recurring echoes of
Alice in Wonderland and alternative art

The road heading south from
Carfax is called St Aldate's. It
was here, down towards the
river, that the first Oxford settlement
is thought to have been established,
beside the Abbey of St Frideswide.
St Frideswide's Abbey provided the
core of the massive college of Christ
Church, part of whose rich folklore
includes the tales told by one of its
dons, Charles Dodgson (writing as
Lewis Carroll).

Heading down St Aldate's, you
pass the **Town Hall** ❶ on the left, a
fine neo-Jacobean building, opened
in 1897, with Queen Victoria seated
in the apex of the central pediment.
It was built to the greater glory of
the City Council, reflecting Oxford's newly-found status and self-
confidence after it was declared a
county borough in 1889. Above, the
three-tiered belvedere on the roof is
topped by a weathervane in the
shape of a horned ox – for Oxford
was originally called Oxenford.

Tea dances are still regularly held
in the Town Hall Main Hall and
sometimes in the adjoining Assembly Room, beneath a large and
incongruous painting of the *Rape of
the Sabines* by Pietro da Cortona
(1596–1669) and portraits of former
mayors and members of parliament.
The Town Hall contains the city
archives, and as Oxford was never

bombed or burned the records are
particularly complete.

Museum of Oxford

Round the corner, in Blue Boar
Street, is the entrance to the former
library, built at the same time as the
Town Hall and now housing the
Museum of Oxford ❷ (open
Tues–Fri 10am–4pm, Sat 10am–
5pm, Sun noon–4pm; entrance fee).
The museum has an easy-to-digest
history of the city's development.
Displays highlight its history from

Map
on page
148

LEFT: porter and
Mercury's statue in
front of Christ Church.
BELOW:
Saxon exhibit at the
Museum of Oxford.

Museum of Oxford.

prehistoric times to the industrial age, with exhibits ranging from reconstructions of Roman kilns to the legend of St Frideswide, and from the origins of the university to the development of car production at Cowley. Best of all are the reconstructions of Oxford houses, contrasting the working-class district of Jericho *(see page 163)* with the stylish drawing-rooms of North Oxford's villas decorated in the latest William Morris textiles, and the reconstruction of a 1930s living room in the newly-built Morris Motors suburb of Cowley. Other highlights are the Keble College Barge, an example of one of the ornate floating boathouses of the late 19th century from which spectators watched river races during Eights Week. The most macabre exhibit is the skeleton of Giles Covington, an Oxford Freeman who was convicted of murder and executed in 1791.

The Town Hall building enlivens an otherwise dull stretch – the 1879 **post office** on the right is of interest only for the brass-bound wooden posting box in front. **Pembroke Street**, the first turning on the right, provides a better flavour of old

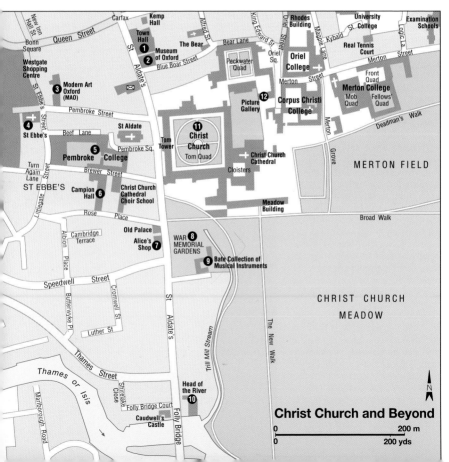

Christ Church and Beyond

Oxford, before Victorian improvers and modern developers set to work – lined as it is with jettied and pastel-coloured bay-windowed houses.

It leads to **Modern Art Oxford (MAO)** ❸ (30 Pembroke Street; open Tues–Sat 10am– 5pm, Sunday 12–5pm, closed Mondays; free), occupying an old brewery warehouse on the right-hand side of the street. MAO mounts highly regarded exhibitions of contemporary work. The **Café Varvara**, in the basement, is a good place to rest the legs.

On the other side of St Ebbe's Street, in **Pennyfarthing Place**, is the **Church of St Ebbe's** ❹, dedicated to a 7th-century Northumbrian abbess. The church was demolished and rebuilt in 1816, but the 12th-century west doorway, ornamented with beakheads, has survived.

Back now to St Aldate's, where the eponymous evangelical church stands back from the main road, in the leafy Pembroke Square, **St Aldate's Church** was virtually rebuilt in 1832, and is the centre of the city's lively young evangelical congregation – services are noisy affairs,

at which hymns are sung with much *joie de vivre* and to the accompaniment of guitars and tambourines.

Pembroke and Campion Hall

The square also provides access, on its southern side, to **Pembroke College** ❺ (visitors wishing to look around should first enquire at the porter's lodge; tel: 01865 276444). The college was founded in 1624 by King James I, and his statue occupies a niche in the tower of the Hall, which occupies the right-hand side of the Chapel Quad and is reached by means of a steep, stone staircase.

The hammerbeam roof and tall Perpendicular windows all look convincingly 15th-century, but the hall was actually built in 1848 by John Hayward. The chapel, on the opposite side of the quad, was completed in 1732.

Opposite Pembroke Square looms the magnificent **Tom Tower** of Christ Church, by Wren. To the north are the first-floor rooms in which Charles Dodgson, creator of *Alice's Adventures in Wonderland*, last resided while at Christ Church.

Map
on page
148

The lexographer Samuel Johnson was a student at Pembroke. He didn't complete his degree there, but was later awarded an honorary degree in recognition of his achievements in compiling the first English dictionary.

BELOW: tutorial at Pembroke College.

The shop's souvenirs relate to Lewis Carroll's Alice in Wonderland.

***

BELOW: "Blue Button" guides are noted for their expertise.

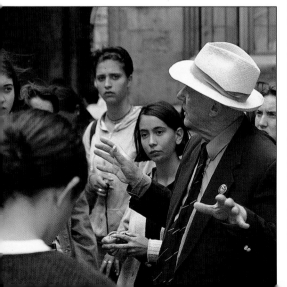

Dodgson, a mathematics don at the college, made friends with Alice, the daughter of the Dean, while taking photographs of the cathedral from the Deanery garden, and together they plunged into their own fantasy world.

Because there is no public access to Christ Church through the entrance under Tom Tower, continue for the moment down the right-hand side of St Aldate's. For another diversion, turn right into Brewer Street.

The buildings on the left house **Christ Church Cathedral Choir School**, and the delightful music of boys rehearsing for evensong is often carried on the breeze.

Further down, on the left, is **Campion Hall** ❻, a rather austere building of 1935 and Oxford's only example of Sir Edwin Lutyens' architecture. Campion Hall was set up in 1895 as a place of study for Roman Catholic priests. The chapel has a striking set of Stations of the Cross painted by Frank Brangwyn.

The friendlier-looking garden wing of Campion Hall, built in Cotswold vernacular style, can be seen by turning left into Littlegate

and left again into Rose Place. At the end of Rose Place, on the right, is the **Old Palace**, built for the first Bishop of Oxford in the 16th century. The oriel windows, supported by carved wooden grotesques, are dated 1628.

Alice's wonderland

Back in St Aldate's, the little shop on the right (No. 83) is **Alice's Shop** ❼ (open 11am–5pm daily). It is here that Alice Liddell used to buy her favourite barley sugar, before setting out on river trips with Charles Dodgson. In *Through the Looking Glass*, Alice visits the shop and is served by a bad-tempered sheep, and it was drawn in that book by Sir John Tenniel as "the Old Sheep Shop".

Directly opposite is Christ Church Cathedral rising beyond the **War Memorial Gardens** ❽. Laid out in 1926, the colourful raised perennial beds provide access to the public entrance to the college, through the **Meadow Building**.

Because of the way the official route round Christ Church is organised, starting at the Meadow Building and finishing in Merton Lane, before entering visitors may first want to continue down St Aldate's towards the Thames.

On the left-hand side, south of the Gardens, a gateway leads to the University Music Faculty, with a sign indicating the **Bate Collection of Musical Instruments** ❾ (open Mon–Fri 2–5pm, Sat during term-time 10am–noon; entrance fee). Established from a donation by Philip Bate in 1963, the collection is an unrivalled survey of woodwind instruments, added to by many donations of brass instruments, pianos and harpsicords, as well as a fine gamelan from Indonesia.

Further down, with the redeveloped district of St Ebbe's on the right, lies **Folly Bridge**, thought to be on the site of the first crossing point ("oxen-ford") over the Thames, created in the 8th century to serve the expanding Saxon community. The present bridge dates from 1827.

From Folly Bridge, visitors can enter through the turnstile gate behind the **Head of the River** pub and walk along the Thames to the **College Boathouses** (*see page 197*). On the other side of the bridge stands Cauldwell's Castle, also known as Isis House, an ornate red-brick folly decorated with white classical statues that was once rumoured to be a house of ill repute.

Nearby is the Aziz Pandesia restaurant, fusing Indian, Bangladeshi and Thai influences and offering great views over the river.

Christ Church

Christ Church (entry through Meadow Building, Mon–Sat 9am–5pm, Sun 12.45–5.30pm; tel: 01865 276150; entrance fee) was founded as Cardinal College in 1525 by Thomas Wolsey, Henry VIII's all-powerful Lord Chancellor, on the site of a priory thought to have been founded by St Frideswide as long ago as 730 (*see margin note*).

The earliest Oxford settlement may have been a lay community serving St Frideswide's; Saxon tools, artefacts and items of clothing have been found during excavations in St Aldate's. But the first truly historical reference comes in a royal charter of Ethelred the Unready, compensating the community for the burning down of its church by the Danes in 1002. A new Augustinian priory, dedicated to the saint, was re-established here by the 12th century, and had been greatly extended by Wolsey's time.

Wolsey dissolved it, using the endowments to found his new college, originally called Cardinal College. But his grand scheme came to an end in 1529 when he fell from grace after failing to secure the speedy annulment of Henry VIII's marriage to Catherine of Aragon. Henry rescued the church and took over the college, refounding it as King Henry VIII's College in 1532. Ten years later, Oxford was made a diocese and the priory was elevated to a cathedral, which Henry then combined with the college, renaming it Christ Church in 1546. Thus

Map on page 148

According to 12th-century accounts of her life, St Frideswide, Oxford's patron saint, refused to marry the king of Mercia and fled to Binsey, where she hid for three years in the woods, working as a servant to a swineherd. When the king tried to take Frideswide by force, he was, it is said, struck and blinded by a lightning bolt.

BELOW: Christ Church.

the church is unique in being both a college chapel and a cathedral.

Tour of the college

Having entered Christ Church, follow the visitors' trail to the **Cloisters**, which date from the 15th century. Wolsey destroyed the west and south sides of the cloisters, as well as three bays of the priory church, to make way for Tom Quad (*see facing page*). Through the first doorway on the right the Old Chapter House, with its Norman doorway and tall Early English lancet windows, now houses a souvenir shop as well as a collection of cathedral and college treasures.

Enter the **Cathedral** via the next door on the right. Begun towards the end of the 12th century, when Norman architecture was giving way to the new Early English style, the old priory church part of the cathedral is rather disappointing from an architectural point of view. The aisles are too squat when compared to the size of the columns, and the small pairs of rounded arches fit too awkwardly into the main ones.

One of Christ Church's custodians.

BELOW: Christ Church's dining hall.

By contrast, the 15th-century **Choir** with its lierne-vaulted ceiling – similar to that of the Divinity School – is magnificent. To the north of the choir is the reconstructed canopy from St Frideswide's tomb.

In the **Latin Chapel**, to the north, is a Burne-Jones window of 1858, depicting the life of the saint, including a depiction of St Margaret's Well at Binsey, the "Treacle Well" from *Alice's Adventures in Wonderland* (*see page 201*). This is one of Burne-Jones's earliest works, and the crowded scenes are full of dramatic detail, though the calamine-lotion colour of the faces is less successful.

In 1877, Burne-Jones also designed the **St Catherine Window** next to the altar, depicting Edith Liddell, sister of Lewis Carroll's Alice, as the saint. Nearby is a monument to Robert Burton (died 1640), author of *The Anatomy of Melancholy*. There is more excellent stained glass around the cathedral, much of it designed by William Morris and Edward Burne-Jones.

St Lucy's Chapel

Further west, **St Lucy's Chapel** contains a wealth of early 14th-century glass, including a scene showing the martyrdom of St Thomas à Becket, the archbishop of Canterbury brutally murdered by King Henry II's henchmen in 1170. He keeps company with a number of lewd and grotesque beasts that inhabit the tracery lights.

Exiting the cathedral by the same door, follow the cloisters round to the left, arriving, just before the opening to the Tom Quad, at the foot of the **staircase** to the Hall. Designed by James Wyatt in 1829, the stairs were built under a splendid fan-vaulted ceiling which had been created in 1640 by Dean Samuel Fell. The best view of the ceiling, and the single slender pillar supporting it, is from the top of the stairs.

Across the landing is the entrance to the **Hall**. With its magnificent hammerbeam roof, this is easily the largest old hall in Oxford, representing the full splendour of the Tudor court. The walls are adorned with portraits of some of the college's alumni, including William Gladstone and Anthony Eden (two of the 13 prime ministers produced by Christ Church) as well as John Locke, the great philosopher, and William Penn, the founder of Pennsylvania. The portrait just inside the door is that of Charles Dodgson.

The cloisters, the staircase and the Hall itself will be familiar to the millions who have enjoyed the film versions of the *Harry Potter* novels. The Hall was used as the inspiration for Hogwarts Hall, with its magically moving portraits, while the staircase featured in the scene in which first-year Hogwarts students are greeted by Professor McGonagall.

Tom Quad

Exit the hall and return to the top of the stairs for a view over the enormous **Tom Quad**, the college's Great Quadrangle. Measuring 264ft by 261ft (roughly 80 metres square), this is by far the largest quadrangle in the city. While considering its size, it is also worth stopping to consider the history of the college and its architecture. Wolsey intended everything about his foundation to be built on the grandest scale. However, all that was completed when he fell from grace in 1529 was the hall, the kitchens behind, and three sides of the Great Quad, including the lower stage of the gate-tower.

The college remained in this half-finished state for more than a century. Building work began again around 1640, when Samuel Fell commissioned the splendid fan vault under which we now stand. Shortly afterwards, Charles I made Christ Church his residence and work stopped during the Civil War.

After the monarchy was restored, the autocratic John Fell (Samuel's son) was appointed Dean. He completed the fourth side of the Great Quad, adding the north range, copying Wolsey's work exactly, even right down to the truncated pillars

Map on page 148

The magnificent Tom Quad tower dominates this part of Oxford.

BELOW: Tom Quad.

Map on page 148

Every night at 9.05pm (Oxford being situated a stubborn five minutes west of Greenwich), Great Tom's bell rings out from Tom Tower, tolling 101 times to signify the number of students admitted to the college at its original foundation. The bell also signalled the hour at which, in theory, all students in Oxford were supposed to be in bed.

BELOW:
Peckwater Quad.

and arches that had been intended to support a vaulted cloister all around the perimeter.

At the western side of the quad and intended to be its focal point, Fell commissioned Christopher Wren to finish the great gate-tower (**Tom Tower**), which he did in adventurous style, adding the bulky octagonal tower with its lead-covered cupola in 1681. Inside the tower, weighing more than seven tons, is the **Great Tom** bell. Recast before being installed, the original bell came from the enormous Osney Abbey to the west of the town, which was completely destroyed at the Dissolution in 1536.

The bell is named not as some people think after Thomas Wolsey, but after Thomas à Becket, whose martyrdom gave him a considerable cult following.

The central fountain, dug originally to supply water to the college, is also contemporary with this work. A statue of Mercury was put up in 1695 but was removed in 1817 after being damaged. The current statue, a copy of Giovanni da Bologna's *Mer-*

cury, was donated in 1928 and is sometimes to be seen clothed in sports kit or academic dress when students play their pranks in the relaxed post-exam weeks of summer.

Follow the eastern range of the quad to the northeastern corner and the **Deanery**. It was here, during the Civil War, that Charles I resided when in the city. The Deanery Garden is just over the other side.

The **Fell Tower**, the castellated tower facing on to the quad, was built in 1876–79, with its statue of John Fell who, for all that he did to improve Christ Church, was a strict disciplinarian and far from popular.

Peckwater Quad

Passing beneath Fell Tower, you pass **Killcanon** on the left, built in 1669 and so called because of the icy winds that blow around the block in winter, and enter **Peckwater Quad**, named after a medieval inn that stood on the site until these grand classical buildings were constructed in 1713. The three enclosed sides of the quad (containing student accommodation) are perfectly proportioned according to all the classical rules.

Opposite stands the college **Library**, built in 1716 and originally designed with the ground floor as an open loggia. Its giant Corinthian columns lend weight and splendour to this side of the quadrangle. The library is not open to the public but you can, with discretion, peer through the windows at the ceiling-high bookstacks, leather-bound volumes and fine stucco ceiling.

From Peckwater Quad, proceed to Canterbury Quad. On the right is the entrance to the **Picture Gallery** ⓬ (open Mon–Sat 10.30am–1pm and 2–5.30pm, Sun 2–5.30pm; entrance fee). It contains a small but important collection of Old Masters, including works by Tintoretto, Veronese and Van Dyck, as well as a famous Holbein portrait of Henry VIII. ❏

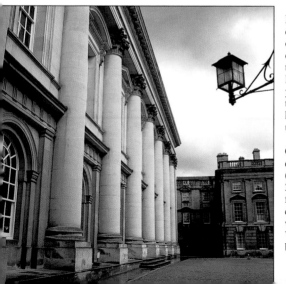

RESTAURANTS, CAFÉS & BARS

Restaurants

Shanghai 30s

82 St Aldate's. Tel 242230.
Open daily ££
A far cry from the normal Chinese take-away, this is an upmarket and sophisticated place, housed in the premises of the former and legendary Elizabeth Restaurant. The emphasis is on seafood, but many other classics, including a large vegetarian menu, are available in a restaurant that succeeds in being both elegant and friendly.

Cafés

Café Loco (85 St Aldate's) is a cheerfully busy café, serving a good range of sandwiches, salads and daily specials. Open every day, it provides good breakfasts and afternoon teas, even if the drinks can seem rather over-priced.

The Café in the basement of **Modern Art**

PRICE CATEGORIES

Prices for three-course dinner per person with a half-bottle of house wine:
£ = under £20
££ = £20–£30
£££ = £30–£45
££££ = more than £45

RIGHT: the Head of the River pub, Folly Bridge.

Oxford (open Tues-Sat 10am-5pm, Sun 12-5pm) is a pleasantly relaxed spot where you can enjoy a wholesome lunch of salads or afternoon tea and cakes. Child-friendly and welcoming, it offers a good alternative to central Oxford's more predictable eateries.

Another good option is **George & Danver's** (1 Pembroke Street), a hospitable café/sandwich bar that specialises in its own brand of ice cream (there is a sister outlet, George & Davis, in Little Clarendon Street).

Further down St Aldate's you will find **Reservoir Books** (84 St Aldate's), something of an intellectual centre, with second-hand books and an exhibition space as well as a well-run café with excellent coffee and cakes. The Café's mission is not only to cater for peckish bookworms but also to preserve the wonderful but dilapidated 16th-century building in which it is housed.

Pubs

Next to MOA, the **Royal Blenheim** pub (13 St Ebbe's Street) is a quiet inner-city local, with none of the youth-oriented atmosphere of nearby competitors. It serves a good range of pub lunches.

The **St Aldate's Tavern** (108 St Aldate's) is spacious, high-ceilinged establishment, with a good mix of Town and Gown custom and an above-average range of real ales.

The **Old Tom** (101 St Aldate's), named after Christ Church's Tom Tower opposite, is a real Oxford institution, but is worth visiting only for the small beer garden.

The enormously popular **Head of the River** (Folly Bridge) draws big crowds in the summer on account of its attractive riverside terrace. Housed in an imaginatively restored warehouse, the pub is a reliable, if pricey, place for lunch, but the views of the river compensate. It has guest rooms that overlook the river.

NORTHWEST OF THE CENTRE

After exploring the Ashmolean, you can enter the
district of Jericho to discover the city's
publishing heritage and end with a drink
in a pub popular with many authors

Looking across from the Martyrs' Memorial, the entrance to Beaumont Street is dominated on the left by the famous, yellow-brick **Randolph Hotel ❶**, a splendid Victorian-Gothic edifice dating from 1863. The Randolph is Oxford's most famous hotel. It is a popular venue for conferences, and at the beginning of the academic year in October you can often see nervous Freshers eating there with their parents – a last meal before a new life begins. The lounge contains paintings by Sir Osbert Lancaster, commissioned to illustrate Max Beerbohm's 1911 satire on Oxford life, *Zuleika Dobson*.

The Taylor Institute

Facing all this gothicry is the **Taylor Institute** and, beyond, the Ashmolean Museum. Built from 1841 to 1845 and a rare example in Oxford of neo-Grecian architecture, the forceful design of the two linked buildings is freely based on the Temple of Apollo at Bassae which the architect, Charles Robert Cockerell, had studied. The four statues standing on top of the columns of the Taylor Institute – that is the east wing, facing St Giles – represent France, Italy, Germany and Spain, for the Institution was founded, under the will of Sir Robert Taylor, mainly for

the study of the languages of these countries. The building now houses lecture theatres and the Taylorian Library, devoted to books published in the principal European languages.

The Ashmolean

Fronting on to Beaumont Street, and surmounted by a statue of Apollo, is the pillared portico of the **Ashmolean Museum ❷** (open Tues–Sat 10am–5pm, Sun 12–5pm, June–Aug until 7pm; donation). Containing the University of Oxford's col-

LEFT:
medieval cottages in
Worcester College.
BELOW: Oxford's
most famous hotel.

Powhattan's mantle (top) and the Alfred Jewel, stars of the Ashmolean Museum.

lections of art and antiquities, the building was originally known as the University Galleries, housing a sculpture collection donated by Francis Randolph.

The name "Ashmolean" was first applied when extensions were built in 1899 to house the collections of the antiquary and scholar Elias Ashmole. These had hitherto been housed in purpose-built premises on Broad Street (now the Museum of the History of Science, *see page 133*), established by Ashmole in 1683. Regarded as the oldest museum collections in the country, their origins go back to before Ashmole's day, and not to Oxford, but to Lambeth, London. There, in a pub called The Ark, the early 17th-century naturalist and royal gardener John Tradescant displayed his extensive collection of rarities and curiosities either gathered by himself on his trips to Europe or given to him by sea captains. After his death in 1638,

Tradescant's son, also called John, infused the collection with items from Virginia, to which he travelled on several occasions.

Meanwhile, Ashmole had befriended the Tradescants and persuaded them that he would be a suitable curator for their curiosities after their deaths. The younger Tradescant left a contradictory will bequeathing the collection to both Oxford and Cambridge, which his widow and Ashmole challenged. Ashmole won, in time, and in return for an honorary degree, he passed it (and his coin collection) to Oxford.

Items from the original "Ark" – or what is left of it after the neglect and sale of many objects in the 18th century – can still be seen in the museum, in the special **Tradescant Room** on the first floor. It is a wonderfully eccentric and eclectic group of objects, including Guy Fawkes' lantern, Oliver Cromwell's death mask and a piece of the stake at

Northwest of the Centre

Radcliffe Observatory **9**
10 St Anne's College
Radcliffe Infirmary
Old Parsonage Hotel
St Aloysius
St Giles
Browns
8 Somerville College Chapel
11
Keble College
6 Oxford University Press
War Memorial
Dartington House
Queen Elizabeth House
St Barnabas **7**
University Offices
JERICHO
Wellington Square
St Benet's Hall
Lamb and Flag
Kellog College
Eagle and Child **12**
Regent's Park College
Pusey House
St Cross College
St John's College
WORCESTER COLLEGE CRICKET GROUND
Worcester Place
Blackfriars
Sainsbury Building
Ruskin College **5**
Oriental Institute
Ashmolean Museum **2**
Taylor Institute
Balliol College
Worcester College **4**
Chapel
Oxford Playhouse **3**
Randolph Hotel **1**
Martyrs' Memorial

0 — 200 m
0 — 200 yds

Worcester College Lake

Map on page 158

which Bishop Latimer was burned, as well as a rhinoceros-horn cup from China, Henry VIII's stirrups and hawking gear, and, as the star attraction, **Powhattan's Mantle**. Powhattan was the king of Virginia, and as any child will tell you, the father of Pocahontas.

Since moving to Beaumont Street, the Ashmolean has developed into one of the world's great museums, hugely enriched by archaeological material, given by such notable excavators as Sir Flinders Petrie, the late 19th-century Egyptologist, and Sir Arthur Evans, who discovered the great palace complex of Knossos on Crete.

The Antiquities Department has a fine Egyptian section, and extensive displays covering Ancient Greece (particularly vases), Rome and the Near East, as well as Dark-Age Europe and Anglo-Saxon Britain.

The Alfred Jewel

It is in the latter section that the museum's most famous artefact is to be found, namely the **Alfred Jewel**. Found in Somerset in 1693, it is regarded as the finest piece of Saxon art ever discovered. Consisting of an enamel seated figure set under a rock crystal in a gold frame bearing the inscription *Aelfred mec heht gewyrcan* ("Alfred had me made"), it isn't in fact an item of personal jewellery but would have been affixed to a pointer for following the text in a manuscript. Such pointers are known to have been given as gifts by Alfred (849–99), along with copies of his translation of Gregory the Great's *Pastoral Care*.

The Department of Eastern Art, which includes some superb examples of Gandharan sculpture, is also impressive, but the other main attraction of the museum is the Department of Western Art on the first floor, which contains a remarkable collection of Italian Renaissance bronzes and paintings. Don't miss the drawings by Michelangelo and Raphael, as well as *The Hunt in the Forest*, painted by the Florentine Paolo Uccello in 1466. There are also more recent works by pre-Raphaelite and Impressionist artists. The Heberden Coin Room, also on

Detail from The Hunt in the Forest *(1466).*

BELOW: the Ashmolean Museum.

TIP

Just round the corner
from the Oxford Play-
house, in Gloucester
Street, is the bijou
Taylor Burton Studio. A
50-seat theatre at the
top of two flights of
stairs, it showcases
student productions
during term and, out of
term, hosts touring
companies or commu-
nity theatre groups.
Tel: 01865 305305.
www.oxfordplayhouse
.com

BELOW:
Regency houses on
Beaumont Street.

the first floor, contains an interesting collection of coins and medals.

Since renovations were carried out in 1995, the public entrance to the museum is no longer through the large blue doors in the centre, but through doors into the west wing. The renovations included the provision of a pleasant café in the vaulted basement, which can also be reached directly from the outside. The museum puts on a range of temporary exhibitions and public lectures.

To the theatre

Opposite the Ashmolean and adjacent to the Beaumont Street side of the Randolph is the **Oxford Playhouse** ❸ (tel: 01865 305305). Opened in 1923, the original Playhouse, opposite Somerville, was known as the "Red Barn" and in 1938 it moved to the present building on Beaumont Street. It has often struggled with financial problems and in 1987 was forced to close after the imposition of new fire regulations and funding cuts. But in 1991 the Playhouse reopened and in 1996 underwent a major refurbishment

project costing £4 million, £2.5 million of which was provided by the Arts Council Lottery Fund.

Early members of the Playhouse company included Dame Flora Robson and Sir John Gielgud, but perhaps its most celebrated supporters were Richard Burton and Elizabeth Taylor, who in 1966 performed *Doctor Faustus* free of charge, earning the theatre enough extra revenue to afford an extension, the Burton-Taylor Studio *(see margin Tip)*. Burton, who had first acted while in Oxford during World War II, kept a strong allegiance to the city and was a generous donor to the Playhouse, and also to St Peter's College and the student newspaper, *Isis*.

Today, the Playhouse offers a broad programme of work that includes drama, dance, opera, musical theatre, popular music and jazz. It has a fledgling youth and education community scheme, plus an attractive bar and coffee shop.

The rest of **Beaumont Street** consists of Regency terraces, several with delicate cast-iron fanlights, verandas and balconies, built between 1822 and 1833. Slightly humbler town houses of the same date line **St John Street** to the right. For anyone wanting to live in Oxford, this is as about as close to the city centre as you can get. Most of the houses serve as college lodgings, or the premises of solicitors, doctors and dentists – but occasionally one does come up for sale.

The western end of Beaumont Street was once occupied by Beaumont Palace, built in the early 12th century by Henry I as his royal residence in Oxford and the birthplace of his sons Richard (the Lion-Heart) and John. Though the palace represented the town's rise in importance during the early Middle Ages, it did not remain here for long; the original door was used by Merton's founders as their library entrance, where it can still be seen (*see page 114*).

Worcester College

At the end of Beaumont Street, cross the road to enter **Worcester College** ❹ (open daily 2–5pm; tel: 01865 278300; free). Worcester is different from most other colleges in that it

has no intimate, enclosed quadrangles. But this in no way detracts from the appeal of the place, for as well as some fine architecture, the college has some of the most beautiful gardens.

Founded in the early 18th century, the origins of the college go back to Gloucester Hall, established on the site for Benedictine monks in 1283, but dissolved in about 1539. After the Dissolution, Gloucester continued as an academic hall, despite several Benedictine changes of ownership, but slid into debt and decline. The doorheads of the west range bear the coats of arms, carved in stone, of the principal abbeys connected with the college: Glastonbury, Malmesbury, Canterbury and Pershore.

Revival only came at the end of the 17th century with funds provided by Sir Thomas Cookes, a Worcestershire baronet. The new Worcester College received its statutes in 1714, but the 18th-century building programme was financed by another man, George Clarke, who is remembered by the college as *tantum nos Fundator* ("almost our Founder").

Map on page 158

The crest of one of Worcester College's founding abbeys.

BELOW:
Worcester College.

*Worcester's library
contains many of the
drawings of Inigo
Jones (1573–1652),
the first great English
architect whose
masterpiece was the
Banqueting Hall in
London's Whitehall.*

BELOW: the 1982
Sainsbury Building
at Worcester College.

Despite this infusion of money, Worcester was never very wealthy, and the original Gloucester Hall **medieval cottages** owe their survival to the fact that the college could only afford the two neoclassical ranges we see today. Of these, the front or west range is the most interesting, for it contains the **Library** (above the cloister), the **Hall** and the **Chapel** (in the two wings).

Designed by Nicholas Hawksmoor, the library was founded on a substantial collection of books and manuscripts donated by George Clarke and includes a large proportion of the surviving drawings of Inigo Jones. The hall and chapel were completed by James Wyatt in the 1770s. Both were transformed internally by William Burges, in the latter half of the 19th century. The hall was, controversially, restored to its 18th-century appearance in 1966, but the chapel remains as a splendid example of Burges's highly unusual style. Sadly, the gloom created by the dark stained glass prevents a full appreciation of the lavish interior, with its Roman-style floor mosaics,

Raphaelesque frescoes and gilded ceiling. Evangelists fill the niches at each corner of the chapel, and the pew ends are carved with a menagerie of animals and birds.

Worcester is sited on a slope, the land dropping away to the west. A tunnel at the end of the Gloucester Hall cottages leads through to the **gardens**, which are as beautiful as any in Oxford, a fact endorsed by Lewis Carroll in *Alice's Adventures in Wonderland* (1865) when he describes the tunnel "not much larger than a rathole" leading "to the loveliest garden you ever saw".

Landscaped like a small park, the gardens are planted with magnificent trees and shrubs and include a lovely willow-fringed lake, where Alice was used to feed the ducks. The lake was reclaimed from the water meadows when the park-like gardens were laid out in the early 19th century, and is now topped up by the overflow from the Oxford Canal, which forms the western boundary of Worcester's grounds. A walk around the lake is recommended.

Looking back through the trees

there are glimpses of the Palladian facade of the **Provost's House**, while at the northern end of the lake is the **Sainsbury Building**. Regarded as one of the best pieces of modern architecture in Oxford, its carefully juxtaposed roof lines and walls descend to a delightful lakeside terrace. Worcester College's playing fields stretch away to the north.

Ruskin College

Exit Worcester and walk north along **Walton Street**. On the corner of Worcester Place stands **Ruskin College ❺**. Not strictly part of the university, this is one of several institutions founded in memory of the art and later social critic John Ruskin, for the education of working men and women. The college has strong links with the trade union movement and the Workers' Educational Association.

Ruskin is appropriately sited on the edge of the former working-class suburb of **Jericho** (*see page 165*), occupying the block between Walton Street and the Oxford Canal. Some say that the name derives from

the insubstantial nature of the jerry-built terraced houses, a few of which date to the 1830s. There was, however, a pub called the Jericho House here as early as 1688, and the name was used in the 17th century for any remote place, by analogy with the biblical town in Palestine.

The area was developed to house the increasing numbers of workers in this part of the city after the arrival of the Oxford Canal in 1790. When the Oxford University Press moved here from the Clarendon Building in 1830, further houses were built to accommodate the print workers.

Around the first corner from Ruskin, also on the west side of Walton Street, the huge, neoclassical **Oxford University Press** building ❻ takes up most of the block between Walton Crescent and Great Clarendon Street. The south wing (left) was originally devoted to Bible printing, the north to learned books. To learn more about the history of this world-famous publishing house, make an appointment to see the OUP Museum (*see page 31*).

It was the print workers who made

Map
on page
158

The OUP has a major presence in the city.

BELOW:
walking in Worcester College's gardens.

St Giles' Fair

The Fair (as it is always called) is one of Oxford's most cherished annual events. Of course, there are those hard-headed citizens who complain that it disrupts trade and traffic, but most people would spring to the defence of an occasion enjoyed by the vast majority.

St Giles' Fair was originally a parish wake, a religious event dating from 1624. The association with St Giles, the patron saint of beggars and cripples, fixed both the date of the Fair (Monday and Tuesday following the first Sunday in September) and the location, the splendidly wide St Giles Street. By the 18th century, the occasion was known as St Giles' Feast, a time for feasting, sporting events, and the selling of "small wares".

The Fair came into its own in Victorian times, when "wonders of art and nature" were added. Menageries and freak shows were the earliest sights: an elephant, the Bear Lady and the Double-bodied Hindoo Boy were regular visitors.

New inventions were a big draw: the photographer with his three-for-a-shilling portraits; the Biograph exhibitions; the miniature railway; the Chairoplane rides. In the late 19th century, the Fair was a dazzling event, with traction engines providing brilliant illuminations. Taylor's Bioscope Show glittered with 4,000 coloured lights, while the rival establishment, run by Jacob Studt, was approached through Corinthian pillars and graced by troupes of lady dancers.

More surprisingly, females also appeared at the Fair as wrestlers, wearing corsets and black tights. Little wonder, with such attractions on offer, that the Fair became, by 1900, the major holiday not only for Oxford city, but the county beyond. The huge caravan of wagons, caravans and engines gathered in Woodstock Road – then open country – on Sunday, and at 5am on Monday morning, the procession moved into the city.

The Fair had its problems, of course. In 1838, the Mayor of Oxford issued an order excluding gypsies from the site because of pickpocketing. Horseplay was firmly dealt with in 1898, when the Mayor decreed a penalty of two months' imprisonment or a £5 fine for anyone found assaulting another with "a Squirt, Scratch-back, Cracker, Whip, or Brush".

Dramatic events occurred in 1830, after trouble on nearby Otmoor, where the locals were opposing the enclosure by landowners of their common land. Matters came to a head in September, when the militia were called in to stop the systematic destruction by the moormen. About 50 were arrested and taken into Oxford for trial. But the crowds gathered for the Fair were sympathetic to the villagers' cause, the soldiers were pelted with stones, and the prisoners were freed to cries of "Otmoor for Ever".

In many ways, the Fair today looks much as it did in Edwardian times. The traction engines still provide power, and a splendid roundabout always occupies pride of place by the Martyrs' Memorial. But much more elaborate and terrifying rides now take the place of the freaks and theatre shows. ❑

LEFT: carousel at St Giles' Fair.

up the majority of the congregation of the massive **Church of St Barnabas** ❼, which was built by the canal in 1868. You can get to the church and take in some of the atmosphere of old Jericho by taking a stroll down Great Clarendon Street. The church is distinctive for its tall, Italian-Romanesque style tower.

Opposite the Press building is the neo-Grecian facade of the old St Paul's Church, built in 1936. It no longer serves as a church today but as **Freuds**, an unusual wine bar and restaurant with live-music programmes specialising in jazz.

If you continue along Walton Street, you will notice away to the north the distinctive octagonal tower of the Radcliffe Observatory (*see page 166*). Passing the **Phoenix Picture House**, which shows foreign and non-mainstream films, and Raymond Blanc's brasserie, **Le Petit Blanc** (an affordable version of the great French chef's Le Manoir aux Quat'Saisons), both on the left, you'll get to Walton Well Road, which leads over the canal and railway line to Port Meadow.

Otherwise, retrace your steps to **Little Clarendon Street**, which links Walton Street with St Giles'. Among various modern administrative buildings of the university are bars, brasseries, cafés, boutiques and gift shops.

Little Clarendon Street emerges at the Woodstock Road end of St Giles. Immediately on the left is **Maison Blanc**, a wonderful patisserie, and adjacent to that is **Browns**, a long-established restaurant whose reputation is not only based on good food but also on its child-friendly attitude, popular with families.

Somerville College

North along Woodstock Road, just after St Aloysius Church is **Somerville College** ❽ (open daily 2–5pm; tel: 01865 270600; free). Founded in 1879 specifically for the education of women, it is now mixed. The first "ladies'" college, Lady Margaret Hall, had been established the previous year, but under the aegis of the Anglican Church. A group of breakaway liberal nonconformists founded Somerville, named after the

Map on page 158

Raymond Blanc, begetter of Le Petit Blanc.

BELOW: the Church of St Barnabas, seen from the canal.

Life in Jericho

Featured as the cholera-ridden slum of Beersheba in Thomas Hardy's *Jude the Obscure* (1895), Jericho's working-class credentials have long expired, for its prime location at the threshold to the city has made it a desirable area to live, particularly for wealthy students and young professionals. House prices have soared and Walton Street is now lined with craft shops, boutiques, delicatessens and restaurants.

Much of Jericho is terraced housing built by speculators and St John's College for the workers of the university, OUP, an iron foundry and the canal. A reputation for seediness in the 1960s led to calls for its demolition.

scientist and suffragette Mary Somerville (1780–1872), to take women of all religious persuasions – or none.

Women at Oxford were at first patronised rather than welcomed. They were not allowed to attend lectures; instead, tuition was provided by the AEW, the Association for Promoting the Higher Education of Women. They were not allowed to take degrees until 1920, and Somerville, along with the other four women's halls founded in the late 19th century, was not recognised as a college until 1959.

Despite this, its students include an extraordinary number of public figures, not least Indira Gandhi and Margaret Thatcher. Although Mrs Thatcher may have had her differences with the university, she was loyal to Somerville, making a large donation to the £4 million Margaret Thatcher Centre.

The buildings of Somerville are small and homely in scale, some built in the "Queen Anne" style of the late 19th century, others in 1930s neo-Georgian.

While she was at Somerville from 1943 to 1947, Margaret Thatcher's main extracurricular activity was the university's Conservative Association; she became its president. She also joined the John Wesley Society and accompanied fellow Methodists on speaking trips to Oxfordshire villages; these aided her public speaking skills.

BELOW: setting up the freshers' photograph at Somerville.

Radcliffe Observatory

Further up Woodstock Road is the **Radcliffe Infirmary**, built from the estates of John Radcliffe, the 18th-century physician, but now surrounded by an accretion of later hospital buildings. The adjacent **Radcliffe Observatory** ❾, completed in 1794, has now been swallowed up by **Green College**, founded in 1979 for graduate medical students.

The Observatory, mostly designed by James Wyatt, does not have the expected dome; instead, it is topped by an elongated octagon, carved with personifications of the four winds and modelled on the ancient Greek Tower of the Winds in Athens. Unfortunately there is no public access to the observatory except for one day a year, the college's open day (tel: 01865 274770 for information).

St Anne's College

St Anne's College ❿, opposite, traces its origins to the Society of Oxford Home Students, an organisation formed in 1879 to provide higher education for the daughters and wives of dons and students from the local girls' high schools. Because they lived at home, rather than in one of the two women's halls of residence (Somerville and Lady Margaret), they were known as "unattached students", and opponents of women's education were fond of referring to the Society as "Soc. mul. Ox. priv. stud." (abbreviated from the Latin name *Societas mulieram Oxoniae Privatum Studentium*).

The Home Students were taught and supervised in the houses of sympathetic Oxford dons and their friends until, in the 1930s, their became so great that more permanent arrangements were needed, and so the library and lecture rooms were added to the existing Victorian houses on the current site. Designed by Sir Giles Gilbert Scott, son of the Victorian Gothicist Sir George, they were completed in 1937.

During World War II, so many Oxford families were involved in war work that it became increasingly difficult to accommodate students at home and find suitable "hostesses" or chaperones; so hostels were built and by 1942 St Anne's had been transformed into a residential institution like any other, achieving full college status in 1959.

A number of buildings were added after the war, notably the **Founder's Gatehouse** (1966), a building in the Modernist idiom reflecting medieval precedents in its polygonal turrets, and the **Dining Hall** (1958–60), with its glass walls and rooftop lantern.

Church of St Giles

Heading back towards Oxford city centre, the **Church of St Giles** sits at the apex of the fork where Woodstock and Banbury roads take their separate ways. The church is largely 13th-century and sits in an island of green, facing down the wide, tree-lined thoroughfare, best seen in early September when the traffic is excluded for the annual St Giles' Fair (*see page 164*). These days the ancient fair is no different from any of those that are held up and down the country, except for the poignant contrast between the flash-

Map on page 158

St Anne's College.

BELOW: the library at St Anne's College.

Map on page 158

The Church of St Giles.

BELOW: the Eagle and Child has been an inn since 1650.

ing lights, candy floss and bingo stalls set against the sedate and ancient college buildings.

The west (right-hand) side of St Giles' is lined with a pleasing mixture of mainly 17th- and 18th-century buildings, many of them owned by religious bodies who, in this century at least, seem to co-exist in neighbourly harmony. They include the Christian Scientists at Nos. 34–6, **St Benet's Hall**, for Benedictine monks, at No. 38, and the Quakers at No. 43.

Beyond Pusey Street is **St Cross College**, a graduates-only college founded in 1965. It has around 220 students and prides itself on its friendliness and the quality of its food.

The Eagle and Child

Perhaps the most interesting building on this side of St Giles' is the **Eagle and Child** pub ⓬, on the corner of Wellington Place, always very popular among students. Its name supposedly relates to the legend of a noble-born baby being found in an eagle's nest, but its fame derives from the fact that, from the 1930s to

the 1960s, it was the meeting place of the informal literary group known as the "Inklings". Led by C. S. Lewis (described by his pupil John Betjeman as "breezy, tweedy, beer-drinking and jolly"), the Inklings included such luminaries as Charles Williams, Nevill Coghill and J. R. R. Tolkien (*see page 135*).

It was here, in these cosy, fireside surroundings, that Tolkien began discussing his saga *The Lord of the Rings* with the assembled company, little realising that it would become such a success that he would be forced, by a torrent of letters, phone calls and visits from fans, to exchange the comforts of Oxford for a life of seclusion in Bournemouth.

Eventually, after his wife died in 1971, he returned to Oxford's womb, taking rooms in Merton and becoming an Honorary Fellow. He died in 1973 and lies buried in Wolvercote Cemetery, just beyond the ring road to the north of the city.

Continuing this literary tradition, the Eagle and Child was a regular watering-hole for Colin Dexter, creator of Inspector Morse. ❏

RESTAURANTS, CAFÉS & BARS

Restaurants

Le Petit Blanc
71-72 Walton Street. Tel 01865 510999. Daily. ££
www.lepetitblanc.co.uk
Oxford's less expensive sister of the acclaimed Quat'Saisons also offers elegant French cuisine, but in the more palatable form of good-value *prix fixe* menus as well as à la carte. The food is a beautifully prepared blend of French regional dishes, served in a pleasantly stripped-down ambiance of modern furniture and wooden floors. Booking is highly recommended.

Branca
111 Walton Street. Tel 01865 556111. Daily. ££
www.branca-restaurants.co.uk
The Italian alternative to Raymond Blanc's French cuisine, Branca is a well-established but still refreshingly modern place specialising in authentic Italian cooking. Dishes include all of the pizza, pasta and antipasti classics, but with a strong emphasis

on fresh local produce and attractive presentation. The decor is spacious and welcoming, and the staff helpful.

The Big Bang
124 Walton Street. Tel 01865 511411. Daily. £
www.thebigbangoxford.co.uk
A new initiative, this cheerful restaurant appeals to aficionados of bangers & mash, offering a range of sausages including the famous and eponymous Oxford Sausage. If you don't like sausages, there are various pies, and vegetarians will be relieved to learn that there are several suitable sausage options. A good-value and up-beat establishment, it draws a big student crowd.

Porters
1-2 Little Clarendon Street. Tel 01865 511442. Open daily. ££
Competing with several chain-style eateries, this is a friendly and welcoming restaurant/bar, which covers most requirements from large breakfasts (weekends only) to an economical pre-theatre dinner menu. The food is locally sourced, generous and served in an agreeably stylish dining area with a bar to one side.

Browns Restaurant & Bar
5-11 Woodstock Road. Tel 01865 511955. Daily. ££
The first of Oxford brasserie-style venues, Browns maintains its combination of good simple food and attentive service. It offers everything from a drink or snack to a three-course dinner, with excellent salads, pasta dishes and traditional classics such as steak & Guinness pie. At weekends the queues can be long.

Cafés

The bright and airy café in the basement of the **Ashmolean Museum** provides drinks, snacks, excellent tea and cakes and a range of hot meals at lunchtime.

The **St Giles'** (52 St Giles) is an above-average "greasy spoon" establishment, with big cooked breakfasts and other fried treats.

Bars & Pubs

The **Morse Bar** in the Randolph Hotel is a civilised place for an early evening drink or afternoon tea and a good way to sample the hotel's Victorian elegance.

The **Eagle and Child** is a literary landmark in

its own right and a good old-fashioned pub serving traditional dishes such as fish and chips or sausage and mash.

Freuds (119 Walton Street), housed in a converted church, is one of several trendy cocktail bars in the area; it specialises in jazz and student social life.

Raoul's (32 Walton Street) is another fashionable watering-hole with an impressive cocktail list and an emphatically cool clientele.

The **Duke of Cambridge** (5-6 Little Clarendon Street) stands out as the most stylish establishment in this stylish street. Prices reflect the status of its upmarket clientele.

RIGHT: St Giles' Café, known for its cooked breakfasts.

ST JOHN'S AND THE NORTH

Apart from St John's, this area was developed
after the great university reforms in the
mid-19th century, and includes two
remarkable museums

S tarting in St Giles', follow the
east side along the long Balliol
facade to the point where it
meets the considerably more varied
frontage of **St John's College** ❶
(open daily 1–5pm; tel: 01865
277300; free).

This college, one of the richest in
Oxford, was originally founded by
Archbishop Chichele, in 1437, for
Cistercian monks and named after St
Bernard. After the Dissolution of the
Monasteries, it was re-founded, in
1555, by Sir Thomas White, a
wealthy member of the Merchant
Taylor's Guild. A statue of St
Bernard, flanked by the two foun-
ders, occupies a niche on the gate-
tower. The niche on the inner side
contains Eric Gill's splendid *St John
the Baptist* (1936).

The Baylie Chapel

The buildings of the Front Quad survive from the original St Bernard
College. The hall, though, was
remodelled in the 18th century and
given its stone screen, designed by
James Gibbs, in 1742. The chapel,
on the left, was comprehensively
spoiled, internally, in the 19th century. More interesting is the **Baylie
Chapel** to the north, with its plaster
fan-vault. This was built in 1662 and
houses the monument of Richard
Baylie (died 1667), the Royalist

President (head) of St John's, who
was forcibly ejected from the college
by Parliamentary troops during the
17th-century Civil War but was reinstated at the Restoration.

In remaining staunchly loyal to
Charles I, Baylie was following the
example of his predecessor, Archbishop Laud, who was president
from 1611 to 1621 and Chancellor of
the University from 1629. During
his time as chancellor, Laud drew up
a long list of rules governing the
behaviour of Oxford scholars,

Map
on page
172

LEFT:
University Museum.
BELOW:
St John's College.

*Charles I in
Canterbury Quad,
St John's College.*

which, for all that Laud was strongly opposed to the Calvinist doctrines of his day, could have been written by a staunch Puritan.

Under the Laudian Code, as it is known, professional actors were forbidden to enter the university and scholars were forbidden to hunt, gamble, smoke, drink or wear their hair long or in curls – these rules remained the basis of university discipline until 1854.

Canterbury Quad

It is all the more remarkable, therefore, that Laud also financed the construction of the **Canterbury Quad** at St John's – a group of buildings unmatched in Oxford for their showy exuberance. The passage linking Front Quad and Canterbury Quad is fan-vaulted, a last touch of late Gothic before the Baroque splendours beyond.

We emerge to face a bold, two-storey portal containing a bronze statue of Charles I (by Le Sueur) under the royal coat of arms. To either side, the delicate arcade, carried on slender Tuscan columns, has medallion busts of female figures (by Anthony Gore), representing the

Virtues and the Liberal Arts, beneath a running frieze of foliage. Crossing the quad and, turning round, we find that the opposite range is similar but with a statue of Queen Henrietta Maria, wife of Charles I, in the niche. For long the design was attributed to Inigo Jones or Nicholas Stone, two of the greatest architects of their day, but now the credit goes to Adam Browne, a craftsman-architect so obscure that you will search in vain for his name in architectural reference books.

When the quad was completed in 1636, Charles I and his Queen were invited to view the buildings and watch a play in the hall (despite the Laudian Code!). It's said the king's entertainment cost almost more than the buildings.

Posthumous move

The library on the south side of Canterbury Quad (not open) contains memorabilia of both Laud and the monarch, both of whom died on the scaffold – Charles, famously, in 1649 and Laud in 1645, accused by the Long Parliament of high treason.

Originally buried in Barking, his bones were quietly re-interred in St John's chapel in 1663.

The east side of Canterbury Quad leads out to the college gardens. Like neighbouring Trinity College (*see page 132*), St John's was built outside the city walls and so the gardens are very spacious. The path around the lawn twists and turns between carefully tended shrubs and groves of trees that were first planted in 1712, providing a wonderful blend of the formal and the naturalistic.

Visitors can extend their walk by taking a side path to the north, past rockeries and shady lawns, catching glimpses of more modern college buildings to the north, including "The Beehive", built in 1958, so called because the plan is based on clusters of interlocking octagons, and the Sir Thomas White Building of 1975.

Through to Keble

From St John's turn right, up St Giles', and look for a passageway on the right, by the **Lamb and Flag ❷** – a tavern that opened in 1695 and

Map on page 172

The student unrest of the early 1970s didn't impinge on Tony Blair, one of St John's law students at the time. The future prime minister, then more interested in forming a rock band, didn't even join the Labour club. "I went through all the bit about reading Trotsky and attempting a Marxist analysis," he said later. "But it never went very deep."

BELOW: St John's College.

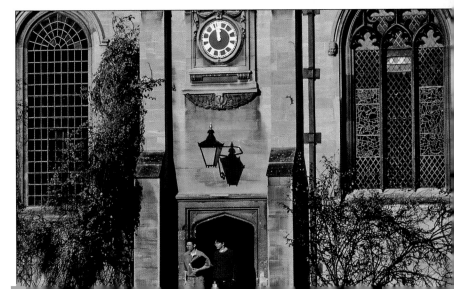

takes its name from the St John's College coat of arms. The passage takes you, in a matter of a few yards, from medieval Oxford straight into the 19th century, leading as it does to Museum Road, lined with 1870s villas, and out into Parks Road, first laid out in the 1830s.

Keble College

Directly opposite stands the mighty neo-Gothic facade of the University Museum (*see opposite page*). Before crossing the road, turn left to arrive at the unmissable bulk of **Keble College 3** (open daily 2–5pm; tel: 01865 272727; free). At a time when the other Oxford colleges were becoming more liberal and preparing to abolish ancient rules that excluded all non-Anglicans from membership, Keble set out to be assertively different. Committed to turning out clergymen formed in the strict High Church mould, Keble demanded that its students lead an almost monastic life of poverty and obedience.

Fortunately for the students, this objective, the antithesis to intellec-

The mixed voice choir of Keble College not only sings in the Chapel at services on Wednesday and Sunday evenings but also tours in Britain, Europe and the US, and has recorded several CDs.

BELOW:
Keble College.

tual freedom, was soon modified and, while remaining primarily a theological college, Keble adopted more progressive attitudes – accepting, for example, that Darwin's evolutionary theories were not necessarily incompatible with Christian teaching.

The Tractarian founders of the college chose one of their own, William Butterfield, as the architect, who proceeded to produce a riot of Victorian Gothic on a scale hitherto unseen. Contentious from the very start, Keble continues to attract its fair share of criticism. It was built not of Oxford stone, but brick, and in addition to the dominant red, Butterfield used different colours to create his hallmark polychromatic patterning.

Nowhere are the aspirations of the college's creators more evident than in the enormous **Chapel**. But the interior here could only appeal to connoisseurs of kitsch, for the stained glass is lifeless and the mosaics of biblical scenes around the walls (inspired by Giotto's great fresco cycle at Assisi!) are sickly sweet, like illustrations from a child's *Life of Jesus*.

A small side chapel to the south was added in 1892, specifically to house Holman Hunt's famous painting *The Light of the World*. Butterfield refused to allow the picture to be hung in the main chapel on the grounds that it is "a place of worship, not a gallery". Holman Hunt, on the other hand, was so angry when he learned that the college was charging visitors to see the picture that he painted another and gave it to St Paul's Cathedral in London. The side chapel also contains a painting by William Keys, *The Dead Christ Mourned by His Mother*.

Brick remains the preferred building material at Keble. Though much derided by Keble critics, the new Arco building along Keble Road, both blends in with its brick surroundings and sets new dynamic accents of its own.

The University Museum

Opposite Keble is another assertive Victorian building, a cross between a French château and London's St Pancras railway station, that houses the **University Museum ❹** (open daily noon–5pm; free). This, however, is in an entirely different class, a delightful and innovative building with many ingenious, half-humorous, half-serious details.

The museum began in 1855 at a time when Oxford was beginning to teach experimental science. Unlike the old humanities, which could be taught in a room, or even while strolling around the river meadows, science teaching required laboratories, and the block of land to the east of Parks Road was set aside for this purpose.

The museum was the first building to be erected, together with the Inorganic Chemistry Laboratory alongside – curiously enough designed to resemble the medieval Abbot's Kitchen at Glastonbury Abbey. The aim of the museum was didactic and all-embracing: to tell the history of life on earth. Its construction was supported by numerous progressive thinkers of the age, including John Ruskin.

Such an objective was bound to be controversial in an age that still clung to biblical ideas of Creation – and when the building was completed in 1860, it was inaugurated by the now-famous debate between the Bishop of Oxford, Samuel Wilberforce and Professor Thomas Huxley on Darwin's evolutionary theories.

The Bishop, according to contemporary accounts, thought that he had won the day when he asked Huxley "was it through his grandfather or his grandmother that he claimed his descent from a monkey?" At least one lady fainted and the meeting degenerated into a near-riot when Huxley said that he was "not ashamed to have a monkey for his ancestor, but he would be ashamed to be connected with a man who used great gifts to obscure the truth".

Controversies of a different nature

Map on page 172

University Museum.

BELOW:
University Museum's
dinosaur collection.

surrounded the building itself. Critics called the design "indecent" and "detestable", because to them the Gothic architectural style should be reserved for religious buildings, not one devoted to a secular purpose. The Dublin firm of builders employed to erect the museum hired as stonemasons two brothers who have passed into Oxford legend. The brothers O'Shea, who carved all the animals and birds of the corbels and window surrounds, were not only renowned for their fondness for drink but also for their irascibility. Dons who continually interfered with the brothers' work, objecting to the subjects portrayed, were likely to find themselves featured in unflattering caricature in stone. Sadly, the brothers were ordered to destroy this work.

The interior of the museum is lit by a glass roof, supported by slender columns and a wrought-iron vault that makes you feel as if you are inside the rib cage of one of the great dinosaurs displayed on the floor below. Slender iron columns, ornamented with representations of trees and shrubs, divide the hall into three bays; the arcade columns around the perimeter of the main hall are each hewn from a different British rock, all clearly labelled.

Statues of eminent scientists line the walls, looking down on cases of stuffed animals and skeletons of creatures living and extinct. At the centre of the hall are the Oxford dinosaurs – not reactionary dons, but fossil skeletons found in the Jurassic rocks of the Oxford area as the city began to expand in the 19th century. The focal point is the fine skeleton of an iguanodon.

Apart from the dinosaurs, a famous attraction of the museum is the painting by John Savery of the Dodo in the northwest corner of the building (*see below*). The bird in question, described as an over-sized flightless dove with a hooked beak, was brought to England in 1638 and formed part of the Tradescant and subsequently Ashmolean collections. This same painting inspired Lewis Carroll's famous character in *Alice in Wonderland*.

It is also worth visiting the upper gallery for its collections of insects,

The O'Shea brothers at work on the University Museum in 1906.

RIGHT: detail from John Savery's painting of the ill-fated dodo.

Dead as a Dodo

John Savery's remarkable painting of the dodo in the University Museum is now considered to be something of an exaggeration, for experts agree that the ill-fated bird was not nearly as grotesque as the depiction suggests. What is beyond dispute, however, is that the dodo was the unfortunate victim not only of hungry sailors, who were easily able to capture the flightless creature, but of evolution itself. First sighted around 1600 on the Indian Ocean island of Mauritius, the dodo (*Raphus cucullatus*), a close relative of the pigeon, was a large bird with a heavy, ungainly body and short, useless wings. Because it could not escape, it rapidly fell prey to the Dutch sailors who first visited the area and to imported cats, rats and pigs which destroyed its nests. The destruction of the island's forest – and hence the dodo's food supply – was another factor in its rapid extinction. The last living bird was sighted in 1681. Today, scientists believe that the dodo actually evolved from a bird capable of flight into a flightless one. Having discovered in Mauritius a habitat with plenty of food and no natural predators, the dodo did not need to fly and over the generations lost the ability to do so.

butterflies and birds. There are great views across the main hall; notice the scale model of the sun, moon and earth attached to the balustrade.

Pitt Rivers Museum

If you're impressed by the University Museum, then you'll be staggered by what lies through the doors to its rear. The **Pitt Rivers Museum of Ethnology** ❺ (open daily noon–4.30pm; free) was built in 1885 to house the collection of Lieutenant-General Augustus Henry Lane Fox Pitt-Rivers (1827–1900), built up during his service in exotic lands with the Grenadier Guards.

Pitt-Rivers pioneered a sociological approach in archaeology and ethnology and emphasised the instructional value of common artefacts. His original collection consisted of some 15,000 objects, but since then the number has swelled to well over half a million, of which some 400,000 are on permanent display. The museum is literally packed with case after case of splendid objects from all corners of the earth – scarey demons, potent fertility figures, colourful totem poles and exotic masks – as well as practical objects such as boats, tents, saddles and snowshoes.

A remarkable theme of the museum is the continuity and similarities that exist between cultures; illuminating parallels are drawn between the use of magical charms among the tribes of Asia and similar practices among Christians in "civilised" Europe. To help achieve this, and in accordance with Pitt-Rivers' wishes, the objects are displayed not by region but by type, so model Chinese junks are to be found next to African dug-out canoes, and so on. The museum's extraordinarily eclectic range of exhibits stresses themes of everyday problem solving from every conceivable culture. With plenty of outlandish objects to examine, children will be fascinated by such items as the witch-in-a-bottle.

Flanking the south side of the lawn in front of the museum is the **Radcliffe Science Library**, the science department of the Bodleian, which receives free copies of all British scientific publications (in-

Parents with bored children can ask one of the obliging attendants at the Pitt Rivers Museum to point out some of the more bizarre exhibits. These include shrunken heads, a witch in a bottle, and drawers full of giant toads.

BELOW:
The Pitt Rivers Museum of Ethnology puts on a show.

A Cyclist's City

Cycling has always played an important part in Oxford's transport system. William Morris, the car magnate, began his career building and racing bicycles, and in 1922 Morrell's Brewery produced a *Hunting and Cycling Road Map of Oxford and District*, overprinted with a list of hotels and inns representing distances from Oxford. Today, as the authorities seek to reduce car use, 20 per cent of short journeys in the city are made by bike, compared with 4 percent nationally.

But thieves like bikes too, and some of the theft is on an industrial scale. Forty cycles can be fitted into a large van and smuggled out of the city by night. Thames Valley Police assigned three full-time officers solely to bike theft and began fitting tracking devices to decoy bikes in order to trap thieves. Oxford City Council, one of the first local authorities to provide for the needs of the urban cyclist, installed hundreds of "Sheffield" stands. These tough steel hoops are impossible to break, and together with the increased use of U-bolt steel locks, they helped bring about a decline in the number of reported thefts,

down by a third in the past 15 years to around 3,000 a year today. About a third are recovered.

Cycle security has been studied so intensively that you almost expect it to be part of a degree course. A normal bike chain can be cut with a bolt cropper in less than five seconds and even a steel shackle can be hacksawed in a couple of minutes. Many thieves prefer the wheel swap trick: they remove the front wheel from a bike whose rear wheel is secured and fit it to an adjacent bike as a replacement for a front wheel that has been chained or padlocked. Few people bother to secure both wheels.

To counter theft, the Police Cycle Department, attached to the Central Police Station, keeps records of all bikes and can produce serial numbers, colours, decoration, modifications and accessories for almost every model. Bikes are kept in two cycle stores: one for the "found" and "miscellaneous" and the other for "crime" bikes (pending court cases). The cleverly designed store holds 200–300 cycles. The "found" bikes are kept for at least six weeks. Unclaimed cycles are auctioned.

The university also launched a cycle registration scheme, encouraging students and staff to attach hologram security stickers (part of a 50p security kit) to their bikes and use an ultra-violet pen to mark a registration number on them. The police routinely give all recovered cycles a UV scan.

Safety first

Safety is an issue too. Cycle lanes are designed to give cyclists space from motorists, and cyclists are allowed to use all bus lanes. The junction with Parks Road and Broad Street has one of the highest cycle flows in the country. To ease congestion, the Advanced Stop Line, the first to be introduced in Britain and now commonplace, allowed cyclists to wait at the traffic lights in front of motor vehicles.

Racing is popular and there are three local clubs for national and international races. The Oxford University Cycling Club is Britain's oldest surviving cycling club. ❑

LEFT: objects of desire that need to be secured.

cluding popular and children's publications). Access to the library – an unmatched resource for any kind of scientific research – is possible with a Bodleian Library reader's ticket.

University Parks

Just to the north of the museum, bright summer days in particular attract locals and visitors alike to the huge expanse of the **University Parks** . Dotted with magnificent trees and shrubs and bordered on its eastern side by the River Cherwell, the park is a wonderful place for a stroll. It is also the home of the **Oxford University Cricket Club**, and this is one of only two places in England where first-class matches can be watched free of charge. If you're not there for the Australians or the Pakistanis, there may be a county fixture going on.

Detour to North Oxford

The University Museum was part of the 19th-century expansion of the university, particularly in the field of science. Since that time, the area around it has developed into the University Science Area, consisting of a not always harmonious jumble of buildings ranging from 1930s functionalism (clearly visible in the Inorganic Chemistry faculty building from University Parks) to 1960s concrete and glass structures, each housing different faculties, ranging from Mathematics to Applied Physics to Microbiology.

As the university grew beyond its old medieval core, new accommodation was required for increasing numbers of professors and their families, as well as wealthy merchants and traders. This demand helped spawn the development of the affluent district known as North Oxford, which begins just north of the University Parks and extends out along the Banbury and Woodstock roads.

Just to the north of University Parks, **Norham Gardens** was laid out from 1860, and although Italianate villas feature in early plans, neo-Gothic was all the rage by the time the estate came to be developed *(see margin note)*.

Map on page 172

Built of brick, with high gables, ornate stone dressings sculpted with fruits and flowers and the occasional turret, Norham Gardens' houses were praised by Ruskin as "human and progressive". But the Rev. W. Tuckwell complained that professors, tutors and fellows now lived family lives in the "interminable streets of villadom", rather than residing in college "celibate and pastoral".

BELOW:
University Parks.

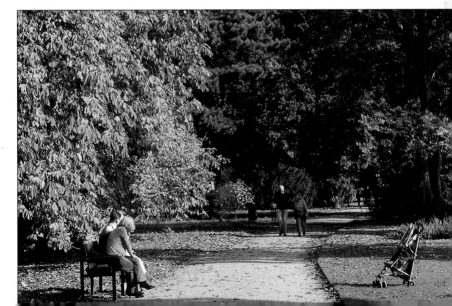

Public executions used to be carried out not only in Oxford's prison (which has now been turned into a luxury hotel and restaurants) but also close to Park Town. When the University ran the town, it would carry out executions in St Margaret's Road.

Lady Margaret Hall

At the end of Norham Gardens (also reached via an alley from University Parks) is **Lady Margaret Hall ❼** (check at the porter's lodge for visits), founded in 1878 as a women's hall of residence (it is now mixed) and itself occupying one of the newly built villas. Strong connections with the Church of England distinguished this college, named after Lady Margaret Beaufort, the scholarly mother of Henry VII, from its contemporary, Somerville.

The original villa, Old Hall, is the undistinguished yellow-grey brick building to the right of the entrance. Better by far is the Queen Anne-style red-brick extension, designed by Basil Champneys and similar to the splendid work he did at Newnham College, Cambridge.

For the chapel, yet another style was employed – Byzantine – with an external octagon that forms a dome inside. It was designed by Sir Giles Gilbert Scott in 1931. The beautiful triptych was painted by Burne-Jones around 1863. The Hall is also blessed with gardens that stretch to the River Cherwell, where remnants of old water meadows are carpeted with daffodils, cowslips, fritillaries and primroses in spring.

Opposite the Balfour Building on Banbury Road (now no longer open to visitors) is the glass-covered conservatory of **Gee's** restaurant, and immediately north of that is **North Parade**, which offers a variety of good restaurants, and has a definite "villagey" atmosphere in comparison to all the grand neo-Gothic residences round about. There are two good pubs in North Parade, the Gardeners' Arms and the Rose and Crown. The latter was built in 1867 on the site of a small market garden, evidence of the area's semi-rural character at the time.

Park Town

Further north, entered from the east side of Banbury Road, is the elegant residential enclave known as **Park Town**, interesting from an architectural point of view because its houses are much admired examples of late Regency style – so late (built from 1853 to 1855) that they might

North and South Parades

One of Oxford's many eccentricities in the realm of street names is the strange fact that North Parade lies to the south of South Parade. Officially called North Parade Avenue (although the Avenue part is never used), its name is widely believed to hark back to the English Civil War of 1642–51 when Oxford was periodically besieged by Paliamentarians. North Parade, it is said, was the north patrolling ground of the defending Royalists, while South Parade (a mile or so further north along Banbury Road), was the south patrolling ground of the Parliamentarians. Christopher Hibbert's *Encyclopedia of Oxford* dismisses this as a myth.

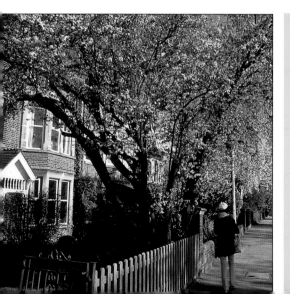

almost be called neo-Regency. Built around crescents, these stucco-fronted houses, with attractive iron railings, remind us more of Cheltenham than of Oxford.

The next street on the right beyond Park Town is Bardwell Road. Just around the corner beyond the famous Dragon School, where Bardwell Road merges with Chadlington Road, a path on the right leads down to the River Cherwell and the **Cherwell Boathouse ❽**. This is a popular base for punting (*see page 200*) as well as home to the Cherwell Boathouse restaurant, a small, intimate and elegant place, with river views, good food and local artists' work displayed on the walls.

Continuing up Banbury Road, one reaches the suburban shopping area of **Summertown**, home to Oxfam before the charity's move to the new business park in East Oxford. Here are a handful of good restaurants, especially on fashionable South Parade, and some traditional and not so traditional shops catering to North Oxford's traditionally well-heeled residents.

The heart of Oxford is easily reached again by returning down Parks Road towards Broad Street, stopping first to admire the 18th-century gates, on the right, that separate the road from the long vista of Trinity College Gardens.

Wadham College

Wadham College ❾ (open only to visitors booked on a tour at the Oxford Information Centre; tel: 01865 277900; entrance fee) is regarded as the youngest of the "old" (pre-Victorian) foundations. Nicholas Wadham, a retiring and obscure Somerset landowner, left his considerable wealth for the foundation of a college at his death in 1609. Wadham's widow, Dorothy, proved an energetic executor, despite being over 75 years old, and by 1613, less than five years later, the college was virtually complete. Thus Wadham is the only ancient college to have been built at one go, and it has scarcely changed.

The buildings are strictly symmetrical and were designed by the West Country builder William Arnold, who borrowed motifs from other Oxford

Map on page 172

Wadham College.

BELOW:
Regency-style crescent in Park Town.

Map on page 172

Wadham College's chapel, noted for its 17th-century stained glass.

BELOW:
the Rose & Crown pub in North Parade.

Jacobean-Gothic buildings, but put them together in a highly accomplished manner. The Front Quad is entered through the fan-vaulted gate-tower.

The chapel is entered by the passageway on the far left (northeast) corner of the quad, and has some of Oxford's finest 17th-century stained glass. The east window, depicting the Passion and Resurrection, is the only one in Oxford painted by Bernard van Linge (dated 1622), brother of the more prolific Abraham, whose work is found in several college chapels. The other significant object is the fine screen of 1613, with its strapwork, slender columns and cresting.

Fellows' Garden

To the left of the chapel is the **Fellows' Garden**, filled with rare and ancient trees, including a striking copper beech, planted in 1796. The garden completely surrounds the chapel, and the **Cloister Garden**, to the rear, contains a modernistic bronze statue of Sir Maurice Bowra by John Doubleday. Bowra, a literary scholar who presided over Wadham as Warden from 1938 to 1970, was renowned for his ascerbic and often bawdy wit. ("Awful shit, never met him" is one of his renowned judgements. Of the Master of Balliol, he once remarked: "He has been ill but unfortunately is getting better. Otherwise deaths have been poor for the time of year.")

Famous alumni include the architect Christopher Wren and chemist Robert Boyle, who, having finished their studies, went on to pursue their careers in London and to found the Royal Society.

The southeast side of Wadham's Front Quad is an exact match of the northeast, with the hall a mirror of the chapel but with a splendid hammerbeam roof. The garden of the adjacent Back Quad contains a giant lime tree of considerable, though unknown, age. The heady scent of its summer flowers is not only irresistible to bees but spreads to fill the air as far as the city centre, which, for all that it seems a long way off in Wadham's quiet precincts, is only a few steps away. ❑

RESTAURANTS & BARS

Restaurants

The Old Parsonage Hotel

1 Banbury Road. Tel 310210. Open daily. ££
www.oldparsonage-hotel.co.uk
A surprisingly rural feel reigns within this beautifully restored ancient building, where the food ranges from generous English breakfasts to elegant post-theatre dinners. The old-fashioned club-like atmosphere attracts an older crowd, and the emphasis is on good, unfussy cooking using local ingredients.

Gee's

61 Banbury Road. Tel 553540. Open daily. ££
www.gees-restaurant.co.uk
Housed in a former florist's conservatory, this is a very atmospheric restaurant, beautifully light during the day and cosy in the evening. The food is simple, with an emphasis on locally sourced ingredients, and features a good deal of delicious fish as well as Italian-influenced salads and meat dishes.

PRICE CATEGORIES

Prices for three-course dinner per person with a half-bottle of house wine:
£ = under £20
££ = £20–£30
£££ = £30–£45
££££ = more than £45

Chez Gaston

6 North Parade. Tel 311608. Open daily. £
One of several eating places in trendy North Parade, Chez Gasto stands out for its exuberant decor – with its colourful exterior and eclectic interior – as well as its irresistible crepes, savoury and sweet. Other dishes, ranging from snacks to pasta and French plats du jour are on offer in a relaxed and rather Bohemian atmosphere.

The Cherwell Boathouse

Bardwell Road. Tel 552746. Open daily. ££
www.cherwellboathouse.co.uk
This long-established restaurant has one of Oxford's most enviable locations, right on the banks of the Cherwell and next door to a punt-hiring station. You can eat outside in summer or, when cold, admire the river through large windows. The food is "modern English" with a strong Italian accent, and set lunchtime menus represent very good value. The wine list is unusually varied.

Saffron

204-206 Banbury Road. Tel 512211. Open daily. £
www.saffronoxford.comk
Conveniently situated at the southern end of the Summertown shopping strip, Saffron offers the unusual choice of Indian or (to a lesser degree) French food. The Indian menu covers the usual range of biriani, dupiaza and tandoori dishes, but cooked with a good deal of subtlety. The French menu includes good salads and chicken.

Cibo Restaurant and Café

4 South Parade. Tel 292321. Open daily. £
www.ilovecibo.co.uk
Cibo is one of a cluster of more or less trendy restaurants on Summertown's South Parade, and its menu is authentically Italian, highlighting pasta, risotto and salads alongside meat and fish dishes. It has bright modern decor and friendly staff, but the quality of the food can be variable.

The Lemon Tree

268 Woodstock Road. Tel 311936. Closed Mon-Wed for lunch. ££
www.thelemontreeoxford.co.uk
It's at the far northern end of Woodstock Road, but local gastronomes like the Lemon Tree for its heavily mirrored Moroccan-style ambiance and its tastefully presented English-French food, which features such delicacies as scallops, sea bass and confit duck leg.

Pubs

There are several good pubs in North Oxford. The **Lamb & Flag** (12 St Giles'), next to St John's, is an atmospheric old inn that serves robust lunches and good beers. The **Rose & Crown** (North Parade) is a charmingly traditional pub, full of nooks and crannies, and serving generous bar lunches to a regular clientele. There is a pleasant outside seating area. The **Gardeners' Arms** (north Parade), almost opposite, is another old-fashioned hostelry, frequented by North Oxford locals. The **Dewdrop Inn** (258 Banbury Road) is Summertown's most popular pub, attracting a mainly young crowd and serving above-average lunches.

BELOW: Chez Gaston.

WEST TO THE CANAL

In medieval times the western part of the city was crowded with wharves unloading cargo from the Upper Thames. Today it gives an insight into Oxford's industrial past

This route includes a journey into Oxford's industrial past. When the canal arrived from the Midlands in 1790, the area around Castle Mill Stream became a bustling inland port. Activity declined with the arrival of the railway in 1844, but the brewing industry was to continue until the closure of Morrell's Brewery in 1998.

From Carfax walk along **Queen Street**, lined by chain stores and every bit as busy as Cornmarket Street, but perhaps more chaotic with buses nudging nose to tail through the crowds of shoppers.

In the summer, some light relief is provided by **Bonn Square ❶**, named after Oxford's twin city in Germany, and a popular meeting place; it is also site of a memorial to men of the Oxfordshire Regiment who died in various campaigns on India's northwest frontier. There is often live music in the form of buskers playing on or near the square.

Nuffield College

On the opposite side of Queen Street is the sprawling Westgate Shopping Centre, one of numerous ugly modern buildings erected in this part of the city centre during the 1970s.

Continue on into **New Road**, whose construction across the castle bailey in 1769 marked the beginning

of local road improvements which were formalised by the creation of the Paving Commission two years later. On the left you'll see an imposing, fortress-like building. Formerly the prison entrance, this is now part of **County Hall**. Down the hill on the right is the unmistakable sturdy tower of **Nuffield College ❷**.

The site and funds for the college were donated to the university in 1937 by Lord Nuffield, alias William Morris, who began life repairing bicycles in the High Street (*see page*

Map on page 186

LEFT:
Nuffield College from the canal.
BELOW:
Nuffield's tower.

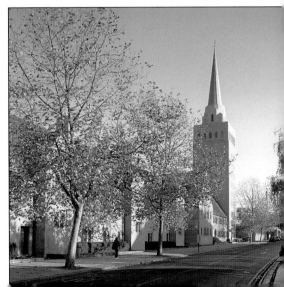

28), progressed to designing the "Bullnose" Morris in Longwall Street and ended up by establishing the first ever mass production line for cheap cars at Cowley (whose successor continues to thrive, albeit under BMW ownership).

Having achieved his manufacturing goals, Nuffield was determined to use part of his vast fortune for good causes, including hospitals and charities. As far as the university was concerned, he had originally envisaged establishing a college specialising in the practical skills of engineering and accountancy, but was persuaded instead to fund a post-graduate college devoted to the study of social, economic and political problems.

Formal agreement was reached in 1937, but progress was slow because Nuffield disliked the original "un-English" designs for the college, and, by the time new designs were completed, war had been declared.

In the event, work did not begin until 1949, and this Lutyens-inspired, Cotswold-style college, very much a product of 1930s architectural thinking, was not completed until 1960. Nuffield had devoted the best part of his wealth to the project, but still referred to it as "that bloody Kremlin, where left-wingers study at my expense". Committed to providing a bridge between the academic and the non-academic worlds, Nuffield College has been the source of some major research developments in British social science.

Attractive to some, plain ugly to others, the Stalinesque **tower** houses the library, which contains 70,000 books on its 10 floors. It was intended to be part of a large college chapel, but this plan was altered as a consequence of the delays and financial problems surrounding the whole project. Except for the tower, Nuffield is much like a Cotswold country house on a large scale, with

Nuffield accepts only 25 postgraduate students a year, specialising in research into social, economic and political problems. Visiting research fellows from the fields of business, politics and the trade unions engage in work that the college describes as making "a bridge between the academic and non-academic worlds".

two courtyards in the pattern of traditional colleges, linked by steps, surrounding lily ponds and rose beds.

The chapel of Nuffield, scaled down from its original grand proportions because of escalating costs, is now no more than a room on the top floor of "L" staircase, entered from the lower quad. John Piper, the artist, designed the glass and simple wooden box pews, modelled on those of Ivychurch in Kent's Romney Marshes.

Oxford Castle

The green mound on the other side of the road is what remains of the **Castle ❸**, built by Robert d'Oilly, Oxford's Norman governor, in 1071. The mound was originally topped with a wooden keep (later rebuilt in stone), and the outer bailey was surrounded by a moat with water from one of the branckes of the Thames used to power the castle mills – hence Castle Mill Stream.

Many historic figures are associated with the castle. In 1142, Matilda (the Empress Maud) was holed up here for three months while battling to gain the English throne from King Stephen after the death of her father, Henry I, in 1135. She escaped in the depths of winter down the frozen Thames, camouflaged against the snow in nothing but a white sheet. She never became queen. From the mid-12th century, the castle was used to house prisoners, and although the fortifications were torn down after the Civil War, it remained the site of a prison.

The present forbidding structure was built in the 19th century. The last public execution took place here in 1863; the last prisoner moved out in 1993.

The role of the prison was dramatically transformed in 2005 with the long-awaited opening of the 94-room **Malmaison hotel**. The exterior of the Grade I listed building was largely preserved and the interior was entirely refurbished to create an unusual and elegant ambiance. The hotel's rooms are essentially the former cells, but in most cases three have been combined to form spacious en-suite accommodation. The prison project was the first of its sort in Britain. The complex also includes a range of restaurants and bars, not least the stylish Living Room Brasserie.

The recently opened heritage centre, **Oxford Castle Unlocked ❹**, explains the history of the castle and its absorption into the former prison. The centre gives access to the castle mound, the crypt of St George's Church and the forbidding-looking Debtors' Tower as well as St George's Tower *(see next page)*. With more than £5 million of public funding, the project was the realisation of a 60-year dream for the Oxford Preservation Trust, which back in the 1940s had pressed for the rescue of the city's medieval heritage as the prison faced closure and perhaps demolition.

Continue along New Road until the next turning on the left, into Tid-

In 1142 King Stephen laid seige to Oxford Castle, where Henry I's daughter Matilda, a claimant to the throne, was holed up.

BELOW: Oxford Castle.

Canal boats provide a restful holiday.

BELOW:
swanning around
on Lower Fisher Row.

marsh Lane. At the very end, the view is dominated by **St George's Tower ❺**, which Robert d'Oilly built at the southern side of the castle bailey in 1074, above the chapel of St George which he founded within the walls. It was the Secular Canons of St George who established here what is regarded as the first learning establishment in Oxford.

Follow the road round to the right, across Quaking Bridge and into St Thomas Street. On the opposite side of the road stands the former **Morrell's Brewery** which closed in 1998. An independent, family-run concern that had belonged to the Morrell family since 1792, this was the last brewery in Oxford. At one time no fewer than 14 breweries thrived in this part of the city, drawing their water from wells deep beneath the Thames and using the river and the canal for transport. The first brewery here in Tidmarsh Lane was established in 1452 by the monks of neighbouring Osney Abbey. The Morrell's premises have been sold, but the adjoining **Brewery Gate** pub remains open.

Canalside

Return to the Quaking Bridge. On the corner of **Lower Fisher Row** is the house lived in by Edward Tawney, who ran the brewery prior to its takeover by the Morrell family in 1792. Follow the attractive Fisher Row which leads north along the Castle Mill Stream. The original fishermen's and canal bargees' cottages have gone, but it remains a pretty spot, overhung by a pendulous willow and often frequented by swans.

Emerging at the end, cross Park End Street to Hythe Bridge Street and the present-day terminus of the **Oxford Canal ❻** on **Upper Fisher Row**, where a sign headed **Oxford Canal Walk** indicates the distances to towns further up the waterway. While visitors might find the 83 miles (134 km) to Coventry somewhat ambitious, a short walk along the canal towpath, lined with colourful narrowboats, is worthwhile. The canal runs along the back of Worcester College (*see page 161*), past the district of Jericho and then Lucy's Ironworks, where steps up to the bridge provide access to Port Meadow.

To the west along Hythe Bridge Street and Park End Street is **Oxford railway station**. Park End Street, until recently an undistinguished row of offices and shops, is now filled with bars and restaurants – a continuation of George Street. The original station was deliberately kept well out of the centre of Oxford because, among other reasons, the railway was thought likely to corrupt young students – making it easy for them to travel to places of ill-repute, such as Ascot racecourse. The existing station lies on the Great Western Railway line to London.

Another line, closed in 1967, terminated at the junction of Park End Road and Hythe Bridge Street: part of the old station, painted red, white and blue, stood on the site until 1999, when it was demolished to make room for a new road scheme and the new Saïd Business School, built by the university from funds donated by various businesses and benefactors, notably Wafic Saïd.

The demolition of the old railway station created considerable controversy, especially when environmental activists occupied the site in an attempt to save a row of trees. The listed building was eventually dismantled and carted off to the nearby Quainton Railway Centre.

The **Said Business School** (open by appointment, 01865 288800), which specialises in prestigious MBA courses and research into business organisations, combines a classically simple symmetry with an exotic copper-clad ziggurat. Its serene gardens, lecture theatre and airy library create an atmosphere that combines modern corporate chic with a traditional monastic feel.

Beyond the railway line lies the district of **Osney** (*see page 199*).

Gloucester Green shopping

To the east, Hythe Bridge Street leads back towards the city centre.

Opposite, fronting on to Worcester Street, is an adventurous brick building, with three lead-covered angle towers enclosing Gloucester Green, which is entered a little further up Worcester Street, on the right.

Opened in 1989, **Gloucester Green ❼**, is a large pedestrianised shopping square. It has been a welcome addition to the Oxford townscape, tidying up an area that had served as a windswept and litter-strewn bus station ever since 1932, when the cattle market on the site was closed down. The present bus station has been integrated into the scheme.

Before you get into the main square, look out for the Old School House, once Oxford's first boarding school and now a popular pub. Continue under the arch into the square itself, which is surrounded by shops and eating places and is the scene every Wednesday of an **open-air market**, with stalls selling everything from pots and pans to brooms and doorknobs. Every Thursday there's a popular **fleamarket**.

Of the pubs that once served the

Map on page 186

A mural in Gloucester Green.

LEFT: the Said Business School.
BELOW: Gloucester Green's Wednesday market.

Map on page 186

The view along St Michael's Street to New Inn Hall Street.

thirsty cattle drovers, only the Euro Bar (formerly the Welsh Pony), in George Street, now survives, transformed into a fashionable continental-style café-bar. Further up, the **Old Fire Station** has been redeveloped to house a theatre as well as a bar/restaurant which is transformed into a disco in the evenings.

Opposite, the delicate neo-Jacobean Social Studies Faculty was originally built in 1880 as the City of Oxford High School, and numbered T. E. Lawrence among its pupils.

George Street is now lined with pubs and restaurants, ranging from the more traditional inn (The Grapes) to the Lebanese Tarbouch Restaurant. Some of the most popular pubs are Copa and the Cock and Camel, whose strange name seems to verge on pastiche.

Along New Inn Hall Street

Proceed up George Street to **New Inn Hall Street** on the right, past the cinema. This street marks the eastern boundary of the medieval city, and was once just inside the walls. The original New Inn Hall has gone

but St **Peter's College** ❽, halfway up on the right, now occupies part of the site. St Peter's was founded in 1929, and did not achieve college status until 1961, but the buildings are much older.

The college is entered through **Linton House**, built in 1797 as the headquarters of the Oxford Canal Company which then moved, in 1828, to the neo-classical **Canal House**, which now serves as the Master's Lodge. The college chapel is the former church of St Peter-le-Bailey, which was built in 1874 to the design of Basil Champneys on the site of the original Norman church.

Opposite St Peter's, **Frewin Hall** ❾ is an attractive house, set well back from the street, dating to the 16th and 18th centuries, and converted into student accommodation in the 1970s. Next to the entrance, a plaque indicates a house that was the first Methodist meeting house in Oxford, used for the first time in 1783, eight years before the death of John Wesley, who had sown the seeds of Methodism while at Lincoln College. ❏

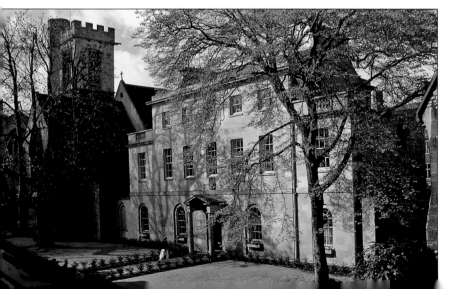

RESTAURANTS & BARS

Restaurants

Café Opium
67–69 George Street. Tel: 01865 248680
Open: L & D daily ££.
www.opiumdengroup.co.uk
An airy, bustling Chinese restaurant with dramatic, stylish decor and quality food. Ideal for a quick meal or a group outing.

Chutney's
36 Michael's Street. Tel: 01865 724241. Open: L & D daily. ££.
Among the Indian restaurants in the centre, Chutney's stands out. The extensive menu includes many good vegetarian dishes. The decor is simple and modern but the tables are somewhat cramped and it can get crowded at weekends. There is also a good-value lunchtime buffet.

The Living Room
1 Oxford Castle. Tel 662223.
Open daily. ££
www.thelivingroom.co.uk
Part of the flagship Castle redevelopment, the Living Room is part of an upmarket chain of bar/brasserie venues. Its interior is pleasingly retro chic, with plenty of black leather and chrome, while its menu offers an elegant selection of English, French and Italian dishes. The large bar area, complete with white piano, pulls in

a large, mostly fashionable crowd at weekends.

Sojo
6-9 Hythe Bridge Street. Tel 202888. Open daily. ££
Situated in what one might, with some exaggeration, call Oxford's Chinatown, Sojo certainly attracts a lot of Chinese diners. The atmosphere is refreshingly modern, and the food, including homemade Dim Sum and Shanghai local specialities, is a cut above the average. The place doubles as a bar, and karaoke entertainment is available (should anyone want it).

Samad's
25 Park End Street. Tel 250244. Open daily. £
With friendly staff and a bright, welcoming interior, Samad's is one of Oxford's better Indian restaurants. It has an extensive vegetarian menu, supplies all the standard favourites, and offers a brisk service for anyone going to or returning from the nearby station.

Tarbouch
29 George Street. Tel 251911. Open daily. £
A more than welcome antidote to the themed mediocrity of most George Street venues, Tarbouch deals in real

Lebanese cooking, with most Middle Eastern staples as well as a few original dishes on offer. Part of the Victoria House Hotel, the restaurant has a good-value set-price lunch menu, but the wine is less of a bargain.

Pubs & Bars

There are countless pubs and bars in and around the George Street–Park End Street area, but many of these are blandly themed establishments, aimed principally at Oxford's youth. There are, however, several notable exceptions.
Antiquity Hall (1-2 Hythe Bridge Street) retains a more authentic pub atmosphere and provides a good range of pub food. **Rosie O'Grady's** (1 Park End Street) successfully creates an Irish ambiance with frequent live music as well as the inevitable Guinness. The **Euro Bar** (48 George Street), formerly the Welsh Pony, has a successfully continental atmosphere and serves good meals throughout the day. The **Cock and Camel** (24 George Street) has a reputation for good food and a lively atmosphere

as well as good beer from London's Youngs brewery. Tucked away in Friar's Entry, a small alley joining Gloucester Green to Magdalen Street is the **Far from the Madding Crowd**, an eminently civilised pub that hosts art exhibitions as well as dispensing good food and beer. The **White House** (2 Botley Road) has appetising food, a pool/sports TV room and a garden.

PRICE CATEGORIES

Prices for three-course dinner per person with a half-bottle of house wine:
£ = under £20
££ = £20–£30
£££ = £30–£45
££££ = more than £45

RIGHT: the Living Room.

OXFORD'S GREEN CORRIDOR

Neglected for much of its 200-year history, the Oxford Canal might easily have been lost forever after World War II. Now it enjoys renewed esteem

When the Oxford Canal was completed in 1790, it had a huge and immediate impact. After centuries of academic and religious privilege, Oxford suddenly found itself confronted by a rapidly changing industrial world. Those who welcomed this workmanlike intruder were not disappointed. Investors soon saw the demand for their principal product of coal turned into massive profits.

Within a decade the Canal Company expanded its original city centre wharves just south of Hythe Bridge Street to encompass the site now occupied by Nuffield College. The labour for this work came from the conveniently located Oxford Castle Gaol, whose governor, Daniel Harris, also found time to grace Oxford's waterways with his skills as an engineer, surveyor and architect.

Benign neglect

Until the mid-19th century Oxford treated the canal as an honoured guest. When the railway arrived in the 1840s, however, a decline set in, and although it took another century before the Company conceded the struggle to carry freight in any volume, the canal suffered a kind of benign neglect. The Company withdrew from the city centre in the 1930s, and the entire canal could easily have been lost forever. But it survived thanks to the efforts of enthusiasts who foresaw the waterway's leisure potential.

ABOVE: Narrowboats are popular for holidays, but some people call them home, enjoying the freedom to vary their views. However, as they are less than 7 ft (2.2 metres) wide, there's little room for the material comforts of a land-bound existence.

LEFT: The origins of traditional canal art are obscure, but the style remarkably enduring. This post-box indicates a permanence of location that the old boaters could never have imagined.

WHAT LIFE'S LIKE ON THE CANAL

A step along the Oxford Canal towpath from Hythe Bridge Street brings an instant sense of relief. The noise, pollution and traffic are forgotten as you enter a calmer, gentler world of boats, anglers and swans.

It's the boats which make the scene really special, and in Oxford there is an unusually high number which are year-round homes. Distributed along the 3 miles (5 km) of canal between Wolvercote and the city, they form a single linear community, united by shared dependence on and responsibility for the same stretch of water, and by an unspoken awareness of common chores and comforts, pleasures and problems.

The canal residents have had to struggle to gain acceptance, perhaps a throwback to the prejudices against working boatmen. Today they provide interest in a quiet part of the city.

They are not alone. Dotted around Britain's (2,000 miles/3,200 km) of inland waterways are other pockets of residential boats. The national Residential Boat Owners' Association (RBOA) gives these "floating voters" a collective voice.

E: In 1898 the canal was 'bed as "an arcadian scene storal beauty." The continuity intained as a distinctive wboat passes through y along the Thames.

: Children were once tial crew for the working han. Nowadays a boating ay provides kids with ise, fun and an appreciation th history and nature.

W: Apart from a foundry in Jericho, the canal has always defied the trial stereotype. People are today's cargo, sustaining the original nercial intent of the Canal. Oxford's busy hire fleet and floating urant operate from Jericho.

BELOW: A rare day off for this boatman and his family, pictured around 1900. The last horse-drawn cargo boat on the canal ceased trading in the 1950s.

RIVERS, MEADOWS AND ABBEYS

The rivers Thames and Cherwell and their surrounding meadows provide a playground not only for energetic oarsman, but also for walkers, picnickers and punters

For many towns and cities built by a river, the water is simply an obstruction to be bridged, or a convenient sewer. For Oxford, the rivers **Thames** and **Cherwell** (pronounced *charwell*) have historically played a vital role in the development of the city. Early signs of human habitation are to be found on Port Meadow, while the Thames and its various arms were also the site of some of the earliest monastic foundations in Oxford, which spawned the development of the university. They include Osney Abbey (now a Victorian terraced-house community) to the west, and Godstow Nunnery, beyond Port Meadow to the northwest of the city.

Christ Church Meadow

Less sensitive souls have often mooted plans to tame or use these "wastelands": a four-lane highway, crossing Christ Church and providing an inner-city relief road, was first proposed in 1933 and revived in 1968. W.H. Auden penned a poem in protest at the proposals ("may the Meadows be only frequented by scholars and couples and cows"). The combined efforts of Oxford's townspeople and the academics brought a halt to these plans, proving with what affection everyone in the city holds their river landscape.

Christ Church Meadow ❶ borders the River Thames to the south of the city. It is not actually possible to walk on the meadow itself because it is fenced off to contain its herd of fine cattle. However, a walk around it is highly worthwhile, not only for giving the feeling of country so close to the city, but also for the magnificent views of the spires and towers of the colleges to the north.

There are several ways of reaching the meadow: either through the War Memorial Gardens past the

Map on page 196

LEFT:
strong-arm tactics.
BELOW:
cows grazing in front of Christ Church.

Meadow Buildings of Christ Church (*see page 151*); from Merton Lane through to Merton Grove and on to the Broad Walk (*see page 115*); or via the turnstile gate behind the Head of the River pub (*see page 155*).

Approaching from the north, joining the Broad Walk just opposite the Meadow Buildings is the **New Walk** ❷, which leads along the west side of Christ Church Meadow towards the river. The New Walk is lined with tall trees planted by the head of Christ Church, Dean Liddell, in 1872, turning a muddy pathway into an avenue. The Dean's daughter, Alice, came this way with Lewis Carroll in July 1862, on the way to a boat trip during which he began to tell the stories that resulted in *Alice's Adventures in Wonderland*.

The New Walk leads to a wide, straight stretch of the Thames – also called the Isis within Oxford. This Latin name was first coined in 1535 by John Leland, who seems not to have been at all happy with the pre-Roman Celtic name (from *tam*, meaning "broad" and *wys*, meaning "water"). Moored on the other side of the river you will see a variety of cruise boats run by Salters Bros, which ply the river between Oxford, Dorchester and Abingdon.

Transport options

If you want to explore the rivers yourself, there are punts, rowing boats, pedalboats and motorboats for hire next to the Head of the River pub (reached by turning right and through the turnstile gate).

To continue the walk, head downstream (southeast) along the river. During term-time you will probably see rowing crews training along this stretch of the river. Activity gets particularly frenetic during the Trinity term in May, when it is the scene of Eights Week (*see page 127*) – also a lively social event, with partisan crowds either celebrating or drowning their disappointment in wine, depending on their team's success.

College Boathouses

College members and their guests watch the races from the verandahs of the bankside **College Boathouses** ❸, situated beyond the arched bridge at the confluence of the Thames and an arm of the Cherwell. The best way to see the excitement of Eights Week races is the stand on the towpath downriver from the boathouses, near Donnington Bridge.

Until the turn of the century, ornate floating barges were used instead – the last of these, Keble College barge, remained in use until 1958 and part of it is now displayed in the Museum of Oxford (*see page 147*). In his satirical novel, *Zuleika Dobson*, Max Beerbohm has the entire student population of Oxford commit mass suicide by leaping from their barges into the river, all hopelessly in love with Zuleika – not, perhaps, so far from the truth as one might think, since romantic emotions still run high as the summer term draws to a close and final-year students either cement or break their Oxford liaisons on these banks.

The path stops just beyond the boathouses, so if you want to see any more of the Thames, go back along the path, through the turnstile, and cross Folly Bridge to the south bank of the river. It is possible, from here, to follow the Thames path for some 2 miles (3 km) down to the lock at **Iffley** (*see page 206*).

The Cherwell

Returning to the Thames at Christ Church Meadow, there are further possibilities for walkers. Just before the arched bridge that leads to the boathouses, take the leftward path that follows the bank of the River Cherwell from its confluence with the Thames. The Cherwell rises in Northamptonshire, to the northeast. It is narrow and shallow, used for punting rather than races, with many a tree-hung peaceful backwater, rich in birds and plants.

From the area around the confluence, the **views** across Christ Church Meadow, with the spires of Oxford in the background, are magnificent,

Map on page 196

TIP

The drink of choice during Eights Week is Pimms. Now owned by drinks giant Diageo, the cocktail was invented in the 1840s by James Pimm, owner of a London oyster bar, who mixed gin, quinine and herbs in a small tankard (No. 1 Cup). Variations are No. 3 Cup, made with brandy, and No. 6 Cup (vodka).

BELOW: a Thames narrowboat.

The distinctive Oxford Centre for Islamic Studies, on George Street, was set up by the university in 1985 to encourage the scholarly study of Islam and the Islamic world.

BELOW: Oxford's rivers and meadows are rich in wildlife.

particularly the towers of Christ Church, Merton and Magdalen. After a short stretch, the River Cherwell divides – the right hand (southernmost) branch is the **New Cut **, dug during the 1640s Civil War as part of the city defences, intended to halt Parliamentary troops approaching from the London side.

The Cherwell path eventually returns to meet Broad Walk, on the left, and Rose Lane to the right, which leads to the Botanic Garden (*see page 116*).

At the other side of Magdalen Bridge, visitors to Magdalen College can explore the Cherwell along Addison's Walk (*see page 104*).

If you want to see more of the Cherwell, you don't have to reach it via Magdalen College. Exit the Botanic Garden and walk down to the Plain (*see page 106*). The road to the left, off The Plain, forms the main street of the suburb of **St Clement's**. A few 17th-century, tim-

ber-framed buildings survive from the time when St Clement's was a village, but most now date to the early 19th century, when speculative developers laid out a network of new streets. The area now has many characterful pubs and unusual shops.

Mesopotamia Walk

Where St Clement's Street divides, take the left-hand fork into Marston Road and look for the lane that leads to the river, past the new **Oxford Centre for Islamic Studies** with its landmark minaret and opposite the government buildings. This path leads to **Mesopotamia Walk **; the name derives from the Greek, meaning "between the rivers", as in the ancient kingdom that lay between the Tigris and Euphrates. Here the path follows a narrow strip of land between two branches of the Cherwell, a popular stretch of the water for punting and picnics. The path crosses a number of bridges, before reaching

River Cherwell map

a weir where punters have to disembark and manhandle their boats over the metal rollers to one side.

From the weir, a path to the left crosses a concrete bridge to merge with South Parks Road and Linacre College. On the right we meet again the huge expanse of **University Parks** (*see page 179*), with its magnificent trees and shrubs and lovely walks by the river. Here it is possible to continue north along the banks of the River Cherwell, over bridges and across fields towards the northern edge of the city.

St Ebbe's

From Folly Bridge, the path along the Thames also leads west. The north side of the river at this point is occupied by recent residential developments with attractive terraces and walkways along the river. These mark the southern boundary of St Ebbe's. Once a working-class suburb of Oxford, **St Ebbe's ❻** was chosen as the site for the town's new gasworks in 1818, and the arrival of the railway in Oxford in 1844 further stimulated speculative building.

Not much of the original St Ebbe's remains today, most of its Victorian houses having been pulled down in the 1960s and the population rehoused at the purpose-built Blackbird Leys estate in east Oxford.

If you continue along the south bank of the river, you soon leave the residential district of Grandpont behind and once more enter a riverscape flanked by green, with the occasional used or disused bridge as a reminder of past industrial progress. **Grandpont nature park** is just a step away from the river, a popular recreation area for local residents. Note the wooden sculpture of a giant hand emerging from the grass.

Osney

Continue beyond the railway bridge to a long, straight section of the river,

beyond which lies Osney Lock and the suburb of Osney **❼**. Also reached from Botley Road over a bridge built in 1888, the main part of Osney is an island surrounded by arms of the River Thames. The district has nicely preserved 1850s terraces and characterful waterside pubs. In summer the river is usually busy with narrowboats and cruisers.

It may seem difficult to imagine today, but back in the Middle Ages the whole island was occupied by one of the largest Augustinian monasteries in England. Founded in 1129, but completely destroyed at the Dissolution in 1536, **Osney Abbey** was among the first major centres of learning in Oxford. Once the third-largest church in England, Osney Abbey housed Great Tom, the huge bell that chimes in Christ Church's Tom Tower (*see page 154*). Nowadays, only the remnants of a 15th-century outbuilding can be glimpsed through the gates of the Osney Marina at the end of Mill Street (second left after the railway bridge heading out of town).

From Ferry Hinksey Road there is

Maps:
pages
196, 198

The 270 households on Osney Island have maintained a notable community spirit, and the active Osney Sustainable Island Group makes news for its efforts to improve energy efficiency and maximise recycling. Its aim: to become the world's first 100% renewable energy island.

BELOW: a narrowboat berthed at Osney.

Messing About on the Rivers

Punts, as much a feature of Oxford as bicycles and spires, have come to embody the timeless romance of the privileged university world. Yet long before the first student ever skipped lectures in favour of punting up the slow-flowing Cherwell, the punt played a vital part in the lives of watermen up and down the Thames. River dredging, fishing, ferrying, transporting and delivering were all duties once carried out by this humble craft.

Decline in river transport in the mid-19th century could have led to the disappearance of the punt altogether. Fortunately, the Victorians, recognising the delights of punting, claimed it as their leisure craft. Punts were modified from broad pontoons that could carry cattle to the slender "saloon" comprising two back rests for passengers – a design still in use today.

Increased use of power craft on rivers has resulted in a sharp decrease in punting and it has survived as a feature almost unique to Oxford and Cambridge. As a Thames craft, the punt was not introduced to Cambridge until the early Edwardian era, when it was imported from Oxford. The Oxford tradition is to punt from the slope, stern first, whereas in Cambridge, punting from the deck end is the norm.

Some Oxford colleges have their own punting fleets and most have private hire arrangements. Punts can be hired in the summer from 10am to sunset from three points: Folly Bridge, Magdalen Bridge and the Cherwell Boathouse. They cost £10 to £12 an hour (US$17–$20) and can take up to six people, but their use is restricted to swimmers. Paddles are provided in case poles get stuck in the mud. Rowing boats can also be hired.

Newcomers might find that the Cherwell provides fewer hazards than the Thames and doesn't have rowing crews and powerboats. It is navigable by punt up to Islip. The Thames will be congested with university rowers below Iffley Lock.

Numerically, rowing is by far the most popular sport among students and a large proportion of rowers are women. The Participants range from non-competitive waterlovers who are exploring the river to the elite university team. Each college has its own rowing society and the societies are brought together under the umbrella of Oxford University Boating Club (OUBC), founded in 1939.

From early morning until dusk throughout the year, Eights, Fours and Sculls can be seen accompanied by coaches who cycle or run along the towpath, megaphone in hand. On the stretch of river beyond Christ Church Meadow are the college and OUBC boathouses. Just before Iffley Lock is the Isis Tavern, watering hole for many a rower and home to much boating regalia. The two main events in the rowing calendar are Torpids and Eights Week (*see page 127*).

By far the most glamorous event in rowing is the inter-Varsity race, first staged in 1829. Oxford "dark blues" take on Cambridge "light blues" in the annual Putney-to-Mortlake race. The prestigious Blue is awarded in rowing and other sports to those competing in a university team against Cambridge. ❑

LEFT: punting is a major summer attraction.

an attractive short walk over the meadows, via a bridge over the Thames to the village of **North Hinksey** . This village, with its thatched cottages, riding stables, Norman church of St Lawrence and pub, retains a rural feel. John Ruskin is commemorated on one of the picturesque cottages. In 1874, Ruskin organised teams of undergraduates to work on road improvements in the village – with the intention of convincing his students (who included Oscar Wilde) of the "pleasures of useful muscular work".

Binsey

Back in Osney, the church of St Frideswide on Botley Road contains a door panel, with a relief of the saint praying by the Thames, carved by Alice Liddell, herself a pupil of Ruskin's, in 1890. Other reminders of the saint as well as the heroine of *Alice's Adventures in Wonderland* can be seen in the remote church of St Margaret in **Binsey** ⑨. The church is reached down Binsey Lane on the other side of Botley Road, and, once past the messy builders'

yards, the suburbs give way to a patchwork of small fields surrounded by high hedges and tall trees.

Binsey itself is a tiny farming hamlet but with a renowned pub, **The Perch**, beside the Thames, a favourite lunchtime retreat for weekend walkers, with a good playground for children.

Beyond the village, a single-track road leads to the little late-Norman church. Just beyond the west end is the **Treacle Well** that features in the story told by Lewis Carroll's Dormouse at the Mad Hatter's Tea Party. In Middle English "triacle" meant any liquid with healing or medicinal powers – only later did it come to mean a syrup.

This well is said to have sprung up at the command of St Frideswide. The king of Wessex, her enforced and self-appointed suitor, was struck blind by thunder when he tried to carry the saint away forcibly. Frideswide agreed to cure him on condition that he leave her in peace; the well appeared miraculously and its waters restored the king's sight.

Hundreds of pilgrims used to visit

Peeking into the Treacle Well at Binsey.

LEFT AND BELOW: North Hinksey's Norman church in summer and winter.

Map
on page
196

*It was in Godstow
Nunnery that
Rosamund Clifford,
mistress of King
Henry II, was buried
in 1175. According
to legend, "fair
Rosamund" was
murdered by the
jealous Queen
Eleanor, but the
truth is probably less
melodramatic, since
she seems to have
retired to the nun-
nery when Henry
grew bored with her.*

BELOW:
canoeing and walking
in Port Meadow.

the church. Few come now and the rustic nave, lit only by oil lamps, has been colonised by bats. The simple wooden pulpit has a carving of St Margaret trampling on a dragon. Inside is another relief of St Margaret on the inner face – not by Eric Gill, as has been claimed – with clearly delineated breasts. Regarded as rather too sensual, she is condemned to face the feet of the incumbent preacher rather than risk arousing the passions of the congregation.

Port Meadow

Binsey seems remote from all the bustle of central Oxford, even though the nearest suburbs are only half a mile (1 km) away. It sits just to the west of the Thames, while to the east, sandwiched between the river and the city, is the great expanse of **Port Meadow** ❿. Used continuously for grazing ever since its first mention in the *Domesday Book* (1087), the meadow is a rare piece of Old England; it has never once been ploughed over, and is still used for grazing horses and cattle.

In winter, when the flooded meadow freezes over, skaters come out to test the strength of the ice. The birdlife is rich at all times of the year, and in summer you can often make out the outlines of Iron Age farming enclosures and hut circles, delineated by the buttercups that grow taller over buried features such as ditches and foundation trenches.

A pleasant walk crosses the meadow and the bridge over the Thames, and follows the west bank of the river past Binsey to Godstow, where a 15th-century bridge leads to the scant remains of the medieval **Godstow Nunnery** ⓫. Founded in 1138 by Benedictine monks, the nunnery is now a romantic ruin.

Nearby, the **Trout Inn**, originally a fisherman's cottage, was rebuilt in 1737, and is famous for the peacocks that wander around the attractive riverside garden. It is a popular place on long summer evenings, and in winter has roaring log fires.

For the route back, it is possible to take the Godstow Road until it meets the Oxford Canal, and follow the towpath all the way to its end at Hythe Bridge. ❑

RESTAURANTS & PUBS

Restaurants

Fishers

36-37 St Clement's Street. Tel 01865 243003. Open daily. ££

An exuberantly colourful exterior and nautically themed interior give this adventurous fish restaurant a welcoming feel. Fresh fish, delivered daily from London's Billingsgate market, is served in generous portions. Popular in the evenings with a student-oriented clientele, it is a very good bet for lunch.

Moya

97 St Clement's Street. Tel 01865 200111. Open daily. £

In a city full of cosmopolitan eateries this really is an original: apparently the UK's one and only Slovakian restaurant. In fact, Moya is as much a stylish cocktail bar as anything else, specialising in sophisticated but not overpriced concoctions. The food is Central European and filling: goulash, dumplings and potatoes, but also plenty of vegetarian and less robust options.

The Fishes

North Hinksey Village. Tel 01865 249796. Open daily. £

RIGHT: the Trout Inn, seen in TV's *Inspector Morse*.

Now more of a restaurant than a pub, The Fishes has won plaudits for its interesting menus and good, locally sourced ingredients. This gastro-pub is set in a lovely, shaded streamside setting, with a tolerant attitude towards children and genuinely friendly service. Traditional Sunday roasts are complemented by more exotic dishes and an exceptional choice of desserts.

Pubs

Many of Oxford's finest pubs are close to water. The **Angel & Greyhound** (30 St Clement's Street) is a busy and friendly place, serving good Youngs beer and specialising in traditional pub games. The nearby **Half Moon** (18 St Clement's) is probably Oxford's most authentic Irish pub, with a great reputation for folk music, poetry readings and local *craic*. On Osney Island, a characterful enclave of terraced houses, the **Waterman's Arms** (South Street, Osney Island) stands out as a traditional local, where the menu features simple home cooking in large portions alongside well-kept real ales. **The Perch** (Binsey Village) attracts large crowds of Sunday walkers, especially in fine weather when even its large garden can become overcrowded, but at other times it's a reliable place for decent pub food and Port Meadow atmosphere. **The Trout Inn** (195 Godstow Road, Lower Wolvercote), enormously popular with locals and tourists alike, has been much restored over the centuries and now contains a spacious and atmospheric bar and restaurant areas with good food and open fires.

PRICE CATEGORIES

Prices for three-course dinner per person with a half-bottle of house wine:
£ = under £20
££ = £20–£30
£££ = £30–£45
££££ = more than £45

OXFORD'S OUTSKIRTS

Beyond Oxford's suburbs, which include Cowley, the
birthplace of Morris Motors, there are
some stunning views of the
"City of Dreaming Spires"

Large houses line the complex of narrow lanes that lead to **Boars Hill ❶**, and such was the pressure of development that the Oxford Preservation Trust purchased the remaining land in 1928 to ensure that the views would not be destroyed.

One Boars Hill resident, Sir Arthur Evans, famous for his archaeological discoveries at Knossos, worked with the Trust to build an artificial mound at the summit of the hill. Evans' intention was partly to provide work for the local unemployed during a period of economic depression, and partly to create a vantage point from where to admire Oxford's dreaming spires.

The tumulus that Evans built, known as **Jarn Mound ❷**, rises to 50 ft (15 metres), and the summit is 530 ft (162 metres) above sea level. It was completed in 1931 and the surrounding area planted with trees to create a wild garden.

Now it is overgrown with bracken and scrub, and the topograph on the summit has gone, the column on which it stood broken. Even so, the views are unchanged: to the northeast the ancient buildings of Oxford appear, framed between ancient trees that seem deliberately planted to hide the modern suburbs – if you go at dusk, the setting sun adds its own rich colouring to the scene. Turn round and you see another extensive view, stretching southwest over the Vale of the White Horse to the Berkshire Downs.

Map
on page
206

Happy Valley

Heading clockwise around the ring road, Chilswell Valley, better known as **Happy Valley ❸**, is reached by turning off the southern by-pass (A34) at a well-signposted garden centre and following a footpath to Chilswell Farm. The view from this

LEFT:
the view of Oxford
from Boars Hill.
BELOW: The Fox
pub at Boars Hill.

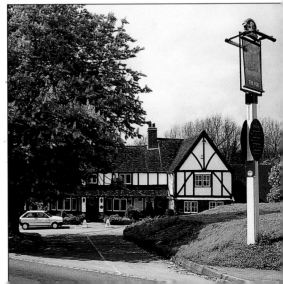

southern hillside is almost as perfect a picture of the celebrated dreaming spires as you will find, remarkably unobstructed by power lines and other modern-day eyesores. What is striking is how small Oxford seems from this vantage-point, its towers and steeples encircled by hills.

From the same exit from the ring road you can also visit the **Hinksey Heights Golf and Nature Park**, where the view is, if anything, even more beautiful. Here the golf club welcomes visitors (as long as they keep off the golf course itself) and you can use the bar and restaurant.

A well-marked trail takes you through woods and over streams until you come to a fishing lake, stocked with six types of coarse fish (day angling permits available for £5 from the golf club). The surrounding countryside is inhabited not just by golfers, but also by foxes, badgers and deer as well as a wide range of birdlife.

Iffley Lock.

Iffley and Cowley

From this point, it is 2 miles (3 km) by the thundering ring road to **Iffley** ❹, a village on the southern edge of the city worth seeking out simply for its **parish church of St Mary the Virgin**. In the whole of England there is scarcely a more complete example of the late 12th-century Romanesque style. The rose window of the west end is later (inserted in 1856), but most of the remaining doorways, windows and arches – covered in sawtooth ornament and carved with beakheads, the signs of the zodiac, fighting horsemen and symbols of the Evangelists – date from around 1180.

After Iffley comes the extensive suburb of **Cowley** ❺, dubbed "Motopolis" by John Betjeman who hated this industrial town on the doorstep of his beloved Oxford because it was devoted to producing the motor car that "roars down the lanes with its cargo of cads, poisons

Oxford's Outskirts

0   2 km
0   2 miles

the air, deafens the ears and deadens the senses".

Cowley was responsible for a massive 43 percent increase in the population of Oxford between 1921 and 1939, as the success of the Morris motor attracted labourers from the depression-hit Midlands and South Wales. They were accommodated in what John Betjeman called "strips of shoddy houses... indistinguishable from Swindon, Neasden or Tooting Bec".

St Bartholomew's Chapel

A small, historical gem is to be found hidden on Cowley Road, away from the suburban grime. Up a small pathway opposite the former Bingo Hall is **St Bartholomew's Chapel**, flanked by a row of almshouses. Built in the early 14th century, the chapel was connected to a leprosy hospital, situated at a suitable distance from the medieval city. The buildings are still there in a special Conservation Area, a world away from the main road just a few hundred yards distant. There's a stillness about it, making it, believers say, a good place to pray.

This main artery is the epicentre of alternative and multicultural Oxford as well as a popular area for students to live. It contains countless ethnic restaurants and grocery stores as well as a good range of independent retailers.

In Cowley itself, the car plant, the successor to the Morris Motor Works and now owned by Germany's BMW, lies either side of the eastern by-pass, with the woodland of Shotover Country Park rising behind. The car factory can be visited by appointment *(see margin)*.

Shotover Country Park

The eastern and southern perimeter of the city, delineated by the busy ring road, offers some spectacular views of Oxford from surrounding hills as well as some interesting nature walks.

To reach **Shotover Country Park** **❻** by car, it is best to drive along Old Road from Headington, cross the ring road and climb up through a wooded residential area. The park itself comprises 250 acres (100 hectares) of mixed natural habitat, including grassland, heath, wetland and woodland. Recognised by English Nature as a Site of Special Scientific Interest, it has good views over the eastern part of Oxford.

Walks are clearly laid out and area is a favourite with dog owners and mountain-bike enthusiasts. Some conspicuous hollows in the ground are what is left of what used to be a yellow ochre mining works. The area was also once the haunt of highwaymen, as the old London road passed over the hill, and carriages containing the well-to-do were an irresistible temptation for Oxford's equivalents of Dick Turpin.

Headington

Headington **❼** consists of several distinct "villages". **Headington**

Map on page 206

TIP

You can see Minis being made by visiting the BMW car plant at Cowley. Children under 14 are not allowed on site. Booking essential. Details from Public Relations and Employee Communication Office, BMW Group, Oxford OX4 6NL. Tel.: 01865-825842. Email: oxford.plant-tours @mini.com

BELOW:
beakhead carvings at the entrance to the chuch of St Mary the Virgin, Iffley.

TIP

One of Oxford Brookes University's more unusual features is Brookes Restaurant *(see opposite page)*, run by the college's catering students. Parking is difficult, though. You can book one of three parking spaces at the restaurant's Gypsy Lane location or else take a Park and Ride bus to Thornhill or Pear Tree car parks.

BELOW:
the controversial shark at Headington.

Quarry ❽, as its name suggests, originally supplied the limestone and roof tiles from which much of medieval Oxford was built. The current suburb developed around the quarrymen's cottages, some of which still remain, dating from the 17th and 18th centuries. This village is home to a well-known team of Morris dancers, the Quarrymen.

Old Headington lies on the opposite side of the London Road, and was once the resort of undergraduates seeking illicit pleasures in alehouses, beyond the jurisdiction of the Proctors or Bulldogs. In the 18th and 19th centuries, wealthy tradesmen built large houses on the leafy hillside. One of them, Bury Knowle House, is the Headington Library and occupies attractively landscaped grounds. Just to the north, restored 17th-century cottages surround St Andrew's Church, which has a Norman chancel arch and 15th-century chancel roof.

Headington Hill ❾, which plunges steeply into central Oxford, was built up mainly in the 19th century. Oxford United used to have its football ground here until the club moved in the 1990s to a purpose-built stadium beyond Blackbird Leys, leaving the ground to be redeveloped as hospital facilities. Further down is Headington Hill Hall, once part of Robert Maxwell's publishing empire, Pergamon Press, but now owned by Oxford Brookes University. Opposite is the modern Gipsy Lane campus of Brookes *(see page 61)*, the growth of which has resulted in several blocks of student facilities and accommodation in and around Headington.

South Park

At the bottom of Headington Hill is the lower part of **South Park** ❿, a large expanse of green stretching sharply upwards. There is usually a bonfire and fireworks in November. From the top of the park, where there are playing fields and a children's playground, you can look down on to the surprisingly compact city centre, picking out the major landmarks such as Magdalen Tower and Tom Tower. The view is particularly lovely at dawn or sunset. ❏

Shark!

One morning in August 1986 the residents of New High Street in Headington awoke to find a 25-ft (8-metre) fibreglass shark plunging through the roof of one of its houses. Its owner, US-born entrepreneur and radio presenter Bill Heine, said the shark, the work of local architect John Buckley, symbolised the arbitrary horror of the nuclear age. The Council said it infringed planning regulations, but eventually, the shark's aesthetic merits were recognised with an award from the Southern Arts Council. You can see its tail from the London Road, but it's worth taking a detour down New High Street to get a better view.

RESTAURANTS & BARS

Restaurants

The Aziz

228–230 Cowley Road. Tel 794945. Open daily. £

Perhaps the best of Cowley Road's many Indian restaurants, the Aziz is a welcome escape from flock wallpaper and predictable menus. With its spacious and tasteful atmosphere, it is the ideal place to sample the subtle variations within Asian cuisine at a very reasonable price. "Specials" change regularly and there is plenty of scope for vegetarians.

The Hi-Lo Jamaican Eating House

70 Cowley Road. Tel 725984. Open daily. £

A distinctive taste of the Caribbean in East Oxford, this eccentric institution allegedly charges customers what it thinks they can afford. True or not, the food includes classic Jamaican staples like rice'n' peas, ackees and saltfish and curried goat. Service may be slow, but that is part of the experience, enhanced by Red Stripe lager and Jamaican rum. Guest rooms.

Door 74

74 Cowley Road. Tel 203374. Open L&D every day except Monday. ££

One of Cowley Road's new breed of stylish restaurant, this attractive and fashionable venue serves locally sourced, often organic, food in a fusion of British and Mediterranean influences. The desserts are particularly good, and there is a popular weekend brunch.

Kazbar

25-27 Cowley Road. Tel 202920. Open daily. £

Probably Oxford's premier tapas bar, Kazbar has lots of Moorish atmosphere, with ochre walls, benches and cushions and suitably attired staff. The generous portions of Andalucian-inspired food, including fish, spicy potatoes and delicious tortilla, are matched by a good selection of Spanish beers and house wines.

Brookes Restaurant

Gipsy Lane, Headington. Tel 483803. Open Mon-Fri (except Mon out of term) for lunch; last orders taken 1.30pm. £

Excellent value 3-course lunches as well as single dishes are on the menu at what is essentially a training school for chefs and other hospitality workers. The food is often better than that on offer from the professionals and is very reasonably priced. The cookery school also runs one-day classes for the public.

Pubs

The **Fox Inn** (Fox Lane, Boars Hill) is a welcoming place all year round, with a pretty garden in summer and real fires in winter. Good food and an unusually extensive wine list.

Iffley boasts the riverside **Isis** with a lovely garden and good lunchtime menu, as well as the **Prince of Wales** (73 Church Way), a busy and friendly establishment on the village's pretty main street. The **Tree Hotel** (63 Church Way) contains the Annora restaurant/bar, serving an acclaimed mix of British, Indian and Thai dishes. **The Bullingdon** (162 Cowley Road) is a lively student-oriented pub with a good-value menu and a large backroom used for folk evenings and other musical events. The **City Arms** (288 Cowley Road) provides very good food at reasonable prices in a welcoming, student-dominated atmosphere. Across the road, **Baby** (213 Cowley Road) is the closest the street comes to chic, with retro decor, cocktails and a young crowd. Many move from there to the **Zodiac** (190 Cowley Road), where the atmosphere is less chic and more down-to-earth.

Its range of music is unmatched in Oxford.

There are several good cafés on Cowley Road, not least **Café Coco** (23 Cowley Road), a bright and cheerful place offering good pizzas, salads and cocktails all day, Vegetarian and vegan-friendly. **Joe's** (21 Cowley Road), a great choice for burgers and/or cocktails, and **Café Baba** (240 Cowley Road), a North African-themed bar/café specialising in tapas.

Of Headington's many pubs, the **Royal Standard** (78 London Road) stands out as a friendly single-bar establishment with an extensive menu of home-cooked lunches and good beer. The 17th-century **Black Boy** (91 Old High Street) is in Headington's picturesque old district and despite its politically incorrect name attracts a mixed crowd of students and regulars with its traditional pub atmosphere.

PRICE CATEGORIES

Prices for three-course dinner per person with a half-bottle of house wine:
£ = under £20
££ = £20–£30
£££ = £30–£45
££££ = more than £45

Trips out of Oxford

TRIPS OUT OF OXFORD

Within easy reach of Oxford are the lovely Cotswolds, alluring riverside towns, Stratford-upon-Avon's Shakespeariana, Warwick's popular castle, and celebrated stately homes such as Blenheim

Drive for just a few miles outside Oxford and you will be immersed in countryside that you didn't realise was so close to the busy city. To help you explore its beauties, the following chapters are divided into routes, beginning with the road to Stratford-upon-Avon. First on the route is Woodstock, famous for the splendid Blenheim Palace and its associations with Winston Churchill, and a charming market town. The road on from Woodstock leads to the pretty villages of Great Tew and Hook Norton before reaching the ancient Rollright Stones. The final stretch to Stratford offers some more delightful villages with names like Compton Wynyates and Clifford Chambers.

Stratford-upon-Avon is a shrine to the playwright William Shakespeare, and visitors from all over the world come to see what all the fuss is about. The tour around the town takes in all the important sights, such as his birthplace, his home at New Place, his school, the Guild Hall, and his burial place, Holy Trinity Church. It's even possible to take in one of the Bard's plays at the Shakespeare Memorial Theatre. There are other sights as well, such as the Garrick Inn and Harvard House, both 16th-century, the canal and beautiful Bancroft Gardens.

From Stratford you can detour to Warwick, dominated by its Castle, a very popular attraction, packed with history. Other highlights of the town are St Mary's Church and a Doll Museum.

The north Cotswolds, one of England's most alluring landscapes, are filled with typical Cotswold towns, such as Chipping Norton, Moreton-in-Marsh, Chipping Camden, Broadway, Bourton-on-the-Water and Stow-on-the-Wold. Although the area lies beyond the scope of this book, you can also follow the lower Thames past medieval Abingdon and 7th-century Dorchester to commuter-land at Goring and Streatley, the regatta-centre of Henley-on-Thames, and back to Oxford via the famous houses of Cliveden and Hughenden Manor. ❏

PRECEDING PAGES: the impressive facade of Blenheim Palace at Woodstock.

THE ROAD TO STRATFORD

It would be a shame to rush to charming Stratford-upon-Avon along the busy main highways, missing out the memorable sights along the route

Map on page 212

BELOW:
the Marlborough Arms Hotel in Woodstock dates back to the 14th century.

Stratford-upon-Avon lies about 60 miles (100 km) northwest of Oxford and exerts a magnetic attraction, having acquired international status as the most important literary shrine in England. Its environs are fascinating, too.

Woodstock and Blenheim

Leaving Oxford on the A44, it is only a matter of minutes before you reach the handsome market town of **Woodstock ❶**. The main street (Park Street) lies off the main road and is flanked by fine Georgian-fronted houses and a collection of pubs, cafés and boutiques.

The town derived much of its former prosperity from glove-making, and while all the factories in Woodstock itself are now closed, gloves are still made in surrounding villages and sold at the Woodstock Glove Shop, next to the town hall.

Also in Park Street, the Oxfordshire County Museum in Fletcher's House provides an overview of the region's archaeology, agriculture and domestic life, and the gardens to the rear are used to display contemporary sculpture. Opposite, the church of St Mary Magdalene was lavishly restored in 1878, but the best part is the 18th-century tower, carved with swags of flowers around the clock and parapet.

At the far end of Park Street, a triumphal arch announces the entrance to **Blenheim Palace** (house: Mar–Oct daily 10.30am–5.30pm; park: all year daily 9am–4.45pm). There is still half a mile (1 km) to go before you reach this monumental building, for it lies at the heart of a vast estate, covering 2,700 acres (1,100 hectares) – the palace alone occupies an area of 7 acres (2.8 hectares). Not for nothing is it called a palace, rather than a mere manor, although that is what it was originally.

Royal blood

Woodstock was, as far back as records go, a royal manor, frequented by a succession of monarchs for deer hunting, when the land was still part of the great forest of Wychwood. Henry II installed his mistress, Fair Rosamund Clifford, at Woodstock, until Queen Eleanor discovered her hunting lodge hideaway. By the 16th century the original royal palace was decayed, and the last remaining buildings were demolished after the Civil War.

In 1705, Queen Anne gave both the manor and the funds to build the palace to John Churchill, 1st Duke of Marlborough and forefather of Winston Churchill. This was his reward for defeating the French army at Blenheim, on the Danube, the previous year, a major victory that temporarily thwarted Louis XIV's desire to dominate Europe.

The Queen made it quite clear that the palace was to be no mere private house, but a national monument, a symbol of Britain's supremacy – by implication, a building to outshine even Louis XIV's own splendid palace at Versailles. Consequently, the best architects of the day were consulted. Christopher Wren was the obvious candidate, and many of his masons, men who had worked on St Paul's, were employed on the project. But Wren was rejected in favour of John Vanbrugh, whose designs for Castle Howard were greatly admired by Churchill. Vanbrugh is therefore credited as the architect of this baroque masterpiece, but his assistant, Nicholas Hawksmoor, ought to share the credit – for it was he who supervised much of the work.

A true folly

In the event, it is remarkable that the building was completed at all, let alone on such an heroic scale. Parliament quibbled about the cost, funds ran out, and the Duchess of Marlborough constantly opposed the grandiose scheme, declaring "I mortally hate all gardens and architecture", and insisting that all she wanted was "a clean, sweet house and garden, be it ever so small".

The Duke ended up bearing a great deal of the cost himself, and such was

Classical detail at Blenheim Palace.

BELOW:
Blenheim Palace.

*Statuary at
Blenheim Palace.*

the enmity between architect and client that Vanbrugh never saw the finished building; when he tried to visit in 1725, the Duchess refused him entrance.

Even when completed, Blenheim continued to be controversial: Horace Walpole called it "execrable" and Alexander Pope, ever with an eye to practicalities, quipped "'tis very fine; but where d'ye sleep and where d'ye dine?"

Yet now Blenheim excites the imagination and invites superlatives. The skyline, with its bizarre chimneys, its pinnacles resembling stacks of cannon balls and its ducal coronets, creates a wonderful silhouette, viewed across the lakes and avenues of the park, landscaped by "Capability" Brown.

Symbols of soldiery

Everywhere you look there are symbols of military prowess – over the main entrance, Britannia stands supreme in armour above the Marlborough coat of arms. Chained slaves writhe on the upper pediment, and the gates to the side wings have carvings of the cock of France being savaged by the British lion.

Inside, the gilded state rooms are rich in furniture and portraits of the Marlboroughs. Tapestries, woven in Brussels, celebrate the 1st Duke's victories. In the magnificent saloon, life-size *trompe l'oeil* figures, representing the peoples of the four continents and painted by Louis Laguerre in 1719–20, lean over balconies as spectators to the state banquets that still are, on occasion, held in this huge, unheated room (for the sake of symmetry, there are no fireplaces).

Despite its scale and discomforts, Blenheim also serves as a home, and the small room where Sir Winston Churchill was born in 1874 attracts as much attention as the state apartments. Like his ancestor, the 1st Duke, Sir Winston is remembered as a great war leader. Unlike the 1st Duke, who is commemorated by a monument of exaggerated proportions in the palace chapel, Sir Winston is buried in a simple grave in the parish church of **Bladon ❷**, on the southern periphery of the estate.

Sir Winston Churchill

Churchill was born on 30 November 1874 in a simple room to the west of Blenheim's Great Hall. Once used by the 1st Duke's domestic chaplain, Dean Jones, the room now forms the core of a permanent exhibition of Churchilliana, including manuscripts, paintings and personal belongings. Visitors can also see letters written by Sir Winston, mostly to his father, Lord Randolph Churchill, as well as a piece of shrapnel that narrowly missed him in World War I.

It was at Blenheim that Churchill proposed to his future wife, Clementine, in the Temple of Diana. The house acted as inspiration for several of his paintings, some now on show.

Great Tew

Some 6 miles (10 km) further north, the B4022 meets the A44, just outside Enstone, and the right turn leads to the picturesque village of **Great Tew** ❸. Dubbed "the place where time stood still", this estate village contains scarcely a modern building, simply because the late landlord permitted no new development; indeed, as the number of labourers employed on the estate steadily declined, the stone and thatch cottages were simply left to rot. One visitor, in 1972, described the derelict houses surrounding the green as "one of the most depressing sights in the whole country".

Now, thanks to new ownership, the cottages have been fully restored to their appearance in the early 19th century, when, as part of a model farm, the village was carefully landscaped. Quite a number of the cottages were given Gothic embellishments at the time, though many date to the 16th century. Set back behind colourful gardens, they present the kind of picture that calendar and chocolate-box manufacturers find irresistible.

The church of St Michael lies south of the village, just within the grounds of the park, and the church-yard is entered through a 17th-century stone gateway. Inside is a noteworthy monument to Mary Anne Boulton (died 1829) by Francis Chantrey. The Boultons, descendants of Matthew Boulton, the Birmingham engineer who made his fortune manufacturing steam engines as a partner of James Watt, acquired the estate in 1815 and gave the 17th-century house its current neo-Gothic appearance.

Hook Norton

The B4022 continues north for just over a mile (2 km) to the A361. If you turn left, and then right via Swerford, a pretty village on the River Swere, you will reach **Hook Norton** ❹. Real-ale lovers will know this as the source of "Hooky", a beer made by traditional methods in the red-brick Victorian brewery at the west end of the village. This prominent building is surrounded by cottages built of the local orange-coloured ironstone – as is the church

Map on page 212

May Day festivities in Hook Norton and other Cotswold villages include morris dancing. Often derided as folkloric kitsch, this strenuous dance may date back 800 years and celebrates the coming of spring. The colourful costume includes dozens of bells attached to the legs and the dancers wield sticks or handkerchiefs.

BELOW: traditional hostelries have been restored in villages such as Great Tew.

Shipston on Stour's High Street.

BELOW:
the Rollright Stones.

of St Peter, commanding the hilltop at the centre of the village. The lively Norman font inside is carved with a charmingly rustic Adam, with his hammer and spade, and a flirtatious Eve, holding her apple, as well as signs of the zodiac.

The Rollright Stones

Three miles (5 km) west of Hook Norton, through the village of **Great Rollright** and across the A3400, you will find the remains of a prehistoric stone circle.

Standing on the high ridge of the northern Cotswolds, the **Rollright Stones** ⑤ form a henge 100 ft (60 metres) in diameter. They date to around 3500 BC. The stones of the circle itself are known as the King's Men, while the solitary stone on the opposite side of the road is the King and the five further east, once the burial chamber of a long barrow, are the Whispering Knights.

The names refer to a legend, first recorded in 1586, that the stones represent petrified men who will one day wake to rule the land. They were tricked, according to the story, by a local witch who promised their leader that he would be king of England if he could see Long Compton, the village in the valley below, from this spot. This simple task proved impossible – some say that the witch conjured up a mist – and so she transformed them with the words: *Thou and thy men hoar stones shall be/And I myself an elder tree.*

Other legends about the stones abound – to their detriment, since they have often been chipped away by visitors (including Civil War soldiers on their way to battle) believing in their magical properties.

The Rollright Stones are too close to the busy A3400 to make a good resting spot, but an ideal place for a peaceful picnic is along the unclassified road back to the main road, across and left towards the Sibfords. This high road, with fine views all round, drops, after 4 miles (7 km), into the Stour Valley at **Traitor's Ford**. Nobody seems to remember now who the traitor was; but the ford, with its clear stream and woodland either side, makes a perfect spot for relaxing on a hot summer's day.

From the ford, an ancient track, **Ditchedge Lane**, leads directly to **Compton Wynyates**, accessible only to walkers – motorists have to take the longer route through Sibford Gower. Compton Wynyates, a romantic Tudor mansion of rose-coloured brick, is no longer open to the public; but you can glimpse it, nestling into the wooded hillside, from the road to the west.

Windmill Hill, rising beyond to the north, is crowned by a stone tower mill, complete with its sails, while on **Compton Pike**, to the south, is a pyramidal structure, dating to the 16th century, built to be lit in the event of an invasion.

Some 5 miles (8 km) west is **Shipston on Stour** ⑥. The name (originally Sheepston) is a reminder that the town was once host to one of

England's largest sheep markets. It is home to many handsome former coaching inns.

Honington Hall

Two miles (3 km) north, **Honington Hall ❼** (open June–Aug, Wed and Bank Holiday Mondays 2.30–5pm) is a 17th-century brick house that could pass for the ordinary domestic manor of some country squire, but for a series of busts all around the facades, depicting 12 Caesars. Even more extraordinary is the sumptuous plasterwork inside.

The house was built in 1685 by Sir Henry Parker who, having made a fortune as a London merchant, had the village church remodelled in the style of Wren's elegant City of London churches. The monument to Parker and his son Hugh is the best of several splendid pieces of carving, in both marble and stone, inside.

Stylish church

From Honington, continue up the A3400 to Newbold-on-Stour and then, if you want to avoid the main road, take the minor road left that runs parallel to the pretty, winding River Stour.

At **Preston on Stour ❽** you will find another stylish 18th-century church, this time in the Gothic style, and an east window made up of 17th-century glass from diverse sources, all illustrating the theme of death. The village has several ornate 16th- and 17th-century timber-framed houses and even the red-brick Alscot housing estate, an early example of its kind, dating to 1852, has a certain undeniable charm.

At **Clifford Chambers** attractive cottages line the single street that leads to the manor house, restored – or rather rebuilt – by Sir Edwin Lutyens in 1919. Here, too, is the first of many buildings associated with Shakespeare, for the 16th-century timber-framed rectory was the home of one John Shakespeare during the 1570s. Since William's father was called John, biographers have speculated whether this might possibly have been his childhood home.

From Clifford Chambers continue on the B4632 and A3400 to reach **Stratford-upon-Avon ❾**. ❑

Map on page 212

Old-world house at Preston on Stour.

BELOW: Compton Wynyates House.

STRATFORD-UPON-AVON

Stratford-upon-Avon

● Oxford

London

Basking in Shakespeare's enduring fame, Stratford remains one of England's most crowded tourist destinations. To go or not to go? That is the question

Map on page 222

The Shakespeare industry dates to the mid-19th century, when a pub called the Swan and Maidenhead, in Henley Street, came on the market. This had long been considered Shakespeare's birthplace, and in 1847 a public appeal was launched to buy the building as a national monument. A trust was formed and, between 1857 and 1864, the property was restored to its "original" appearance, a process that involved virtually rebuilding the house that is seen today.

BELOW:
Shakespeare's
Birthplace.

Shakespeare's Birthplace

The best starting point for a tour of Stratford is **Shakespeare's Birthplace** Ⓐ (open Mar–Oct, Mon–Fri 9am–5pm, Sun 9.30am–5pm; winter to 4pm). The rooms are furnished as far as possible in late 16th-century style, as well as having small-scale displays on aspects of family history and William's work. The room in which Shakespeare is supposed to have been born, on 23 April 1564, is lit by a window inscribed with the signatures of illustrious guests such as Sir Walter Scott, Thomas Carlyle and Isaac Watts.

You can, however, learn much more about Shakespeare at the **Shakespeare Centre** Ⓑ just along the street (opening times as above). Here is an excellent exhibition entitled "William Shakespeare – His Life and Background", which gives a concise and visually appealing account of the context of the playwright's life in Stratford, then London, and finally Stratford again. There are displays on the town of Stratford itself and on the countryside which inspired so much of Shakespeare's imagery. As well as original documents and copies of such items as his marriage licence bond, there are portraits, furniture, a wonderful model of the Globe Theatre in London, and a reconstruction of "Shakespeare's Study", the kind of room he may well have worked in.

Beyond the Shakespeare Centre, the pretty garden has been planted with many of the trees, shrubs and flowers mentioned in his plays.

A short distance away, at 19 Greenhill Street, old and valuable children's toys are on display in Giles Brandreth's excellent **Teddy Bear Museum** **C** (daily 9.30am–6pm, closes 5pm Jan and Feb) – a good place to take children when they are bored by their parents' preoccupation with stuffy old poets.

This museum faces on to the broad expanse of Rother Street, mostly a car park but the venue on Friday for the town market. The **American Fountain** was given to Stratford for Queen Victoria's 1887 Jubilee by the Philadelphia newspaperman George C. Childs.

Wood Street, to the left, leads to the town centre and has a sprinkling of those heavily timbered properties that we associate with the ancient heart of England, when the extensive Forest of Arden, which once covered the country north of Stratford, provided a ready supply of materials.

The **High Street** has some of the town's most ornate buildings, many now stripped of 18th-century brick and stucco facades to reveal the original timber framing.

Harvard House

Overlooking the little paved open space at the first crossroads, the **Garrick Inn** and **Harvard House** **D** make an eccentric and flamboyant pair of buildings. Both date to about 1596, built just after a fire destroyed much of the town. Harvard House is elaborately carved with flowers and grotesque heads, and was the home of Katherine Rogers. She married Robert Harvard of Southwark, and their son, John Harvard, died in Massachusetts in 1638, a year after he emigrated to the New World. He bequeathed much of his estate to Harvard College, which now owns this house and uses it to display material relating to the Harvard family. The house (open May–Sept daily 10am–4pm) also contains the Neish Collection of

TIP

"Shakespeare's Life in Stratford" is an informative two-hour walk led by a Shakespearian actor and director at 10.30am Thur and Sat. Book at the Swan Theatre, where the walk starts and ends. Tel: 01789-412602.

BELOW: where the Bard was born.

Who was Shakespeare?

Part of the lure of Shakespeare's birthplace is that so few details of the playwright's life can be authenticated. It is known that his father, John, was a successful glove-maker and wool merchant, and that his mother, Mary Arden, was the daughter of a well-to-do farmer. William went to school in Stratford. Having got a Shottery girl, Anne Hathaway pregnant, he married her in 1582, when he was 18 and she 26; they had three children. Most of his professional career in the theatre, however, was centred in London, though he spent the last five years of his life in Stratford, where he died in 1616. The rest is largely speculation.

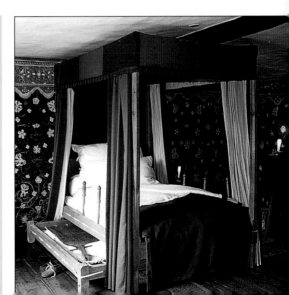

pewter, with pieces ranging from Roman times to the 19th century.

Originally called the Reindeer, the Garrick Inn was renamed after the great 18th-century Shakespearian actor David Garrick. He was greatly influential in the revival of interest in Shakespeare's dramatic works and helped to organise the first festival in his honour, the Garrick Jubilee, in 1769. The festival was a great social occasion, patronised by royalty – hence the bold slogan "God save the King" painted in the same year across the Chapel Street facade of the **Town Hall** Ⓔ, a solid neo-Palladian building marking the end of High Street, completed in 1768. The statue of Shakespeare, on the Sheep Street frontage of the Town Hall, was presented by Garrick. Opposite the Town Hall, there is a mosaic portrait of the Bard over the doorway of the Victorian redbrick **Old Bank**.

In Sheep Street you will find

An Old Bank mosaic pays tribute to the town's most famous tourist attraction.

BELOW:
an inn that catches Stratford's mood.

numerous souvenir shops and restaurants not only flanking the street but also running up the alleys behind. The **Shrieve's House** Ⓕ (40 Sheep Street) is an interesting example of a 16th-century merchant's house, with a cart entrance and long, cobbled back yard, lined with buildings that would have been used as workshop and warehouse space – now converted to shops.

New Place

Chapel Street continues the timber-framed theme, first with the magnificent many-bayed and gabled **Shakespeare Hotel** Ⓖ, and then, at the corner of Scholars Lane, the **Falcon Hotel**, the lower two storeys of which date from around 1500. Opposite is another property of the Birthplace Trust, **Nash's House** Ⓗ and the **Site of New Place** (open Mar–Oct, Mon–Fri 9am–5pm, Sun 9.30am –5pm; winter to 4pm). The former belonged to Thomas Nash,

Stratford-upon-Avon

who married Shakespeare's granddaughter, Elizabeth Hall. It is now a museum of material relating to the history of Stratford. New Place was one of the town's largest houses, and Shakespeare was wealthy enough to purchase it in 1597. He later retired to the house and died there on his 52nd birthday, in 1616.

A later owner, Rev. Francis Gastrell, had little respect for the poet's memory. He was so annoyed by the constant stream of visitors wanting to see the mulberry tree in the garden, planted by Shakespeare, that he cut it down. In 1759 he demolished the house itself, rather than pay rates. Sensibly, no attempt has been made to reconstruct it. Instead, the foundations are exposed and paths thread through delightful gardens.

The **Knot Garden** is planted with flowers known to have been grown in the 16th century, and the Great Garden beyond, originally the orchard and kitchen garden to New Place, has box and yew hedges.

The **Guild Chapel ①** opposite served as the chapel of the Guild of the Holy Cross, a body of local worthies who regulated trade in the town, fixing prices, collecting levies and allocating funds to charitable purposes. A wealthy member, Sir Hugh Clopton, later Lord Mayor of London, paid for the rebuilding of the nave in 1496. Just visible on the chancel wall is a *Last Judgement* painting.

The Guildhall

Adjoining the chapel is the 15th-century former **Guildhall ①**, part of which was used as the town Grammar School. It is conjectured, reasonably, that Shakespeare was a pupil here. The delightfully named "Pedagogue's House" in the courtyard behind was probably the schoolmaster's dwelling. Beyond, 15th-century almshouses, still used as such, stretch for a distance of 50 metres, an impressive range with massive studs and a jettied-out upper storey.

Further down Church Street the character of the buildings begins to change, as timber gives way to the brick of elegant townhouses. **Mason Croft**, an early 18th-century building, was the last home of Marie

Map on page 222

The town's name, "street ford", indicates that this was the point at which a Roman road crossed the River Avon. But Stratford's real history goes back only to Saxon times, when a monastery flourished here, probably located where the parish church now stands.

BELOW: the Knot Garden.

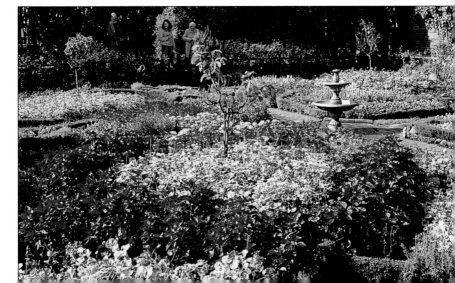

Corelli (1855–1924) – real name Mary Mackay – the prolific novelist who, despite critical derision, was as popular in her heyday as Shakespeare was in his. The house is now an international centre for Shakespearian research, owned by Birmingham University.

Turning left, into Old Town, you reach **Hall's Croft** (Mar–Oct, Mon–Fri 9am–5pm, Sun 9.30am–5pm; winter to 4pm). Of all the buildings associated with Shakespeare, this is the least altered and most atmospheric. It dates to the late 16th century and was the home of Dr John Hall, husband of Shakespeare's daughter Susanna. One room is equipped as an apothecary's dispensary, and the walled garden has ancient mulberry trees and perennial borders.

Holy Trinity Church.

Further down, an avenue of lime trees leads to **Holy Trinity Church** **L**, idyllically sited by the River Avon and a fine example of a 13th-century church. You have to pay to visit the most interesting part of the church – the chancel – where Shakespeare's monument is the chief attraction.

BELOW: the Royal Shakespeare Theatre.

The poet's son-in-law, Dr John Hall, took a wax impression of Shakespeare's face at his death, and this was used by the Dutch mason Gerard Jansenni, or Johnson, as the basis for the painted alabaster bust of Shakespeare. It is thus the best likeness we have of the poet; other portraits, based on this, have tried to make him look less self-satisfied.

The nearby tomb slab, covering Shakespeare's grave, is famously inscribed: *Good Frend For Jesus Sake Forbeare/To Digg the Dust Enclosed Heare:/Blese Be Ye Man (that) Spares Thes Stones/And Curst Be He (that) Moves My Bones*. These words have often been interpreted as implying that the grave contains evidence of the "true" authorship of Shakespeare's works – for, despite substantial evidence to the contrary, many people still believe that Shakespeare was only a front for some other writer. All requests to investigate the tomb have been refused.

Burial places

Other Shakespeare family tombs are found nearby: namely, those of his wife Anne (*née* Hathaway), his daughter Susanna, and those of Thomas Nash and Dr John Hall. The misericords should not be missed; they date from around 1500 and provide an amusing commentary on contemporary domestic life.

Just north of Holy Trinity churchyard, back in Old Town, a gate on the right leads to the **Avonbank Garden** **M**, with its 19th-century summerhouse (now a brass-rubbing centre) and paths that follow the River Avon to the **Royal Shakespeare Theatre** complex **N**. The first part of the complex to come into view is the **Swan Theatre**, with a curved end and sweeping lead-covered roof, like some romantic mid-European castle. Partly used as a museum, displaying costumes, props and theatrical mementoes, this incor-

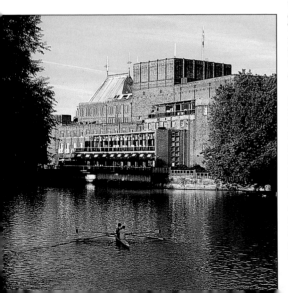

porates all that remains of the original theatre, built in 1879 but damaged by fire in 1926.

The main theatre, completed in 1932, was a radical building in its time – shaped like a stack of bricks and almost windowless – but seemed somehow inadequate. Now it is being given a £100 million remodelling, due to be completed in 2010. Until then, the plays will be staged in The Courtyard, a 1,000-seat temporary theatre built in the former car park.

In front of the theatre, the **Bancroft Gardens ⊙** surround a large canal basin, marking the point where the Stratford Canal joins the River Avon. The 1888 **Gower Memorial** has the alert figure of Shakespeare seated on a plinth, surrounded by statues of Hamlet, Prince Hal, Falstaff and Lady Macbeth. The **nine-arched bridge** was built in 1823 for the tramway whose horse-drawn carriages and goods wagons once rattled their way between Stratford and Shipston-on-Stour. It was converted to pedestrian use in 1918 and is a good place from where to get a grandstand prospect of activities on the river. Further north,

the **Clopton Bridge** was built in the late 15th century.

The **Stratford Canal**, completed in 1816, runs north to the Grand Union. As an alternative to travelling by car, you can follow the canal tow-path for 3 miles (5 km) through the town and out, past a long flight of locks, to the hamlet of **Wilmcote**. Here, the Shakespeare Birthplace Trust has restored the 16th-century home of Mary Arden as a museum of country life in Tudor Warwickshire.

Anne Hathaway's Cottage

For the return journey you could visit **Anne Hathaway's Cottage ⊙** (open Mar–Oct, Mon–Fri 9am–5pm, Sun 9.30am–5pm; winter to 4pm) in the suburb of **Shottery**. This 15th-century thatched farmhouse was once the home of Shakespeare's wife, and stands in a delightful cottage garden. Furnished with Hathaway family heirlooms, pride of place is given to the famous bed that Shakespeare bequeathed to his wife – the only thing he left her in his will, fuelling speculation that their marriage might not have been happy. ❑

Map on page 222

The Gower Memorial to Shakespeare.

BELOW: Anne Hathaway's Cottage.

WARWICK

The city of Warwick is best known for its magnificent castle, but there are many other sights here, including the glorious Beauchamp Chapel, which was built for earls but is fit for kings

Maps:
Area 212
City 228

BELOW:
Beauchamp Chapel
in St Mary's Church.

One of the most delightful old towns of the English Midlands with a wealth of late medieval and Georgian buildings, **Warwick** ❿ is built on a rise above the Avon. From much of the surrounding countryside, the town, whose origins date from the 10th century, seems to be dominated by the majestic tower of St Mary's Church, but it is above all the great castle – often described as England's finest medieval stronghold – on its rocky bluff overlooking the river that draws visitors here.

The basic layout of the town is that of a cross formed by High Street, Church Street, Jury Street and Castle Street. Their meeting point is marked by substantial edifices all dating from the time of the town's rebuilding, including the **Court House** Ⓐ of 1725 whose ground floor is occupied by the Tourist Information Centre and which also houses the Town Museum and the Warwickshire Yeomanry Museum.

Lord Leycester's Hospital

Lined with dignified Georgian buildings, the High Street leads to the 12th-century **West Gate** with its massive archway partly cut into the rock. Above it is St James' Chapel and the beautiful timber-framed almshouses of **Lord Leycester's Hospital** Ⓑ (open summer, Tues–Sat and Bank Holiday Mondays 10am–5.30pm, winter 10am–4pm), founded in 1571 as a home for old soldiers. A highlight is a magnificent mid-15th century **Guildhall**, and the atmospheric **St James' Chapel**, lit by a 15th-century candelabrum.

Modern life in Warwick centres on the area around the Market Place with its fine stone-built **Market Hall** Ⓒ of 1670. The building, its arches now blocked in with windows, houses the **Warwickshire Museum** (open Mon–Sat 10am–5pm, Sun in summer 2–5pm). It has displays on local natural history as well as the striking mid-16th century **Sheldon tapestry map** of Warwickshire.

St Mary's Church

The 174-ft (53-metre) tower of **St Mary's Church** rises above Church Street and can be climbed, the reward being superb views. Highlights include the Norman crypt with its massive columns, the Dean's Chapel with lovely fan vaulting, the 14th-century chancel, and the **Beauchamp Chapel**.

The gilded **brass effigy of Richard Beauchamp**, Earl of Warwick, was made 15 years after he died in 1439 and is rightly famous. The great magnate lies with his head resting on a helmet, his hands raised in supplication. At his feet are a bear and a griffin; around the tomb are figures of weepers and angels.

Follow Church Street back to its junction with High Street and Jury Street. The latter leads to the charming 15th-century **East Gate** topped by a chapel dedicated to St Peter and now only used by pedestrians. Beyond is Smith Street, at the far end of which is **St John's**, a fine early 17th-century stone building now part of the **Warwickshire Museum** (open Good Friday–late Sept, Fri, weekends and Bank Holidays 10am–1pm, 2–4pm) and includes reconstructions of a Victorian classroom and kitchen. The **Museum of the Royal Warwickshire Regiment** shares the building.

St Nicholas' Church overlooks **Castle Bridge**. This handsome 100-ft (30-metre) single-span structure was built in 1793 to replace the medieval bridge. Now a cul-desac, **Mill Street** completely escaped the effects of the fire and contains a fine array of timber-framed houses. From the **Mill Garden** at the far end is a fine view of the castle's Caesar's Tower high above.

The castle can be approached via its Stable Block at the foot of Castle Street. One of the prettiest of the town's streets, Castle Street also has one of the prettiest houses in Warwick, a timber-framed early Elizabethan building named after its owner, Thomas Oken, a prosperous

Warwick's Courthouse proclaims its authority.

BELOW: Lord Leycester's Hospital.

The long bow demonstrated at Warwick Castle.

mercer and benefactor of the town. His home is now the delightful **Doll Museum** (open Easter–late Sept, Mon–Sat 10am–5pm, Sun 1–5pm, winter Saturdays until dusk), inhabited not only by dolls but also by other toys and games.

The Castle

Warwick Castle ❶ (open Apr–Oct 10am–6pm, Nov–March 10am–5pm), which is owned by Madame Tussaud's, was once described as "the most perfect piece of castellated antiquity in the kingdom". The natural potential of the site – on a sandstone spur above the Avon – has been fully exploited by successive owners and builders and there are few views more emblematic of England's historic heritage than that of Warwick's walls and towers rising above luxuriant parkland and reflected in the river.

The castle's history stretches over a period of more than 1,000 years, beginning with the fortification built by Ethelfleda. It was only two years after the Conquest, in 1068, that King William ordered the castle to be re-founded, a standard Norman motte and bailey construction which was succeeded in the 12th and 13th centuries by a more permanent stone structure. Much of the fabric of this castle was replaced in the mid-14th century by Thomas Beauchamp, Earl of Warwick.

Eventually it became the property of the Greville family. The Grevilles, who became Earls of Warwick in 1759, were responsible for the conversion of the medieval fortress into a princely palace. Walls and towers remain as reminders of medieval might, and basements, dungeons and undercroft preserve their ancient character, but the habitable part of the castle consists of a sumptuous series of state rooms of Jacobean and later date. In the 18th century, the grounds were re-landscaped by Ca-

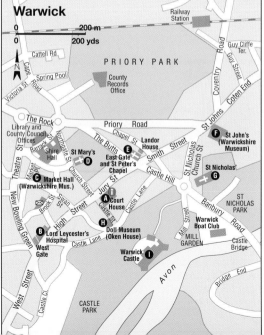

pability Brown and extended north.

From the **Stable Block** entrance, a curving pathway makes a dramatic approach to the **gatehouse and barbican** with **Guy's Tower** rising up splendidly on the right to a height of 128ft (40 metres).

Once within the great circuit of walls, the visitor has various choices. Beneath **Caesar's Tower** are the **Armoury**, **Torture Chamber** and **Dungeon**.

Further underground chambers and passageways of the medieval castle house an entertaining tableau, "Kingmaker". This is a convincing evocation of the preparations which preceded the Battle of Barnet in 1471. As well as armourers and others at work, there are children larking about, a horse giving off a powerful stable smell, and living costumed figures barely distinguishable from the waxworks.

A very different epoch is evoked in the tableaux of the **Royal Weekend Party of 1898**. Towards the end of the 19th century, Warwick had become a great social centre, largely due to the influence of the Countess of Warwick, born Frances but universally known as Daisy. Among the guests populating some of the former private apartments are the young Winston Churchill, the future George V lighting a cigarette, and Edward Prince of Wales, a frequent visitor and rumoured lover of Daisy.

The Chapel, Great Hall and State Rooms are reached by stairs. The early 17th-century **Chapel** has medieval stained glass and superbly carved wooden panels. The 18th-century Dining Room has splendidly framed royal portraits, including a famous study of Charles I on horseback. The **Great Hall** exudes the atmosphere of the Middle Ages with its displays of arms and armour. The **State Rooms** compete with each other in magnificence: the Red Drawing Room has bold red lacquer

panelling; the Cedar Drawing Room a superb plaster ceiling; the Green Drawing Room mementoes of the Civil War; the Queen Anne Bedroom a bed intended for that royal personage but never used; while the Blue Boudoir has a portrait after Holbein of Henry V.

Next to the so-called **Ghost Tower** the great **mound** rises to a surprising height. Topped by mock fortifications, it offers a magnificent prospect over the castle grounds, the river, and the lush countryside.

Kenilworth

If Warwick is one of England's finest castles, then **Kenilworth ⓫**, barely 4 miles (6 km) to the north of Warwick (open Apr–Oct 10am–6pm, Nov–March 10am–5pm), must rank as one of its finest castle ruins. It was destroyed after the Civil War, but the original Norman keep still stands, as does the shell of the Great Hall. The castle's natural defences were strengthened by flooding the surrounding marshland. The lake is no longer there, but Kenilworth remains an evocative place. ❑

Maps:
Area 212
City 228

Kenilworth Castle.

BELOW:
the past re-created
at Warwick Castle.

THE NORTH COTSWOLDS

The remarkable beauty of the Cotswolds, a prominent range of hills to the west of Oxford, owes much to the distinctive architecture of entire golden villages built of durable Cotswold stone

Map on page 212

The soils of the Cotswolds are shallow, not easy to cultivate but ideal pasture for grazing sheep, and it was wool that kept the area's landowners affluent for centuries. This former wealth is visible everywhere in the landscape, characterised by opulent manor houses, cathedral-like barns and splendidly ornate parish churches.

Chipping Norton

Chipping Norton ⓬, 12 miles (20 km) northwest of Oxford, is a prime example: a typical Cotswold town on the northwest limits of the limestone belt. Market Square was once the venue for an important sheep fair. Gabled almshouses – typical of Cotswold vernacular architecture, with their stone-mullioned windows and drip mouldings to channel rain away from the face of the buildings – line the path to St Mary's Church. To the north of the church are the extensive remains of a Norman motte and bailey castle.

Chipping Norton also has an imposing tweed mill, visible on the right as you leave the town on the A44 Evesham road. **Bliss Valley Mill**, with its domed tower, was designed in 1872 by the Lancashire mill architect George Woodhouse, to look like a country house – which is what it has ended up as, for after the mill closed in 1980 it was converted into luxury apartments.

Four miles (7 km) on, a minor road leads left to **Chastleton House ⓭**, built around 1605 by another wool merchant, Walter Jones. Shortly afterwards, the family fortunes declined and the house escaped later improvements, surviving as an example of Jacobean domestic architecture. At the top of the house, a long gallery runs the length of the building. Originally intended for indoor games, such as

BELOW:
St Mary's Church, Chipping Norton.

Map on page 212

bowls, like many of the rooms, it is lavishly plastered with bold Flemish-style friezes and ceilings.

Moreton-in-Marsh ⓮ comes next, a busy town on the junction of the Roman Foss Way and the later Oxford to Worcester road. Numerous former coaching inns still do a brisk trade serving cream teas to passing motorists, but there is a cluster of characterful shops at the northern end of the High Street. Where the Oxford road joins the High Street there is a 16th-century curfew tower; the bell in the tower continued to be rung until 1860, reminding householders to "cover their fires" (the derivation of "curfew") before retiring to lessen the risk of a blaze.

Sezincote

Two miles (3 km) out of Moreton, the A44 climbs steeply up the Cotswold scarp, through the pretty but traffic-torn village of **Bourton-on-the-Hill**, and towards the summit a left turn leads to **Sezincote** ⓯ (Garden 2–6pm Thur, Fri and bank holidays Jan–Nov, House 2.30–6pm Thur, Fri, May–Jul and Sept). Here

you will find one of the most curious and delightful houses ever built in the English countryside: an Indian palace made of golden limestone, tucked into the valley of the River Evenlode, which is channelled into a series of canals representing, in Moghul fashion, the rivers of life. Begun in 1805, Sezincote was built for Charles Cockerell who, on retiring from service with the East India Company, wanted to create a rajah's palace, complete with onion domes and peacock-tail windows.

The Prince Regent, on seeing it in 1807, loved it so much that he ordered existing plans for Brighton Pavilion to be scrapped, and new ones drawn up "more like Sezincote". External appearances, though, are deceptive, for guided tours reveal that the interior is elegantly European in the classical tradition.

Batsford Arboretum

Another expatriate returning home created **Batsford Arboretum** ⓰, on the opposite side of the A44. Lord Redesdale, a retired Tokyo diplomat, built his manor house in neo-Eliza-

Bliss Valley Mill, dating from 1872.

BELOW: Sezincote.

bethan style in 1888, but he planted the surrounding path with oriental species and decorated it with Japanese temples and statues of the Buddha. The arboretum is very colourful in spring, when the cherry trees blossom, and in autumn, when the Japanese maples turn a fiery crimson.

The village of **Blockley** ⓱, 2 miles (3 km) west, brings us back to the traditional Cotswolds. Formerly an estate belonging to the bishops of Worcester, the surrounding hillsides once supported vast flocks of sheep, and flourishing villages round about were deliberately destroyed to create further grazing. But Blockley survived, and today's village consists of elegant townhouses occupying the heights and smaller rows of cottages squeezed into narrow terraces all the way down the valley side. At the bottom only one mill survives (now a private house) of the six that produced silk to supply the ribbon makers of Coventry.

Blockley's church contains imposing Renaissance and baroque monuments to the owners of **Northwick Park**. This 17th-century mansion, now converted to apartments, lies just north of Blockley, and the road that skirts the western perimeter of the estate provides a splendid view of nearby **Chipping Campden** ⓲, whose oldest house (in the High Street, opposite Church Street) dates from around 1380.

Chipping Campden

Campden is the Cotswold's most beautiful market town. Certainly, it is the best preserved, thanks to the work of the Campden Trust, established in 1929 to restore and maintain town properties using traditional materials.

Early in the 20th century Campden was "invaded" by craftsmen from the Mile End Road in east London, where C. R. Ashbee, inspired by the example of William Morris, had founded his Guild of Handicrafts, devoted to reviving skills lost to industrial processes. Descendants of George Hart, one of the original 50 craftsmen who came with Ashbee in 1902, still make handcrafted silverware in the Old Silk Mill in Sheep Street.

Chipping Campden.

BELOW:
Batsford Arboretum.

The village church is attributed to William Grevel, described on his memorial brass as "the flower of the wool merchants of all England". He left money for the church to be rebuilt and the work, completed some 100 years after his death, is a splendid example of the Perpendicular style at its best.

A mile (2 km) northwest of Campden, over the summit of Dover's Hill, is a natural amphitheatre on the Cotswold scarp. Worth visiting for the panoramic views over the **Vale of Evesham**, this is also the venue for the "**Cotswold Olympicks**", held every Friday following the Spring Bank Holiday, followed by the Scuttlebrook Wake Fair on the next day. The "Olympicks", which features shin-kicking and stick-fighting among its bizarre events, was founded by an eccentric local lawyer, Robert Dover, in 1612.

Hidcote

Two miles (3.5 km) north of Campden are two of England's finest gardens, standing on opposite sides of the same road above **Mickleton**.

Hidcote Manor Garden , for all its maturity, was begun only in 1948 (open April–end of Oct daily except Tues and Fri 11am–6pm, then June and July Tues). All that existed before was a few walls and 11 acres (4.5 hectares) of windswept Cotswold upland. Major Lawrence Johnson transformed this into one of the most influential gardens of our age, "a cottage garden on the most glorified scale", according to the writer Vita Sackville-West.

Its structure is relatively formal, based on the concept of a series of rooms, walled with yew and planted thematically – yet the underlying discipline is hardly evident as climbers tumble from one room to the next, and happy combinations of self-seeded flowers are left to do as they will. Visitors can also enjoy the fine views.

Kiftsgate Court ❷ (open Apr–Oct daily) is equally renowned in gardening circles for its prolific rambling rose, *Rosa filipes* "Kiftsgate". Having colonised several trees, it must surely be England's largest climbing rose, and is delightful in early summer, cascading down in showers of white blooms. The rest of the garden is full of unusual plants, and the views from the swimming-pool terrace look over wooded slopes to the Vale of Evesham.

Broadway

From Mickleton, the B4632 southwest follows the Vale, with the steep-faced Cotswold scarp rising to the left, all the way into **Broadway** ❷. Packed with tourists throughout the summer, this town of ancient golden houses nevertheless merits a visit.

Many of the ancient and wisteria-clad townhouses in Broadway now serve as teashops, boutiques or art galleries, and the renowned furniture maker Gordon Russell has his showroom and factory at the bottom end of the High Street.

To escape the crowds, you can

Map on page 212

TIP

Broadway's most celebrated restaurant is in the Lygon Arms hotel. Those who can't afford lunch there can at least admire its handsome Renaissance doorway, dated 1620, and the cordon-trained fruit trees growing the full height of the facade.

BELOW: the gardens at Kiftsgate Court.

follow the Cotswold Way long-distance footpath from the centre of the town, up the steep sides of **Broadway Hill**, to the **Tower** at the summit. This folly was built in 1800 and stands 65 ft (20 metres) tall on top of a 1,024-ft (412-metre) hill, giving extensive views which, on a clear day, extend to the cities of Worcester and Warwick. William Morris used the tower as a holiday retreat, and there are displays there about his life and work, and about the Cotswold wool industry.

Less than a mile (about 1 km) to the northeast, along the ridge of the hill, is another picturesque folly, built in the 18th century as a "gaze-about house", now part of the Fish Inn.

At the western end of Broadway, a narrow road signposted to Snowshill Manor passes the Norman **church of St Eadburga**, standing next door to the Court House, whose ancient topiary yews spill from the garden into the churchyard.

Two miles (3 km) on is **Snowshill Manor** ㉒, a popular National Trust property best avoided at busy weekends (daily except Tues 2–5pm Apr

The Lygon Arms, Broadway.

BELOW:
Broadway Tower.

and Oct, 2–6pm May–Sept). It houses a magpie collection of extraordinary diversity: everything from bicycles to Samurai armour. The terraced garden brims with colourful flowers.

Cotswold heritage

From Snowshill, a high and narrow lane crosses the heights of the Cotswold uplands, attractive in summer, but bleak and chill in winter, through Taddington and into the beautiful wooded Windrush Valley. **Temple Guiting** ㉓ (pronounced *guyting*) was once a property of the crusading Knights Templar, and the Windrush, much diminished in size since the stream has been tapped to provide drinking water, used to drive the hammers of fulling mills, used in wool processing.

This industry continued into the 18th century: the tomb of John Mowse (died 1787) in St Mary's Church records that he was a wool dyer, who employed a great number of the poor of the parish in the various parts of his trade. He may also have contributed to the rebuilding of the church, with its fine wooden fur-

Map on page 212

nishings and George II coat of arms, unusually made out of plaster. Two miles (3 km) southeast is **Cotswold Farm Park ㉔** (*see panel below*).

Six miles (10 km) downstream, the River Windrush flows through the centre of **Bourton-on-the-Water ㉕**, crossed by a series of elegant 18th-century stone bridges. Bourton is a village to avoid if you do not like people, for the combination of the Model Village – a one-ninth scale replica of Bourton itself, made in 1937 – a Motor Museum, Model Railway and Birdland all make this a busy spot.

The Slaughters

This same fate has overtaken the nearby hamlets of **Lower** and **Upper Slaughter ㉖**, so named because of the sloughs, or marshes, that once bordered the River Eye flowing through the two villages. Simple clapper bridges, made of huge planks of limestone, cross the stream as it flows between carefully tended banks and in front of the much photographed mill in Lower Slaughter.

Similar in character, but far more peaceful, is the little hamlet of **Upper Swell**, with its 18th-century bridge, watermill and mill pool fed by the River Dikler. Occasionally in summer the **Abbotswood** estate, south of Swell, is open under the National Gardens Scheme. Well worth visiting, Abbotswood is one of the finest works of Sir Edwin Lutyens, who designed the garden, with its pools and water channels, as well as the striking water house, in 1902.

Stow-on-the-Wold

Stow-on-the-Wold ㉗, a mile (2 km) east, sits on the summit of an 800-ft (240-metre) hill and has the reputation for being a chilly place: "Stow-on-the-Wold, where the wind blows cold" is an ancient taunt.

The great Stow Horse Fair is now held at **Andoversford**, near Cheltenham. It was moved because of the nuisance often caused by gypsy horse breeders converging on the town. Stow these days prefers more genteel visitors and caters for them with numerous antique shops, tea rooms and a museum of antique dolls in Sheep Street. ❑

Tranquillity at Lower Slaughter.

BELOW:
Cotswold Farm Park.

Cotswold Farm Park

This is headquarters of the Rare Breeds Survival Trust, home to a flock of the traditional breed of Cotswold sheep upon which the medieval prosperity of the region was based. Nicknamed "Cotswold lions" because of their distinctive long, curly fleece, these big-limbed animals are descended from sheep introduced by the Romans. Another 40 or more rare breeds, such as Gloucester Old Spot pigs and Old Gloucester cows, are protected and displayed at the Farm Park, along with goats, rabbits, ponies and huge shire horses. Most are placid, so the park is suitable for children. Open Apr–Oct, tel: 01451-850307.

TRANSPORT

GETTING THERE AND GETTING AROUND

Note: Unless indicated otherwise, Oxford telephone numbers have a 01865 area code. From outside the UK, dial (44) 1865.

GETTING THERE

By Air

London Heathrow Airport is situated to the west of London on the M25/M4, 45 miles (72 km) southeast of Oxford. From Heathrow central bus terminus and Terminal 4, the Oxford Bus Company operates the X70 Oxford Espress coach service, which departs every half-hour during the day and every 2 hours overnight (80 mins journey time to Terminals 1–3 and 100 mins to Terminal 4). Reserve a seat by booking online at www.oxfordbus.co.uk, or call 01865-785 400.

London Gatwick is situated to the south of London on the M23, 85 miles (136 km) southeast of Oxford. The X80 Oxford Espress coach from Gatwick (north and south terminals) runs hourly and every two hours overnight (journey time 2 hours).

Birmingham International Airport is 65 miles (104 km) from Oxford; there are regular train connections, as well as six

coach services a day operated by National Express (National Express bookings and enquiries tel: 08705-808080).

Oxford airport is located at nearby Kidlington but operates only special charters. A twice-daily scheduled flight to Cambridge (a tedious commute by road) was launched in 2006 using eight-seater Piper Chieftains, but it failed after six weeks owing to lack of demand.

By Sea

Oxford is one of the UK's most inland towns. The nearest port offering a cross-Channel service is Portsmouth (80 miles/128 km). A National Express (*see below*) bus service links Oxford to the south coast every hour daily.
Brittany Ferries, tel: 0870 3665 333, www.brittanyferries.co.uk
P&O European Ferries, tel: 0870 5980 333, www.poferries.com
Stena Line, tel: 0870 5707 070, www.stenaline.co.uk

By Train

There is a regular train service between **London Paddington** station and Oxford. The journey takes about an hour, depending on the number of stops. Travellers can also use the fast services between London

Paddington and Midlands destinations such as Worcester and Birmingham, which stop in Oxford. Trains from London depart regularly about twice an hour during the day. Oxford train station is a 5-minute walk from the centre of the city.

While any train can be boarded with a full-fare return ticket, with all other return tickets restrictions are applied to peak period departures (from Paddington between 4–7pm) on Great Western trains. Travellers should be given a leaflet advising on these restrictions when buying their ticket. Cheap Day Returns between Oxford and London are available from 9.30am and are much cheaper than the normal return.

For fare enquiries and general information, telephone the **National Rail Enquiry Service** on 08457-48 49 50.

By Coach

Regular coach services run between Oxford and London. Stagecoach operate the **Oxford Tube**, and the Oxford Bus Company run **Oxford Espress** services. With fares about half that of a Cheap Day Return train ticket, these services are very popular indeed.

From London, **Oxford Tube**

coaches leave from Grosvenor Gardens (turn left out of the main Victoria British Rail and Underground stations). All coaches stop on request at Marble Arch (10 minutes after departing Victoria), Notting Hill Gate (15 minutes) and the Kensington Hilton at Shepherd's Bush (20 minutes). The service runs every 10 minutes during rush hours, at 20-minute intervals for most of the day, and hourly between 12.15am and 5.10am. For travel information, see www.oxfordtube.com or call 01865-772 250.

The **Oxford Bus Company**'s **Oxford Espress** coach services depart daily every 15–20 minutes from London's Victoria Coach Station (Gate 10) and also pick up at Marble Arch (on Park Lane) and Baker Street (on Gloucester Place). Most journeys take about 1 hour 40 minutes but during peak periods you should allow more time due to traffic congestion in London. For travel information, tel: 01865-785400, www.oxfordbus.co.uk.

Both the above services arrive at and depart from Oxford's Gloucester Green Bus Station in the heart of the city. **National Express** offer a nationwide network of coach services from Oxford and have an office at Gloucester Green. For enquiries and credit card bookings, tel: 08705-808080 or visit www.nationalexpress.co.uk.

The cheapest pre-booked fares are offered by **MegaBus**, who offer Oxford coach services every 20–30 minutes from London (75 minutes journey time). See www.megabus.com or call 0900 160 0900.

By Car

From both London and the Midlands, Oxford is well served by the M40 motorway, which passes within 8 miles (13km) of the city. The journey from central London takes about 80 minutes, except during rush hour when it

can take considerably longer to get out of the city along the A40. Drivers coming from London should exit at Junction 8, while those coming from the Midlands should turn off at Junction 9.

If you are coming from Gatwick or Heathrow airports, join the M40 via the London orbital motorway, the M25. Oxford is accessible from Southampton and Portsmouth by the M3 and A34 and from Bristol by the M4 and A34.

GETTING AROUND

Orientation

The busy city centre is pedestrianised and, as a result, access to motor vehicles is very limited. Cornmarket is closed to all traffic 10am–6pm, as is High Street 7.30am–6.30pm. The western end of Broad Street is closed all day and night, and Turl Street and Market Street are closed to all but delivery vehicles.

Buses in the city run along bus priority routes, closed to other traffic.

Maps

The *Oxford A to Z* is an invaluable map covering the whole city. The Ordnance Survey Landranger Map (scale 1:50,000) provides a good overview of Oxford and the surrounding area. It is an ideal aid to planning walks and drives in the vicinity of the city.

Public Transport

Oxford and the surrounding area are served by local buses, minibuses and the direct buses between the Park-&-Ride stations and the centre. The local services are covered by the Oxford Bus Company and Stagecoach. In addition, Stagecoach operates numerous services to outlying towns. Both bus companies offer

special day-return tickets, family tickets, as well as travel cards with unlimited travel in the city. You purchase your ticket from the driver.

The Zone Freedom Pass allows unlimited travel on Oxford Bus Company services: cost is £3.20 for 1 day or £12 for 7 days. Pick up a copy of the City Bus Guide at the Gloucester Green travel shop or see www.oxfordbus.co.uk, where you can check timetables and download bus route maps.

Taxis

The main taxi ranks are at Oxford railway station, Gloucester Green, St Giles, Broad Street and High Street. There are additional ranks at Carfax and Bonn Square on evenings only.

Due to the one-way traffic system there is no short route across the city to the railway

CYCLING

Cycling is popular in Oxford and, as well as many cycleways, there are clear signs to enable cyclists to avoid the main thoroughfares.

You can hire bicycles from several outlets. All kinds of bikes are available, and they are supplied with a lock. Lights, basket and helmet are optional extras.

Bikes can be hired from: **Bike Zone**, 6 Lincoln House, Market Street, tel: 01865-728877. **Cycle King**, 128–130 Cowley Road, tel: 01865-728262. **Cyclo-Analysts**, 150 Cowley Road, tel: 01865-424444. **Summertown Cycles**, 202 Banbury Road, tel: 01865-316885. **Warlands**, 63 Botley Road, tel: 01865-241336.

For cycle maps see: www.cyclemaps.org.uk www.sustrans.org.uk

station, so fares tend to be high. Some taxi meters start at £1.50, others might have a minimum charge of £2.

A.B.C Taxis,
tel: 01865-770077
Euro Taxis,
tel: 01865 430430
Oxford City Taxis,
tel: 01865-794000
Radio Taxis,
tel: 01865 242424
001 Cars,
tel: 01865-240000
24seven Taxis,
tel: 01865 722799

Driving

Rules of the Road

In Britain you should drive on the left-hand side of the road and observe speed limits. It is strictly illegal to drink and drive, and penalties for drink driving are severe. Drivers and passengers, in both front and back seats, must wear seat belts where fitted. Failure to do so can result in a fine. For further information on driving in Britain consult a copy of the *Highway Code*, widely available in bookshops.

If you are bringing your own car into the UK you will need a valid driving licence or an International Driving Permit, plus insurance cover, vehicle registration and a nationality sticker.

In Oxford there are many cyclists on the road: be extra careful to be bike aware.

Parking

Parking in central Oxford is very limited, and in residential areas you often need a resident's parking permit.

There is a multi-storey car park at the Westgate Centre (pay on return to your car, £1.80/hour). There is an underground car park at Gloucester Green (entrance on Beaumont Street) and pay-and-display outdoor parking at St Clements and at Worcester Street (enter from

Park End Street). Finally, there is metered street parking on St. Giles', Broad Street, Parks Road and Beaumont Street, but during the day it is difficult to find a space. Payment applies per hour 8.30am–6.30pm from Monday to Saturday, after which there is a fixed charge payment until 10pm. Sunday is a fixed charge payment however long you are there.

Visitors should note that traffic wardens in Oxford are extremely vigilant. In the evening (after 6.30pm) city centre parking is much easier.

Park-and-Ride

Major areas of the city centre are traffic-free zones. If you want to avoid the problem of parking, take the reliable Park-&-Ride service offered by the Oxford Bus Company. You can park your car at the following sites on the Oxford ring road (colours refer to codings at bus stops):

Thornhill (yellow square) in the east of the city – for traffic coming in on the A40 from London.
Redbridge (red square) in the south – for those arriving by the A34 from Abingdon or the A4074 from Reading.
Seacourt (pale blue square) in the west – convenient for A420 or B4044 traffic.
Pear Tree (green square) in the north west – for motorists coming in on the A40 from Cheltenham, the A44 from Chipping Norton, the A34, or the A4260.
Water Eaton (dark blue square) in the north east – for traffic arriving by the A34 or A4260.

Parking is 60p (free at Thornhill and Water Eaton) and buses to the city centre leave every 10–15 minutes. Bus fares cost less than the city centre car parks and journeys take only 10–20 minutes. Don't forget to make a note of the colour symbol at your bus stop (e.g. yellow for Thornhill). For more details of locations and bus services see

www.parkandride.net.

A special Freedom travel card allows you unlimited travel on the Cityline and Park-&-Ride network for a day. Services are frequent during the daytime but there are no services on Sunday evening for Redbridge, Pear Tree and Seacourt, and none at all on Sunday on the Water Eaton route.

Breakdown Services

The following motoring organisations operate 24-hour breakdown assistance. They have reciprocal arrangements with other national motoring clubs. All calls to these numbers are free.
AA: 0800-887 766
RAC: 0800-828 282
Green Flag: 0800-400600
Britannia Rescue: 0800-591563

CAR RENTAL

Conditions for car rental state that the driver must be over 21 (over 25 for some companies) and have held a full driving licence for more than a year. Most hire charges include insurance, unlimited mileage, road tax and a 24-hour breakdown service. Ask for special weekend deals. There are vans and minibuses available, too, and some of the companies offer one-way rentals at extra cost. Payment is usually by cash, cheque or credit card.
Avis, 1 Abbey Road, Botley Road, tel: 01865 153 9102; www.avis.co.uk.
Budget, Unit 1, Oxford Business Centre, Osney Lane, tel: 01865 724884; www.budget.co.uk.
Euro Drive, Transport Way, off Watlington Road, Cowley, tel: 01865 715500; www.eurodriveuk.com.
Europcar, Littlemead Business Park, Ferry Hinksey Road, tel: 01865 246373; www.europcar.co.uk.

TRANSPORTATION

ACCOMMODATION

ACTIVITIES

A – Z

ACCOMMODATION

HOTELS, YOUTH HOSTELS, BED & BREAKFASTS

Choosing a Hotel

Accommodation in Oxford is not cheap, and while there are plenty of bed and breakfast places, there is only a limited number of hotels. Not all establishments take young children, so it is worth checking in advance.

Booking ahead is therefore essential, especially in summer, on weekends and during public holidays. For visitors arriving in the city without accommodation, the Oxford Tourist Information Centre (*see page 259*) offers a room-booking service for a modest fee.

The following websites have accommodation-finders:
● www.visitoxford.org – if you require accommodation within the next seven days, call 01865 726871.
● www.stayoxford.co.uk – the Oxford Association of Hotels and Guest Houses.
● www.oxfordcity.co.uk
● www.oxfinder.co.uk
● www.oxtowns.co.uk (for outside Oxford).
● www.abodesofoxford.com offer bed-and-breakfast accommodation and host family stays.

The *Accessible Oxford Guide* (available from the Oxford Information Centre) lists hotels and self-catering accomodation which have good access for people with limited mobility.

Hostels & "Ys"

Ideal for the budget traveller are two hostels situated in the city centre close to the bus and railway stations. Both have internet access, a TV/games-room and luggage storage (see listings).

The **Youth Hostel Association** also offers accommodation for all ages at their new purpose-built hostel just behind the train station with 2-, 4- and 6-bed rooms. Non-members can join on arrival.

A Place of Your Own

If you are planning to stay in the area for an extended period, it may be more economical to choose a short-term rental. For a good selection click on 'Apartments & Self-Catering' at www.oxfordcity.co.uk. Among the agencies that offer this service is Oxford Shortlets, tel: 01865 311696; www.oxfordshortlets.co.uk.

Camping

The Camping & Caravanning Club has a site just over a mile from the centre at 426 Abingdon Road, tel: 01865-244088. You can join online at www.campingandcaravanningclub.co.uk
Cotswold View Caravan and Camping Site, Enstone Road, Charlbury, tel: 01608 810314.
Heyford Leys Camping Park, is a family run park situated on an old 17th-century farm premises: Camp Road, Bicester, tel: 01869 232048; www.heyfordleyscampingpark.co.uk.

For others, see www.visitoxford.org. *Camping Beside the River Thames* is a free leaflet giving details of campsites on or near the River Thames, available from Environment Agency Thames Information: tel: 0845 6015336, www.visitthames.co.uk.

BELOW: the luxurious Randolph.

CENTRAL AREA

HOTELS

Luxury

Macdonald Randolph Hotel
Beaumont Street
Tel: 0870 400 8200
www.randolph-hotel.com
Oxford's most famous hotel is situated in the city centre, opposite the Ashmolean Museum. There are two restaurants, two lounges, a coffee shop and bar. Extensive conference facilities.

Old Bank Hotel
92–94 High Street
Tel: 01865 799599
www.oldbank-hotel.co.uk
Oxford's most stylish hotel, housed in a former bank. Centrally located.

Old Parsonage Hotel
1 Banbury Road
Tel: 01865-310210
www.oldparsonnage-hotel.co.uk
A fine and well-located hotel in the renovated old parsonage next to St Giles' church. Thirty luxuriously appointed en-suite bedrooms. The Parsonage Bar restaurant is open all day, also to non-residents. Excellent afternoon tea.

Paramount Oxford Hotel
Godstow Road
Tel: 01865 489988
www.paramount-hotels.co.uk
Recently re-vamped four-star luxury hotel is two miles (3km) out of town on Woodstock Road. The modern, tasteful rooms have cable TV and internet. Leisure facilities include fitness suite, splash pool, steam room and squash courts. The bus into town stops around the corner in Mere Road.

Expensive

Bath Place Hotel
4–5 Bath Place
Tel: 01865-791812
www.bathplace.co.uk
A family-run hotel situated in the heart of backstreet Oxford, occupying a group of restored 17th-century cottages. Excellent restaurant.

Cotswold Lodge Hotel
66a Banbury Road
Tel: 01865-512121
www.cotswoldlodgehotel.co.uk
Beautiful Victorian building, situated in a quiet conservation area, only a few minutes' walk from the city centre. Bar serving coffee and light meals, as well as a restaurant serving lunch and dinner. Conference facilities.

Holiday Inn Oxford
Pear Tree Roundabou
Tel: 0870 400 9086
www.ichotelsgroup.com
Hotel with indoor pool and health centre on site. Short bus ride into centre.

Linton Lodge Hotel
Linton Road, off Banbury Road
Tel: 01865-553461
www.bw-lintonlodgehotel.co.uk
Restaurant, conference facilities, dinner-dances for 150 and private functions. TV, radio, telephone and en-suite in all rooms.

Macdonald Eastgate Hotel
23 Merton Street
Tel: 01865-400 8201
www.macdonaldhotels.co.uk
Traditional hotel in a central location, adjacent to the site of Oxford's old East Gate and opposite the Examination Schools. Restaurant and bar.

Moderate

The Galaxie Hotel
180 Banbury Road
Tel: 01865-515688
www.galaxie.co.uk
Friendly, family-run hotel near the shopping and leisure facilities of the Summertown residential district.

Marlborough House Hotel
321 Woodstock Road
Tel: 01865-311321
www.marlbhouse.co.uk
Small, luxurious hotel, situated in a residential area about 1½ miles (2.5 km) from the city centre. Continental breakfast in bedrooms, which are all en-suite and have their own kitchenettes.

The Old Black Horse Hotel
102 St Clements
Tel: 01865-244691
www.oldblackhorse.com
Attractive hotel in a 17th-century coaching inn just across Magdalen Bridge. All rooms en-suite; restaurant and bar. Friendly, family-run atmosphere. Secure car

park. Airport and London coaches stop outside.

Palace Hotel
250 Iffley Road
Tel: 01865-727627
Small hotel in a Victorian town house about a mile from the city centre. Parking available.

Parklands Hotel
100 Banbury Road
Tel: 01865-554374
www.oxfordcity.co.uk/hotels/parklands/
This privately-run hotel was originally an Oxford dons' residence built in the Victorian era. Mainly bed and breakfast accommodation but offering meals when required. Parking facilities.

Pine Castle Hotel
290–292 Iffley Road
Tel: 01865-241497
www.pinecastle.co.uk
Small, family-run hotel 1¼ miles (2 km) from

PRICE CATEGORIES

A very approximate guide to current room rates for a standard double per night is:
Luxury = over £150
Expensive = over £95
Moderate = over £70
Budget = under £70

the city centre. Pleasant, personal service and licensed bar.

The Tower House
15 Ship Street
Tel: 01865 246828
www.towerhouseoxford.co.uk
Family-run 17th-century guest house situated in a quiet street only minutes away from the city centre and renowned for its warm hospitality. Comfortable bedrooms furnished with antiques.

Victoria Hotel
180 Abingdon Road
Tel: 01865-724536
www.victoriabalkanlodge.co.uk
Small, friendly hotel, within walking distance of the city.

Westgate Hotel
1 Botley Road
Tel: 01865-726721
Fax: 01865-722078
Very convenient for both the city (5 minutes' walk) and the coach and railway stations. Restaurant and bar.

Budget

Lakeside Guest House
118 Abingdon Road
Tel: 01865 244725
www.oxfordcity.co.uk/accom/
lakeside/
Family-run hotel 15 minutes walk from the city centre and on a major bus route. This former Edwardian rectory overlooks Hinksey Park with its tennis courts and open-air heated swimming pool (in the summer). Satellite TV in all ensuite rooms.

River Hotel
17 Botley Road
Tel: 01865 243475
www.riverhotel.co.uk
Excellent riverside location on the Thames, near bus and railway station. A friendly, small and comfortable hotel.

B & Bs

Beaumont Guest House
234 Abingdon Road
Tel: 01865 241767
www.oxfordcity.co.uk/accom/
beaumont/
Small and friendly guest house in a Victorian family home tastefully decorated to a high standard. Short walk or bus ride into city centre. Reasonable rates and an excellent reputation.

Burlington House
374 Banbury Road
Tel: 01865 513513
www.burlington-house.co.uk
Top-rated guest house in an elegant, comfortable and impeccably maintained, Victorian house in Summertown, North Oxford. Quality, substantial breakfasts.

College Guest House
103–105 Woodstock Road
Tel: 01865-552579
Family-run guest house in a building of considerable character. En-suite rooms available

Cotswold House
363 Banbury Road
Tel/fax: 01865-310558
Highly commended bed-and-breakfast accommodation. Non-smoking.

Eurobar
48 George Street
Tel: 01865 725087
Small hotel located right in the centre. Hotel café-bar open all day.

Head of the River
Folly Bridge
Tel: 01865 721600
Large pub-restaurant in converted warehouse on the Thames. Rooms overlook the river.

Hi-Lo Jamaican Guest House
68–70 Cowley Road
Tel: 01865 725984
Hi-Lo is a Jamaican

restaurant with vegetarian-friendly menu which also has five guest rooms. Open all year.

Isis Guest House
45–53 Iffley Road
Tel: 01865-242 466/8894
www.isisguesthouse.co.uk
Owned by the university's St Edmund Hall, this hotel is open for B&B in July, August and September. Private car park.

Newton House
82/84 Abingdon Road
Tel: 01865 240561
www.oxfordcity.co.uk/accom
/newton/
The closest guest house to historic Christ Church, just half a mile from the city centre. Made up of two handsome Victorian townhouses retaining many original features, with a high standard of decor and period furniture. Special diets are catered for.

Sportsview Guest House
106–110 Abingdon Road
Tel: 01865 244268
www.oxfordcity.co.uk/accom/
sportsview
Family run Victorian guest house overlooking the Queens College sports ground and the Oxford University boat house. Just south of the city centre, near the Thames, canal and an open-air swimming pool.

Youth Hostels

Central Backpackers
13 Park End Street
Tel: 01865-24 22 88
www.centralbackpackers.co.uk
Friendly, smoke-free hostel near the train station (look for the yellow door). Female or mixed-sex dorms with 4 to 12 beds. £14–18 per bed; passport required on check-in. Facilities: TV lounge, self-catering kitchen, laundry service, internet, and lockers. Non-guests can also store luggage (£2 per day).

Oxford Backpacker's Hostel
9a Hythe Brige Street
Tel/fax: 01865-721761
oxford@hostels.co.uk
www.hostels.co.uk
Ideally-situated hostel only two minutes' walk from train or bus station. Self-catering kitchen, licensed bar with pool table. £14–16 per bed; passport required on check-in.

YHA
2A Botley Road
Tel: 0870 770 5970
email: oxford@yha.org.uk
www.yha.org.uk
Budget accommodation for all ages in a new purpose built 4-star Youth Hostel with 2-bed, 4-bed and 6-bed dormitory rooms. Restaurant, garden, games room, common room, TV room and internet. Located directly behind the railway station. Over 18: £20.95; Under 18: £15.95, includes breakfast. Non-members may join on arrival (£10 a year for adults).

OUTSKIRTS OF OXFORD

HOTELS

Luxury

Oxford Spires Four Pillars Hotel
Henley Road, Sandford-on-Thames
Tel: 01865-324 324
www.four-pillars.co.uk
A luxury hotel 4 miles (7 km) from the city centre, incorporating buildings dating back to medieval times. Superb leisure centre and extensive conference facilities. Four Pillars have three other hotels around Oxford.

Expensive

The Westwood Country Hotel
Hinksey Hill Top
Tel: 01865-735408
www.westwoodhotel.co.uk
Comfortable hotel set in woodland and garden. Wheelchair users welcome.

Moderate

Foxcombe Lodge Hotel
Fox Lane, Boars Hill
Tel: 01865-326326
www.foxcombelodge.co.uk
Restaurant and conference facilities. All rooms with TV, radio, direct-dial telephone and computer with internet. Friendly.

Hawkwell House Hotel
Church Way, Iffley
Tel: 01865-749988
Fax: 01865-748525
www.hawkwellhouse.co.uk
Country house hotel set in own grounds. Weddings and conferences catered for.

The Tree Hotel
Church Way, Iffley Village
Tel: 01865-775974
www.treehotel.co.uk
Comfortable hotel in attractive setting, just over a mile from the centre. Bar and restaurant seving Thai, Indian and English cuisine.

B & Bs

Casa Villa
388 Banbury Road
Tel: 01865-512642
www.casavilla.fsnet.co.uk
Modern, detached, family-run guest house. Offers cosy en-suite accommodation, ample car parking. Ten minutes from centre.

Conifers Guest House
116 The Slade, Headington
Tel: 01865 763055
www.conifersguesthouse.co.uk
Family-run B&B in residential area. Ensuite rooms with TV. Large garden.

Gables Guest House
6 Cumnor Hill
Tel: 01865 862153, www. oxfordcity.co.uk/accom/gables
6 rooms. Awarded four red AA diamonds. Vegetarian-friendly.

Highfield West Bed & Breakfast
188 Cumnor Hill
Tel: 01865 863007,
www.oxfordcity.co.uk/accom /highfield-west

Vegetarian guest house, a short walk from the historic village of Cumnor. Swimming pool.

Homelea Guest House
365 Abingdon Road
Oxford
Tel: 01865 245150
www.oxford-guesthouse.co.uk
Friendly, family-run guest house with prize-winning garden.

Tilbury Lodge
5 Tilbury Lane, Botley
Tel: 01865 862138
www.tilburylodge.com
AA four-star sparkling diamond award winner. Excellent facilities include internet and jacuzzi. Self-contained apartment also available.

OUTSIDE OXFORD

HOTELS

Luxury

The Bear Hotel
Woodstock
Tel: 0870 400 8202
www.macdonaldhotels.co.uk
Renowned for its luxurious accommodation and magnificent cuisine. An historic coaching inn with modern conference facilities.

Bay Tree Hotel
Sheep Street,
Burford
Tel: 01993 822791
www.cotswold-inns-hotels .co.uk
Once the home of Sir Lawrence Tanfield, Elizabeth I's Lord Chief Baron of the Exchequer, this 16th-century house has 23 en-suite rooms, some oak-panelled and with four-poster beds. There's also a walled garden and terraced lawns.

Calcot Manor
Tetbury, Gloucestershire
Tel: 01666 890391
www.calcotmanor.co.uk
Calcot Manor, with its 17th-century farm buildings, has been converted into a complex combining one of the area's most popular restaurants, the Gumstool Inn, and a separate hotel with a range of rooms: you can choose between four-posters and antiques, or family

rooms with children's bunk beds and playroom. Calcot Spa has excellent health, beauty, fitness and relaxation facilities.

The Feathers Hotel
Market Street, Woodstock
Tel: 01993 812291
www.feathers.co.uk
17th-century country
town hotel, with cele-
brated restaurant, in
the centre of historic
Woodstock. Some
rooms overlook the
courtyard garden.

**Lords of the Manor
Hotel**
Upper Slaughter,
Gloucestershire
Tel: 01451 820243
www.lordsofthemanor.com
Much-extended 17th-
century rectory in
idyllic parkland. The
trout-filled River Eye
meanders through.

**Lower Slaughter
Manor**
Lower Slaughter,
Gloucestershire
Tel: 01451 820456
www.lowerslaughter.co.uk
This 17th-century
manor, on the edge of
one of the Cotswolds'
prettiest villages, offers tennis courts, a
croquet lawn and
putting green, plus
indoor pool and sauna.

The Oxford Belfry
Milton Common
near junction 7 off
M40
Tel: 01844-279381
www.marstonhotels.com
Sixty bedrooms, all en-
suite with satellite TV,
radio, and telephone.
Specialises in confer-
ences. Leisure club
with swimming pool.

Expensive

The Bell at Charlbury
Charlbury
Tel: 01608 810278
www.bellhotel-charlbury.co.uk
A quiet hotel, where
gliding, fishing and
horse riding can be
arranged.

Burford House Hotel
High Street, Burford
Tel: 01993 823151
www.burford-house.co.uk
The hotel is set in a
mellow Tudor building
full of beams and
maze-like corridors.
Beautiful decor.
Relaxing.

The Swan Hotel
Bibury,
Gloucestershire
Tel: 01285 740695
www.cotswold-inns-hotels
.co.uk
17th-century former
coaching inn on the
banks of the River Coln
in what William Morris
called "the most beau-
tiful village in England".
Excellent food in the
award-winning restau-
rant. Beauty spa.

Weston Manor
Weston-on-the-Green
Tel: 01869 350621
www.westonmanor.co.uk
A 16th-century manor
house set in beautiful
gardens. Excellent cui-
sine in the Baronial
Hall.

Moderate

Bibury Court
Bibury, Gloucestershire
Tel: 01285 740337
www.biburycourt.com
This glorious Jacobean
house fulfils every-
one's idea of the per-
fect Cotswold manor.
Rarely does such a
sense of history come
for such a reasonable
price.

Studley Lodgel
Horton-cum-Studley
Tel: 01865-351235
www.studleylodge.com
Country hotel offering
rural peace, yet close
to Oxford. Restaurant
and lounge bar. Four
poster bedroom is
more expensive.

Budget

**The Coach and
Horses Inn**
Watlington Road,
Chislehampton
Tel: 01865-890255
www.coachhorsesinn.co.uk
On B480, 7 miles (11
km) from Oxford and 5
miles (8 km) from junc-
tion 7 on the M40,
adjacent to farmland in
rural Oxfordshire.
Excellent accommoda-
tion for the tourist or
business person. Oak-
beamed restaurant
and bar.

The Maytime Inn
Asthall, between Burford
and Witney
Tel: 01993 822068
www.themaytime.com
Comfortable accommo-
dation, all on the
ground floor, with pri-
vate bathroom,
shower, TV, radio and
tea-/coffee-making
facilities. Good restau-
rant, with extensive
seasonal menu and
vegetarian dishes at
very reasonable
prices.

Tavern House
Willesley, Tetbury,
Gloucestershire,
Tel: 01666 880444
www.tavernhouse.co.uk
Up-market B&B in for-
mer coaching inn near
the beautiful Weston-
birt Arboretum.

B & Bs

The Bungalow
Cherwell Farm, Mill Lane,
Old Marston
Tel: 01865 557171
Email: ros.bungalowbb
@btinternet.com
Quiet modern bunga-
low set in 5 acres of
land. Within 3 miles
city centre but not on
bus route.

Lewis Lodge
2 Lewis Close, Headington
Tel: 01865 762285
www.lewislodgeoxford.com
Modern and immacu-
late hotel-standard
ensuite rooms in brick
house near The Kilns,
C.S. Lewis's former
home in Risinghurst.
Good value.

Mulberry Guest House
265 London Road,
Headington
Tel: 01865 767114
All rooms ensuite and
with internet connec-
tion.

**Riversdale Bed &
Breakfast**
The Walk, Islip
Tel: 01865 373376
www.islipbandb.co.uk
An 18th-century family
home in the centre of
Islip village 5 miles
from Oxford. Secluded
garden. Double rooms
with en-suite bath-
rooms, and a twin-
bedded room.

Oak Tree Copse
Woodfarm, Worminghall
Tel: 01865 358751
www.oxfordfarmhouses.co.uk
Country farmhouse
B&B 10 miles from
Oxford on the
Buckinghamshire
border. Very reason-
able rates.

YOUTH HOSTELS

**Stow-On-The-Wold
Youth Hostel**
The Square
Stow-On-The-Wold
Tel: 0870 770 6050
www.yha.org.uk

A listed 16th-century townhouse in the centre of the historic market town. Picturesque villages, the Rollright Stones, Cotswold Heritage Centre and Chedworth Roman Villa are nearby. The hostel has been comfortably refurbished, providing smaller rooms, many ensuite. Families are especially welcome. Restaurant, self-catering kitchen, laundry and cycle shed. Adult £14.95, under 18 £10.50.

IN AND AROUND STRATFORD-UPON-AVON

HOTELS

Luxury

Alveston Manor
Clopton Bridge,
Stratford-upon-Avon
Tel: 0870 400 8181
www.macdonaldhotels.co.uk
Large, half-timbered hotel on the far bank of the River Avon from the Royal Shakespeare Theatre. Part of it dates from the 16th century and it is believed to be the site of the first performance of *A Midsummer Night's Dream*.

Welcombe Hotel and Golf Club
Warwick Road,
Stratford-upon-Avon
Tel: 01789 295252
www.menzies-hotels.co.uk
This grandiose, 19th-century, Jacobean-style mansion is set in its own spacious parkland and offers every amenity including its own golf course and gourmet restaurant, named after a former owner, the historian Sir George Trevelyan.

Expensive

Victoria Hotel
Arden Street,
Stratford-upon-Avon

Tel: 01789 271000
www.marstonhotels.com
Centrally located modern 4-star hotel built in Victorian style. Award winning restaurant, gym and spa plus access to leisure facilities at the Stratford Manor hotel. Within walking distance of many attractions and river Avon.

Best Western Salford Hall Hotel
Abbots Salford,
Stratford-upon-Avon
Tel: 01386 871300
www.bestwestern.co.uk
Romantic Tudor manor set in extensive gardens. Log fires, four-posters and an award-winning restaurant. Sauna, solarium and tennis court.

Moderate

White Swan
Rother Street,
Stratford-upon-Avon
Tel: 01789 297022, www.thewhiteswanstratford.co.uk
A key example of Stratford's heritage of half-timbered buildings, the Swan dates from the 16th century and features a wall-painting of that era in its impressive Oak Room. Bedrooms are mostly in later extensions.

Budget

Emsley Guest House
4 Arden Street
Stratford-upon-Avon
Tel: 01789 299557
www.theemsley.co.uk
Victorian townhouse in town centre (5-minute walk to the train station). Attentive staff and excellent breakfasts.

B & Bs

Brook Lodge
192 Alcester Road,
Stratford-upon-Avon
Tel: 01789 295988.
www.brook-lodge.co.uk
Close to Anne Hathaway's Cottage and to open country, this immaculately run little guest house has 7 ensuite rooms.

Firs Cottage
Dorsington,
Tel: 07969 052575
www.firscottage.co.uk
Four hundred-year-old thatched cottage in the quiet village of Dorsington on the Heart of England Way, between Stratford and the Cotswolds.

Heron Lodge
260 Alcester Road
Stratford-Upon-Avon,
Tel: 01789 299169
www.heronlodge.com
A mile from Stratford

town centre, this friendly four-diamond rated B&B is known for its good food. Their ground floor ensuite room is particularly well-suited for those with limited mobility.

Loxley Farm
Loxley
Tel: 01789 840265
www.loxleyfarm.co.uk
15th-century cruck-framed thatched cottage in the village of Loxley, near Stratford and Warwick.

YOUTH HOSTELS

Youth Hostel
Hemmingford House Alveston,
Stratford Upon Avon
Tel: 0870 7706052 (within UK)
www.yha.org.uk
A splendidly refurbished Georgian mansion house set in three acres of grounds in a quiet village 2 miles from Stratford-upon-Avon. Family rooms available.

ACTIVITIES

FESTIVALS, THE ARTS, NIGHTLIFE, SHOPPING, TOURS AND SPORTS

CALENDAR OF EVENTS

Pick up a copy of *In Oxford*, the free monthly guide to what's on. See also www.inoxfordmag.co.uk.

Festivals and Holidays

The Oxford Tourist Information Centre (*see page 259*) will be able to give visitors precise dates and times of events.
Degree Days (days on which degrees are conferred by the University) are listed in the University diary.

February

Torpids: Traditional college rowing races on the Isis. Usually held in the 6th week of Hilary Term. One of the great rowing events in the University calendar. In February or early March a competition is held to introduce freshmen (first-year undergraduates) to the University rowing course between Iffley Lock and Folly Bridge.

May

May Morning (1 May): At 6am, the Magdalen College choir sings from Magdalen Tower. Morris dancing in Radcliffe Square and Broad Street. A not-to-be-missed event. Take up

position half-way across Magdalen Bridge at about 5.30am, and after the chorus wander around town having a boozy breakfast and watching the revellers making merry in all manner of fancy or formal dress.
Lord Mayor's Parade (On Spring Bank Holiday Monday): a parade of decorated floats starts at St Giles and finishes at South Parks.
Eights Week: Held in late May or early June, this is a series of inter-collegiate rowing races. College crews move up and down a league table depending on each day's racing. The race is in a single line and each crew attempts to "bump" or touch the boat in front. Once this has been achieved the race is won.
Beating the Bounds (Ascension Day): Starts at the Church of St Michael at the Northgate at 10.30am.
Artweeks: Artists and crafts-people of all ages open their workshops and homes so that the public can meet them and discover their methods and motivations. From mid-May to beginning of June. See www.artweeks.org
Whitsun: The Headington Quarry Morris Dancers occupy a unique position in Oxford's history and in the story of morris dancing. A chance meeting

between the folk song collector Cecil Sharp and William Kimber's Headington Quarry Morris Dancers, on Boxing Day 1899, led eventually to the national revival of interest in morris dancing. William Kimber was to lead the Headington morris to world fame. He inherited his skills from his father, who in turn had learned his morris from an earlier generation of Quarry dancers. The tradition continues to this day.

June

Encaenia: The ceremony takes place at noon on the first Wednesday in the week following full Trinity term. Honorary degrees are conferred by the University at the Sheldonian Theatre.

July

Sheriff's Races: Held on Wolvercote Common. Amateur horse races, side shows and stalls.

August

Oxford Regatta: Details from the City of Oxford Rowing Club, tel: 01865-242576.

September

St Giles' Fair: Held on the first Monday and Tuesday in September. A once-famous annual enjoyment for town, gown and surrounding countryfolk. It can still be fun, but some see it as an expensive, tacky fair with a dubious safety record and knee-deep litter.

October

Oxford Round Table Firework Display: Britain's firework displays traditionally take place on Guy Fawkes' Night (5 November). This one is held in late October in South Parks, and is a worthwhile spectacle.

November

Christ Church Regatta: Generally held the 7th week of Michaelmas term. All enquiries to the Boat Captain, Christ Church, St Aldate's, Oxford.
New College: End November. Advent Carol Service. See www.newcollegechoir.co.uk.

December

Lord Mayor's Carols: Held in the Town Hall. Date announced in autumn.
Christmas Music: At Christmas the chapel choirs of Christ Church, Magdalen and New College combine their regular liturgical duties with carol concerts that sometimes feature major orchestras and famous soloists. Advance tickets available.
Christ Church: 23 December. Nine Lessons and Carols. Tickets from the Chapter Secretary no later than 16 November. Enclose a stamped, addressed envelope.
Magdalen College: Mid-December. Carols by Candlelight (tickets in advance from the College Office).
New College: Early December. Carol Service (tickets in advance from the Precentor).
The Headington Quarry Morris Dancers' Mummers Play and Sword Dance: Boxing Day.

THE ARTS

Museums & Galleries

Oxford has Britain's oldest public museum, the Ashmolean Museum of Arts and Archaeology (*see page 157*). Britain's oldest purpose-built museum building is also here, housing the Museum of the History of Science. This reputation continues with plans for the new Science Oxford building in the West End of the city.

Other notable institutions include Modern Art Oxford, the Pitt Rivers Museum and the Museum of Natural History – home to the Oxford Dodo and winner of the Guardian's *Family Friendly Museum 2005* award. For more museum information visit www.ox.ac.uk/museums and www.oxfordcity.co.uk

Some museums are closed on Mondays (the Ashmolean, Modern Art Oxford, Museum of the History of Science, Museum of Oxford). Others are open daily (Museum of Natural History, Pitt Rivers Museum, University Museum, The Oxford Story).

Art Galleries

Apart from the permanent and changing exhibitions in Oxford's museums, there are several private art galleries, and the art colleges at the University hold regular exhibitions.

The best time to explore the art scene is during Artweeks, in May and June, when local artists open up their studios to the public.

From May to September local artists display their work along the railings of University Parks, Parks Road (Sunday 2–6pm).

Here are a few venues exhibiting art:
Christ Church Picture Gallery, Oriel Square, www.chch.ox.ac.uk. An important collection of Old Master paintings and drawings, with rotating selection.
Modern Art Oxford, 30 Pembroke Street; Tel: 01865 722733, www.modernartoxford.org.uk. One of the leading modern art spaces in Britain, with a changing programme of exhibitions. Café and shop.
O3 Gallery, Oxford Castle, www.ovada.org.uk. A new gallery at Oxford Castle presenting selling exhibitions of contemporary visual and applied arts by local artists.
Wiseman Gallery, 40–41 South Parade, www.wisegal.com. Commercial gallery showing contemporary art.
University of Oxford Shop, 106 High Street, www.oushop.com. Watercolours and commissions.

There are also regular exhibitions on the walls of the café at both **Freud Café** (119 Walton Street) **Jericho Café,** (112 Walton Street).

Oxford Colleges

The majority of colleges are open to visitors in the afternoon only, usually from 1 or 2pm to 4 or 5pm. Some colleges do open longer, however: Christ Church Mon–Sat 9–5pm, Sun 1–5pm; Magdalen daily 1–6pm; New College daily 11am–4pm; Trinity College Mon–Fri and weekends out of term 10am–noon and 2–4pm.

These colleges charge a fee, with Christ Church being the most expensive; admission to all the other colleges is free, including to St Edmund Hall, which is open daily from dawn till dusk.

The Queen's College is only open to visitors on a tour booked at the Oxford Information Centre with the Oxford Guild of Guides. University College, Oriel College and Green College are generally closed to the public, though it is still worth enquiring at the porter's lodge.

Visitors should note that the above times can only be used as a guide, particularly during exam times. Colleges have a habit of closing as a result of building works or simply at the whim of the all-powerful porter.

Theatre & Opera

New Theatre Oxford
George Street, Oxford OX1 2AG
Tel: 0870 606 3500.
www.getlive.co.uk.
A varied programme of commercial theatre for all ages, including opera and ballet, plays, musicals, pop and classical concerts, comedy, pantomime, and shows for young theatre-goers.
OFS Studio (Old Fire Station)
George Street
Tel: 01865 297170
www.getlive.co.uk.
Contains a fully-equipped (if small) studio theatre and rehearsal space in a complex of bars, restaurants and galleries. Student productions often staged here.
Oxford Playhouse
11–12 Beaumont Street
Tel: 01865 305305
www.oxfordplayhouse.com
A recently renovated premises with a diverse range of productions, including a traditional Christmas pantomime and experimental theatre and dance.
Burton-Taylor Studio Theatre
Behind the Oxford Playhouse, Gloucester Street
Tel: 01865-793797
www.newburytheatre.co.uk
Built in 1973 after a generous donation to the University by Richard Burton and Elizabeth Taylor, and recently refurbished with a new foyer and dressing rooms. Specialises in student and fringe productions with new plays and Edinburgh Festival comedies all year round.
Newman Rooms
Rose Place, St Aldate's
Tel: 01865-722651
The venue for a variety of plays and musicals at reasonable prices.
The Theatre At Headington
Headington School, Oxford.
Tel: 01865 759138 (Box Office)
www.headington.org

A wide-ranging programme of theatre, comedy, music and dance.
Creation Theatre
Tel: 01865 245745
www.creationtheatre.co.uk
Creation put on site-specific theatre in atmospheric locations, including Headington Hill Park and Oxford Castle.
Pegasus Theatre
Magdalen Road, off Iffley Road
Tel: 01865-722851
www.pegasustheatre.org.uk
Youth theatre and dance activities.

Cinemas

Odeon Oxford, George Street, **Odeon Oxford-Magdalen Street**, tel: 0871 2244007; www.odeon.co.uk.
For mainstream film fare in the city centre.
Phoenix Picture House, 57–58 Walton Street, tel: 01865 554 909, bookings: 0870 758 3218; www.picturehouses.co.uk.
Shows some mainstream movies but concentrates on modern cult films, classics and a variety of international productions.
Ultimate Picture Palace, Jeune Street, tel: 0778 6325121; www.ultimatepicturepalace.co.uk.
Atmospheric for classic flicks. They also have Wednesday screenings of films exclusively for parents with babies under one year old.
Ozone Multiplex Cinema, Ozone Leisure & Entertainment Park, Grenoble Road, tel: 08712 240 240, www.ozonemultiplex.com.
Further out from the centre (bus Nos. 5, 5A, 5B, 5C, 106),

Classical Music

Holywell Music Room
Holywell Street
Tickets available through the Playhouse box office, tel: 01865 305 305
www.ticketsoxford.com
The oldest music room in Europe; many famous musicians, including Haydn, have played here since it opened in

1748. Excellent acoustics. Chamber music concerts are held here most Sundays at 11.15am (www.coffeeconcerts.com).
Jacqueline du Pré Music Building
St Hilda's College
Tel: 01865 305 305
www.sthildas.ox.ac.uk/jdp
This hall was created in the memory of the great cellist Jacqueline du Pré and is one of the best modern music venues in the city. A variety of musical styles are performed, as well as music examinations taken.
Sheldonian Theatre
Broad Street
Tickets available through Playhouse, tel: 01865 305 305
www.ticketsoxford.com
Designed and built by Christopher Wren in the style of a Roman theatre, the famous Sheldonian is used for concerts, university ceremonies and other events. Be aware, however, that the seats are mainly wooden with no back rests.

Music At Oxford put on classical concerts at various locations; see www.musicatoxford.com.

Church Music

The world-famous New College Choir performs at New College Chapel. You can find latest concert dates and buy CDs at www.newcollegechoir.co.uk.

For Christmas carol concerts *see Calendar of Events, page 218.*

Rock & Pop Concerts

The main venues for rock and pop concerts are the Zodiac, the New Theatre, Aylesbury Civic Centre and the Cellar. For tour dates in and around Oxford see www.anconcerts.com.

There are also many more pubs, cafés and restaurants with live music. For details of venues and gigs, *see Live Music page 248.*

NIGHTLIFE

Oxford has both many traditional pubs and some trendy bars too. The Jericho area is upmarket, gown and trendy, with an art-house cinema and lots of cool bars and restaurants. East, over Magdalen Bridge, Cowley Road is also lively, trendy and studenty but with a less upmarket vibe.

Oxford has quite a few night-clubs for a small city but they are largely geared to the young and there is a lot of "cheese" (kitsch) and R'n'B about.

Nightclubs

Park End
Park End Street
Tel: 01865 250181
www.parkend.co.uk
Top dog of Oxford clubs. Three dancefloors. Long queues are the norm.
The Bridge
6–9 Hythe Bridge Street
Tel: 01865 242526
www.bridgeoxford.co.uk
Upmarket alternative to Park End. The pre-club Anuba bar inside is one way to avoid the queue.
The Cellar, Frewin Court, Cornmarket Street,
Tel: 01865-244761
www.cellarmusic.co.uk
The cool cognoscenti's choice, offering a range of specialist nights.
Po-Na-Na
13–15 Magdalen Street (at the bottom of St Giles)
Tel: 01865 249171
www.ponana.com
Intimate Moroccan-style decor and cocktails. Alternative, laid-back and catering to fans of funk, soul or anything not cheesy.
The Zodiac
190 Cowley Road
Tel: 01865-420042
www.the-zodiac.co.uk
Considered by many to be Oxford's best club. A variety of

regular and special club nights. Large, dark and popular.
The Coven II
Oxpens Road
Tel: 01865-242770
Much more town than gown, with regular drum 'n' bass, trance and hard house nights.
Escape
9A High St (1 Market Avenue)
Tel: 01865 248480
www.escape-oxford.co.uk
Restaurant, bar and dance area on first floor with chill-out lounge above. Mon–Sat 5pm–late.
Jongleurs Comedy Club
3–5 Hythe Bridge Street
tel: 0870 787 0707
www.jongleurs.com
Comedy/live acts, food and DJs.

Live Music

Having spawned a number of great rock bands, including Radiohead and Supergrass, Oxford is well known for its live music scene. For major Rock/Pop concert venues *see page 247.*
The Zodiac (see above)
Probably Oxford's leading live music venue, with a busy diary of live acts.
The Cellar (*see above*)
Establishing itself as one of the centres of musical life in Oxford. Good sound system.
Exeter Hall, 1 Oxford Road, tel: 01865 776431; www.thex.co.uk. Large friendly pub with very good value live music. On bus routes 1 & 5 towards Cowley.
Jericho Tavern
56 Walton Street, tel: 01865 311775. Birthplace of Radiohead and Supergrass. Gigs on Tuesdays, Wednesdays (jazz) and Saturdays. Gourmet pub food noon–11pm.
The Bullingdon, 162 Cowley Road, tel: 244516. Music or DJs every night (blues on Mondays, jazz on Tuesday).
Wheatsheaf, 129 High Street, tel: 721156.
For a full gig guide see 'What's On' at www.dailyinfo.co.uk.

Gay Scene

Bars

Paradise Street has **The Castle**, (No. 24) and **The Jolly Farmers**, (No. 20), one of the oldest pubs in Oxford. Nearby is the **Brewery Gate** on St Thomas' Street, which is less male-dominated. On Cowley Road there is **Baby Bar & Restaurant** (No. 213) and the **Brickworks Café Bar**, (No. 182). Other gay-friendly bars include the **Angel & Greyhound**, 30 St Clements Street, and the **Kings Arms**, 40 Holywell Street.

Clubnights

Flirt, Mondays at the **Old Fire Station**, George Street, Tel: 01865-297170. Has broad appeal.
Pop-tarts, Tuesdays in Baby-Love bar, 3 King Edward Street.
Loveshack, Fridays at The Coven II (*see above*).
CLOUD 9, Saturdays at The Studio Lounge, 34-35 The Westgate Centre, tel: 01865 245136.

BELOW: a variety of clubs provide the latest sounds

SHOPPING

Oxford offers an intriguing mixture of traditional and modern shops, catering for every taste and pocket. The main shopping area is compact and easy to explore on foot. There are two modern indoor shopping arcades in the centre: the Westgate Centre and the Clarendon Centre. If it is raining, sheltered shopping can also be had in the Covered Market or one of the deparment stores – Marks & Spencer, Bhs (both on Queen Street) or Debenhams (at the junction of George Street and Cornmarket Street).

Most of the shops in the city centre are open Monday to Saturday 9am–5.30pm, although some (increasing all the time) open on Sunday as well, 10am–4pm. There is late-night shopping every Thursday, when many shops remain open until 8.30pm.

Shopping Areas

Oxford's central crossroads is known as **Carfax**, where Cornmarket, High Street, Queen Street and St Aldates meet.

Cornmarket leads north, and is closed to all traffic (including buses) 10am–6pm. Along Cornmarket are many of the Britain's high street chains, including W.H. Smith, Boots, Gap, Miss Selfridge, HMV and Virgin Megastore.

Just off Cornmarket, near the Carfax end, is the historic **Golden Cross Inn Arcade**, which leads to the Covered Market (*see Markets, below*). This small courtyard contains a Puccino's café, a Pizza Express, and a variety of gifts and goods from souvenirs and jewellery to healthfoods. At No. 5 is Scriptum, a tiny shop crammed with Romantic fine stationery, pens, quills, and leather-bound notebooks. There is vintage clothing in Fresh at No. 9.

The **Clarendon Centre**, which you can enter either from Cornmarket, Queen Street or New Inn Hall Street, is a modern arcade with shoe shops, fashion boutiques, sport shops, electrical goods and computer shops. Gap, at the Cornmarket entrance, has a Gap Kids on the first floor.

Broad Street, running east from the northern end of Cornmarket, is Oxford's book street, with no fewer than six bookshops, including Blackwell's. At No. 17 is the first ever Oxfam shop. Professional and amateur artists will be interested in the two excellent art and craft shops, The Brush &. Compass at No. 14 and Broad Canvas at No. 20. Blackwell's Art and Poster shop at No. 27 has a great range of posters, prints and books. There are a few other shops too.

West from Carfax runs **Queen Street**, also a pedestrian area but open to buses. It includes a large Marks & Spencer store, Bhs, Next, Gap and an Early Learning Centre, as well as many smaller shops. At the end of Queen Street is the fully enclosed **Westgate Centre** with numerous stores including Sainsbury's, Alders, and a Disney Store. The fine public Central Library, with a large local history section and a periodicals reading room, is at the entrance to the Westgate Centre. The Westgate is also easily accessible from the multi-storey car park to which it is linked. An ambitious new Westgate centre is slated for development, commencing 2007. Opposite the library is New Inn Hall Street with Argos, Culpeper and Kings Fabrics.

The **High Street** strikes east from Carfax, curving down to Magdalen Bridge. The college buildings which line it are interspersed with small traditional businesses, including antique and print dealers, as well as trendy modern shops. Near the Oxford University Press Bookshop, Shepherd &

Woodward at Nos. 109–114 sells traditional menswear (including Barbour jackets), while Sanders of Oxford at No. 104 sells rare prints and maps. In Wheatsheaf Yard behind No. 128 is Gill & Co, Britain's oldest ironmongers (though this is not the original site). Established in 1530, they stock over 7,000 lines.

There are several modern designer fashion boutiques. Particularly interesting is Sahara at 46 High Street, which donates 50% of the profit from its sales to endangered forest conservation projects and to the support of indigenous people's rights. Other interesting fashion boutiques are Narda Fashion Studio at No. 67–68 and Agnès B fashion at No. 56. And should you need a new pen, Pens Plus at No. 70 is the right place to go. They buy, sell and repair old pens.

High Street is connected to Broad Street by **Turl Street**, where there are a number of traditional shops, including Walters & Co. at No. 10, selling high-class menswear, and Past Times at No. 4 selling historical gifts, including traditional games. Ducker & Son at No. 6 sells high-quality handmade shoes.

The fourth arm of Carfax is **St Aldate's**, which leads south. At 107 St Aldate's is Touchwoods, a sports and outdoor gear shop. A little further down is the main Post Office at No. 102, with a philatelic counter and the post shop, selling a selection of stationery. At No. 83, opposite Christ Church, is Alice's Shop, the little 15th-century "Sheep Shop" said in Lewis Carroll's *Through the Looking Glass* to be "full of all manner of curious things". The real-life Alice, daughter of the Dean of Christ Church, to whom Lewis Carroll told his tales, used to buy her Barley Sugar sweets here. Carroll wove the shop into his story, transforming the old lady who kept it into a sheep who sat at the counter knitting with a multitude of needles. It now sells the largest selection of "Alice" memorabilia in the country, together with Oxford gifts and souvenirs, Oxford University T-shirts and sweatshirts in the University colours.

George Street, with a variety of shops and restaurants, links Cornmarket to **Gloucester Green** (not a green but a square) where the city's open markets are held. The Gallery of shops surrounding the square houses a wide range of shops. Worth a look is Once a Tree at No. 99, with a surprising array of high-quality wooden items, functional and decorative, small and large, from sustainable sources around the world.

Beyond Gloucester Green, **Walton Street**, at the heart of trendy Jericho, has some interesting shops, particularly in the crafts and design variety. There is a print and picture shop and plenty of second-hand books at Jericho Books and Mind. It is quieter than the city centre streets and the numerous cafés and bars allow for a pleasant stroll.

Little Clarendon Street, which cuts through to St Giles, also mixes interesting shops with plenty of places to take a break. There are designer women's clothes at Hobbs and independent boutiques, plus Uncle Sam's vintage clothes store. For a caffeine-free lift, try the Juice café at the Walton Street end. Emerging onto St Giles, there is Taylor's gourmet delicatessen – a great place to buy provisions and a bottle of traditional lemonade if planning a post-shopping picnic, or just for coffee and snacks on the hoof.

Markets

Built in 1774 to provide a permanent home for the many stallholders who had earlier cluttered the city streets, the **Covered Market** is located between High Street and Market Street. There are several entrances from both, plus access through Golden Cross Arcade off Cornmarket Street. It

still has fresh and cooked meat, game, cheese, fruit, vegetables and flowers but now there are also many boutiques and shops. These remain either traditional, foodie, crafty or gift-related, including: traditional shoe shops and a barber, a tea and coffee merchant, a hat shop, leather goods and art prints. Running almost the length of the market, Nothing has a selection of hand-knitted sweaters, jewellery and cards along it's endless, segmented counter. Opposite is Next-To-Nothing with an interesting selection of eccentric t-shirts, some genuinely amusing. Within the market and around its entrances also offers a wide choice of cafés.

The city's **open market** is held every Wednesday in **Gloucester Green** next to the bus station. Stalls sell food and a wide range of other goods. On Thursday mornings there is an antique and crafts market here.

Bookshops

Oxford is the home of bookshops and Broad Street is where most of the bookshops are located, almost monopolised by the name of Blackwell. Blackwell's have always operated a policy of allowing shoppers to browse freely, and this is nowhere more enjoyable than at the main Blackwell's Bookshop at No. 48–51, where there is a café on the first floor.

The main competition to Blackwell's is provided by Waterstones on the corner of Cornmarket and Broad Street and by Borders Books & Music on Magdalen Street – both also have cafés inside. W.H. Smith is at No. 22 Cornmarket and in Templar's Square, Cowley.

Those interested in second-hand and rare books might want to browse in: Thorntons at No. 11 Broad Street; Arcadia Booksellers at 4 St Michael's Street; Classics Bookshop at 3 Turl Street; Waterfields Booksellers at 52 High Street;

Oxfam bookshop on St Giles; or Jericho Books on Walton Street.

Everything published by Oxford University Press can be bought at their outlet at No. 116 High Street, while St Andrew's Christian Book Shop at No. 57c St Clement's sells religious books. Books on the mind, body, spirit and health can be found at The Inner Bookshop, 111 Magdalen Road.

Down St Aldate's you will find St Philip's Books, at No. 82, and Reservoir Books (No. 84) with philosophy, literature, theology, history, anthropology, fine art and architecture collections.

TOURS

Open-top Bus

City Sightseeing Oxford, Railway Station, tel: 01865-790522, www.citysightseeingoxford.com. Operate open-top sightseeing tours daily, year-round. The complete tour lasts approximately one hour, but your ticket is valid all day and you can get off and on the buses at your leisure at any of the 20 marked bus stops in the city. Departures every 10–15 minutes 9.30am–5pm; ticket price £9.50.

Coach Tours

Cotswold Roaming organises half-day and full-day tours from Oxford to Blenheim Palace, the Cotswolds, Stratford and Warwick Castle, Bath, Stonehenge and Avebury. You can book at the Tourist Information Centre (*see page 259*) or tel: 01865 308300; www.oxfordcity.co.uk/cotswold-roaming/

Walking Tours

Walking tours of the City and Colleges, led by qualified members of the **Oxford Guild of Guides** (Blue Badge guides), leave the Oxford Information Centre daily at 11am and 2pm, with additional tours at busy times. There are also walking tours from Carfax Tower on Friday, Saturday and Sunday at 1.45pm.

The Oxford Information Centre also organises special interest tours such as C.S. Lewis and Lewis Carroll tours, Inspector Morse Walking Tours, Spooky Ghost Tours, Pub Tours and Family Tours. Do-it-yourself MP3-guided walking tours are also now available for tours at your own pace. For further information, call 01865-726871 or see website: www.visitoxford.org

Further walking tours, taking in sites of literary and historical interest, are organised by **Blackwell's Literary Walking Tours**; they start from Blackwell's Oxford Bookshop at 53 Broad Street (Apr–Oct Tues 2pm, Thurs 11am, Sat noon; tel: 01865 333606).

Boat Tours

No visit to Oxford is complete without a trip on the water. Punts, canoes, rowing boats and private cruisers can be hired for use on the Thames, Cherwell or the Oxford Canal. *For punting and rowing boats see page 224.* For those who like to take it easy, excursions on the Thames are arranged by:
Salters Bros, Folly Bridge, tel: 01865-243421; www.salterssteamers.co.uk.
May to September there are 40-minute cruises on the Thames and a regular Oxford–Iffley–Sandford–Abingdon service (2 hours duration).
Oxford River Cruises, 7 Rogers Street (over Folly Bridge), tel: 08452 269 396; www.oxfordrivercruises.com. Trips, picnic trips, and charters in Edwardian style craft.
College Cruisers Narrowboat hire, Combe Road Wharf, Oxford, tel: 01865-554343; www.collegecruisers.com. 2-to-12-berth canal boats for short breaks or longer holidays.

Cycle Tours

Gentle Cycle Tours
Tel: 01296 631671
www.capital-sport.co.uk
Sunday guided tours of Oxford and surrounding countryside run from May throughout the summer. Tours leave at 10am and last around 3 hours. Cycle hire is included in the price of £20. You need to book a place by 5pm Friday, by phone, email or online.

SPORT & LEISURE

Participant Sports

Golf

Oxford and its surrounding area is well supplied with golf courses. For more golf clubs consult www.oxford.gov.uk (click on Leisure).
Hinksey Heights Golf and Nature Park
South Hinksey (just off the A34 southwest of Oxford)
Tel: 01865-327775
www.oxford-golf.co.uk
Fairly new course to the west of the city with stunning views of Oxford's dreaming spires. Membership or pay as you play. Lessons available. Also nature park and trail and licensed bar.
North Oxford Golf Club
Banbury Road
Tel: 01865-554415
www.nogc.co.uk
Southfield Golf Club
Southfield, Hill Top Road, Oxford
Tel: 01865-242158
www.southfieldgolf.com
Bicester Golf and Country Club, Chesterton, near Bicester, (10 miles/16 km from Oxford, off the A421)
Tel: 01869 241204
www.bicestergolf.co.uk
With health club, bar, restaurant, hairdressing and beauty salon.
Burford Golf Club
Swindon Road, Burford (19 miles/30 km from Oxford, 1 mile off the A361)
Tel: 01993 822583

www.burfordgolfclub.co.uk
Frilford Heath Golf Club
Frilford Heath, near Abingdon, (7 miles/11 km from Oxford on the A338)
Tel: 01865-390864
www.frilfordheath.co.uk
Haddon Hill Golf Course and Range
Wallingford Road, Didcot
Tel: 01235-510410
www.haddenhillgolf.co.uk
With pro-shop and teaching.

Swimming
Hinksey Open Air Pools
Lake Street or Abingdon Road
Tel: 01865-247737.
Mixed swimming in a range of renovated open-air pools. Open: end May to early September.
There are indoor pools at Blackbird Leys, Ferry, Peers, and Temple Cowley sports centres (*see box below, page 252*).

Ice Skating
Oxford Ice Rink
Oxpens Road
Tel: 01865-467002
www.oxford.gov.uk
Not far from the railway station. Facilities include a 185- by 52-ft (56- by 16-metre) rink, fully licensed bar and fast food cafeteria, professional instructors, ice shows and special events, and a fully stocked skate shop.

Bowling
Bowlplex
Ozone Leisure & Entertainment Park, Grenoble Road, (bus Nos. 5, 5A, 5B, 5C, 106)
Tel: 01865-714100
www.bowlplexuk.com
With 24 lanes, pool tables, video games and a late licence. Open 10am–midnight, 2am at weekends.

Other
You can play some virtual golf at **Golfing2Day**, Threeways House, Gloucester Green (tel: 01865 200233; www.golfing2day.com) where there is also a **LaserQuest** (phone as above; www.laserquest.co.uk).

LEISURE CENTRES AND HEALTH CLUBS

Bourton Mill Health & Leisure Club
6 High Street
Tel: 01865 251261
www.bourtonmill.net
Aerobics studio, resistance training machines and free weights. Personal trainers and various fitness classes. Jacuzzi, sauna, sunbeds, treatments and therapies. Central location.

Arena Fitness
109 Oxford Road, Cowley
Tel: 01865 779115
www.arenafitness.co.uk
Fully equipped gymnasium, computerised fitness assessment, aerobic classes, saunas and crèche. Daily rates for non-members.

Ferry Sports Centre
Diamond Place,
Summertown
Tel: 01865 467060
www.oxford.gov.uk
Off the Banbury Road.
Swimming, fitness suite, racket sports and classes.

Peers Sports Centre
Sandy Lane West, Littlemore
Tel: 01865 467095
www.oxford.gov.uk
Facilities include swimming

pool, fitness centre, gym, badminton, basketball, tennis and table tennis.

Temple Cowley Pools
Temple Road, Cowley
Tel: 01865 749449
www.oxford.gov.uk
The fitness room offers a wide range of modern exercise machines and cardiovascular equipment. Before using the equipment an induction and basic health check is required. Call for details of fitness classes.

Blackbird Leys Leisure Centre and Pool
Blackbird Leys
Tel: 01865 467020
(pool: 01865 467040)
www.oxford.gov.uk
Approximately 5 miles southeast of the city centre. Sports hall with badminton and tennis courts, pitches for basketball, volleyball, football and netball, a snooker room and a fitness suite, plus a café, licensed bar and crèche. Fitness classes and coaching sessions are offered. Booking ahead is essential. Times for general swimming are imited.

Punting & Boating

For messing about on the river in punts, rowing boats or canoes, the following operate Easter to October.

Cherwell Boathouse, at the bottom of Bardwell Road,
tel: 01865-515978;
www.cherwellboathouse.co.uk.
Punts, rowing boats and canoes, £12–£14 an hour (£60 deposit or credit card weekdays, £70 deposit weekends). Also a fine restaurant.

C. Howard & Son, Magdalen Bridge, tel: 01865-202643; www.oxfordpunting.co.uk. Punts and rowing boats. £12 an hour weekdays, £30 cash deposit. Also chauffeured punts £20 per half hour (with free bottle of wine).

Salter's Steamers Boat Hire Station, Folly Bridge, tel: 01865-243421; www.salterssteamers.co.uk. Punts, skiffs and canoes: £15 an hour, £25 deposit, or £45 per hour for chauffeured punts.

Spectator Sports

Athletics

Regular meetings are held at the Iffley Road running ground and at the city-owned track at Horspath Road Sports Ground. www.oxfordcityathleticclub.com

Cricket

Oxford University plays first-class games against county sides in the University Parks, Parks Road; tel: 01865-241335;

www.cricketintheparks.org.uk. Banbury Cricket Club, Bodicote, Banbury; tel: 01295 264368; www.banburycricketclub.co.uk

Football

Oxford United FC (Coca-Cola Football League 2) play at The Kassam Stadium, Grenoble Road; tel: 01865 337500; www.oufc.co.uk
Oxford City FC (Spartan South Midlands League) play at Court Place Farm, Marston; tel: 01865 744493; www.oxfordcityfc.co.uk

Ice Hockey

The Oxford City Stars play home matches on Sundays Sept–April at the Oxford Ice Rink, Oxpens Road; tel: 01865-467002; www.oxfordstars.com.

Rugby

Oxford University Rugby Club plays at Iffley Road; tel: 01865-432000. The Oxford Rugby Football Club plays at the Southern Bypass; tel: 01865-243984; www.oxfordrfc.co.uk.

ACTIVITIES FOR CHILDREN

Indoor Activities

The **New Theatre** (see page 247) often has entertaining productions for children. **Bowlplex**, Ozone Leisure & Entertainment Park (see Bowling page 251), is also a good place to go with kids, as well as bowling there is a video game arcade and American pool. Ozone also has a multiscreen cinema (see page 247, Cinemas). Older children may enjoy shooting each other at **LaserQuest**, Threeways House, Gloucester Green (tel: 01865 200233; www.laserquest.co.uk) or, for the less combative, attempting virtual golf at the same site.

Museums

An ideal place for a rainy day is **Hands-On**, Science Oxford, 1–5 London Place, tel: 01865

728953; www.oxtrust.org.uk; open Saturdays, daily during school holidays, 10am–4pm. A hands-on science gallery with exciting interactive experiments and a changing menu of themed activities. Recommended age 5–12 years. Best to book a 2-hour session in advance (starting at 10am, noon or 2pm).

Children will be particularly fascinated by the **Pitt Rivers Museum** (*see page 177*) where they can ask the attendant to show them the giant toad or even the witch in a bottle. Adjacent is the **Oxford Natural History Museum**, which won the Guardian's *Family Friendly Museum* 2005 award.

As well as the dinosaurs, the **University Museum** (*see page 175*) also has the portrait of the same Dodo that features in Lewis Carroll's *Alice's Adventures in Wonderland*.

Young visitors to the **Ashmolean Museum** (*see page 157*) will be enthralled by its large collection of Egyptian mummies as well as Powhattan's Mantle (Powhattan being the father of Pocahontas).

Displays in the **Museum of Oxford** (*see page 147*) include some interesting finds from prehistoric times, as well as a large placard with a simplified version of the Legend of St Frideswide, the city's patron saint.

The Oxford Story (*see page 130*) provides an unusual ride back in time to show the history of Oxford and its University; a special commentary for children is available.

Outdoor Activities

For kids who prefer to be outdoors, there are plenty of attractions within easy reach of the city.

Shotover Country Park, beyond Headington (*see page 207*), is a delight for all those who like playing hide and seek and climbing trees; there is also a "natural" sandpit.

At **Port Meadow** (*see page 202*) children will enjoy patting the horses and also feeding the ducks, geese and swans at the bridge over the Thames.

To the north of the city, beyond the ring road, **Cutteslowe Park** has an aviary, ornamental carp pond and a refreshment kiosk plus a fine playground, tennis and orienteering (call Park Services on 0800 0521455). On Sundays the City of Oxford Society of Model Engineers operate the miniature train circuit. A bridge links the park to nearby Sunnymead Recreation Ground which includes a new skate park.

Closer to the centre are the **University Parks** – 70 acres (30 hectares) of parkland, sports and landscaped areas on the West bank of the River Cherwell, www.parks.ox.ac.uk.

Outside Oxford

The environs of Oxford also have much to offer children.

Cotswold Wildlife Park near Burford, (tel: 01993 823006, www.cotswoldwildlifepark.co.uk; open daily 10am–6pm or dusk if earlier; *see page 235*), is a half-hour drive from the city (towards Cheltenham on the A40). Even before seeing the wide variety of animals and birds or visiting the Children's Farmyard, children will probably demand a session in the adventure playground as well as a ride on the narrow gauge railway (Apr–Oct only). Penguin feeding takes place at 11am and 4pm. Gift shop and restaurant.

Blenheim Park (tel: 08700 602080, www.blenheimpalace.com; *see page 214*), at Woodstock, 8 miles down the A44 towards Evesham, also has an adventure playground and railway.

At **Cogges Manor Farm Museum** in Witney (tel: 01993 772 602; Tues–Fri 10am–4pm, Sat & Sun 12–4pm, most children will be fascinated by the hand-milking and butter-making, as well as the crafts demonstrations held in the barn.

Young steam buffs should be taken to the **Didcot Railway Centre**, Didcot (tel: 01235 817200, www.didcotrailwaycentre.org.uk; *see page 253*). Call beforehand to enquire when the steam trains will be put through their paces.

BELOW: Port Meadow's animals are popular with children.

A – Z

A HANDY SUMMARY OF PRACTICAL INFORMATION, ARRANGED ALPHABETICALLY

B icycles

If arriving by train you will notice the vast bicycle park at the station, so it should be no surprise to see more cyclists here than you are used to. It is worth making a conscious effort to be bike-aware as both a driver and a pedestrian (to avoid stepping out into the path of cyclists – especially at dusk).

● *For bike hire see page 237; for bike tours see page 251.*

Business Hours

Most of the shops in the city centre are open Monday to Saturday 9am–5.30pm, although many now open on Sunday 10am–4pm. There is late-night shopping every Thursday, when many shops remain open until 8.30pm.

Supermarkets on the outskirts of Oxford tend to be open 8.30am–8pm from Monday to Saturday and 10am–4pm on Sunday, although some are now beginning to open 24 hours from Monday to Saturday.

Offices usually operate 9am–5.30pm Monday–Friday with an hour for lunch.

British pubs are now permitted flexible opening hours, with the potential for up to 24 hour opening, seven days a week. Typically, most still open 11am–11pm. Persons over 18 years may buy alcohol in a bar; children under 14 must be accompanied by an adult.

C ar Rental

For car hire firms *see box on page 238*. For rules of the road, parking and breakdown information see *Driving page 238*.

Children

Children are well catered for in Oxford, especially in recreation centres. During holiday periods, special programmes are designed by theatres, museums and sporting associations – the Tourist Information Centre (*see page 259*) has full details. *See also Activities for Children page 252.*

TRANSPORTATION

Oxford for the Under-Eights, published by the New Parent Network, is available in bookshops, with useful tips for parents with young children in Oxford. Pick up a free copy of the bi-monthly *Families in Oxfordshire* from the Tourist Information Centre (*see* page 259).

Nappy-changing facilities are available at: The Early Learning Centre, 30 Queen Street; and Gloucester Green bus station.

Climate

In addition to the general vagaries of English weather, Oxford is famous for its damp climate, enhanced by its position in the Thames Valley.

Even if the sun is shining in the vicinity, there may well be a pall of mist hanging over the city itself, particularly during the winter months. Most of the summer is cool enough for a jacket. Expect rain at any time of the year.

For recorded weather forecasts (Berks, Bucks and Oxon) call Weathercall 09068 505306.

Clothing

In youthful, cosmopolitan Oxford, you can wear just about anything and not be considered out of place. Students wear very casual clothes – often jeans and sweaters of doubtful age and condition, or the fashions of the day. Older people tend to wear a range from everyday casual wear to smart outfits, depending on the situation. As weather is unpredictable at all times, it is advisable to bring along clothes for both rain and shine.

Even in summer, the weather is variable, so you will need some warm clothing and comfortable footwear for the notably uneven flagstones of some streets. Formal dress is encouraged in some hotels and restaurants and for evening entertainment, particularly in university circles.

University dress code: During Encaenia, the main honorary degree ceremony in June, the Chancellor of the University leads a procession of dignitaries and dons along Broad Street. The magnificent scarlet and pink robes they wear are a reminder of the days up until the Reformation when all members of the university were in holy orders.

This applied to students, too, and their successors today are still required to wear their black and white "subfusc" garments while sitting exams and receiving degrees.

Consulates

Most countries have diplomatic representation in London – a selection is given below. For others telephone a directory enquiries service (e.g., 118 247, or 118 888) or see www.yell.com or www.192.com.

Australia
Australia House, Strand,
London WC2 4LA.
Tel: 0171-379 4334.
Canada
38, Grosvenor Street,
London WIX OAA
Tel: 0171-258 6600.
New Zealand
80 Haymarket,
London SW1Y 4TQ.
Tel: 0171-930 8422.
United States
24 Grosvenor Square,
London W1A 1AF.
Tel: 0171-499 9000.

D isabled Access

The Oxford City Council publishes the booklet, *The Accessible Oxford Guide*, for people using a wheelchair. This, and a list of premises which are accessible to wheelchairs, is available at the Tourist Information Centre (*see* page 259). Another useful leaflet is *Oxford city centre parking for people with disabilities*, which shows all Blue badge parking spaces.

Free wheelchairs or scooters can be borrowed from **Oxford Shopmobility**, a scheme funded by the City Council. Booking is required, tel: 01865-744478. People using wheelchairs are welcome to join any of the guided tours. Stagecoach runs modern easy-access buses on most of the city's bus routes.

The County Disability Information Centre, **DIALability**, can help you find out what's available in Oxfordshire for disabled people. Their information and advice line is 01865-763600; www.dialability.org.uk.

Another useful website is www.oxfordcity.co.uk/info/disability

E conomy

For centuries, agriculture and the wool industry provided Oxford with an economic base as a thriving market town. However, it was only when William Morris started manufacturing cars in 1912 that Oxford became part of mainstream industrial Britain. Morris Motors was born, and Oxford, the city of learning, was transformed into a major industrial centre, increasing its population from 57,000 in 1920 to more than 80,000 in 1930. Since the demise in 2005 of MG Rover Group, formerly one of the city's major employers, the local motor industry is kept going by the BMW-owned Mini factory in Cowley.

Printing and publishing on the

CLIMATE CHART

°C | J F M A M J J A S O N D | mm

30 — 150
25 — 125
20 — 100
15 — 75
10 — 50
5 — 25
0 — 0

☐ Maximum temperature
■ Minimum temperature
— Rainfall
☀ Sunny months
☔ Rainy months

ACCOMMODATION

ACTIVITIES

A–Z

other hand, are almost as old as the university itself: 1478 saw the first book printed in Oxford (just two years after Caxton set up his printing press). The city is the UK's second most important publishing centre, its activities spearheaded by the Oxford University Press, but also including Aldens, Blackwell's, Nuffield Press, Heinemann Educational Books, Holywell Press and more than 100 others.

Electricity

240 volts is standard; plugs have three square pins. Hotels will usually have dual 110/240-volt sockets for razors with two-pin plugs (round pins).

Emergency Numbers

Emergency services (fire, police, ambulance) dial **999**.
Thames Valley Police,
tel: 01865-266000 (burglaries, stolen bicycles and lost property).
Citizens' Advice Bureau, 95–96 St Aldate's, tel: 01865-247578.
Samaritans, tel: 01865 722122 or 08457 90 90 90. Assistance available 24-hours.
Oxford Rape Crisis Line,
tel: 01865-726295. Operates Monday and Thursday 6.30–9pm, Wednesday 3.30–6pm, and Sunday 6–8.30pm. Answerphone at other times.

Gay and Lesbian

Oxford has an active gay scene. For details contact: **Oxford Friend**, Gay and Lesbian Helpline for counselling, advice and help, 111 Magdalen Road (open till 2am, 4am weekends), tel: 01865-726893 (Tuesday, Wednesday and Friday 7–9pm), www.oxford-friend.co.uk.
    Oxford Lesbian and Gay Community Centre, Northgate Hall, St Michael's Street, tel: 01865-200249.
    See also the online gay and lesbian events information directory: www.queeroxford.co.uk. *For gay nightlife see page 248.*

Geology

In few parts of Britain has geology so influenced the landscape and architecture. The underlying rock in the Oxford area is oolite limestone, formed under pressure millions of years ago from the crushed shells of primitive sea organisms. Its small spherical grains vary in colour and texture depending on their location and depth. Wind and rain has moulded the limestone into a rolling countryside and the rock favours the growth of beech trees.
    The stone has delighted builders – from the creators of prehistoric burial mounds to the architects of Oxford's cathedrals of learning. When mellow, it alters dramatically in colour, often from one moment to the next, as a cloud formation shifts. Buildings made from this stone, wrote the novelist J.B. Priestley, can keep "the lost sunlight of centuries glimmering about them".

Government

Oxford County Council is responsible for overall planning policies and large-scale services in the area, such as police, education, fire brigades, libraries and social services. Those services are financed by the council tax, payable by every householder, and by grants from central government.
    Oxford City is divided into 17 wards, which are represented by elected Councillors. The City Council is controlled by the party which wins a majority of the seats at the election. In the case of Oxford this has been Labour for many years but recently they have shared control with Liberal Democrats and Greens.

Health and Medical Care

If you are a national of the EU you are entitled to free medical treatment for illnesses arising while in the UK. Many other countries also have reciprocal arrangements for free treatment. However, most visitors have to pay for medical and dental treatment and should ensure they have adequate health insurance.
NHS Helpline, tel: 0845 4647.

Medical Emergencies
In a medical emergency, either call an ambulance (dial 999) or make your way to the nearest Accident and Emergency department (John Radcliffe Hospital, Headington, *see below*).

Hospitals
John Radcliffe Hospital (with accident and maternity units), Headley Way, Headington, Oxford. Tel: 01865-741166.
Churchill Hospital
Old Road, Headington, Oxford. Tel: 01865-741841.
Radcliffe Infirmary (eye hospital), Walton Street, Oxford. Tel: 01865-311188.
Abingdon Hospital
Tel: Abingdon 01235-522717.

Dental Treatment
Oxfordshire Health Authority Dental Helpline
Tel: 01865-226532
They will give you information on emergency dental services as well as general information.
NHS Emergency Dental Clinics
Tel: 01865-842609.

Pharmacies
There are several chemists all over Oxford open during regular business hours. As well as selling over-the-counter medicines, they make up prescriptions.
The Ten O'Clock Pharmacy 59 Woodstock Road, Tel: 01865-515226 is open daily 9am–7.30pm. The pharmacy counter in Sainsburys, Heyford Hill, is open till 11pm.

Internet Cafés

Mices, 118 High Street and 91 Gloucester Green, tel: 01865-726364, www.mices.com; open daily 9am–11pm.
Virgin Spaces, 18–20 Cornmarket, tel: 01865-723 971.
Budget Internet Café, 196 Banbury Road, tel: 01865-515955.

Lost Property

Enquiries should be made, or lost property handed in, at the Central Police Station, St Aldate's (Mon–Thurs 8.45am–4.30pm and Fri 8.45am–4.15pm, tel: 01865-266226). It is important to inform the police if you recover any property previously reported lost.

Money

Some city centre banks offer bureau de change facilities on weekdays and Saturday mornings, as do some travel agents.

The majority of branches have automatic cash machines (ATM) where cashpoint or international credit cards can be used, with a personal identification number (PIN), to withdraw cash.

International credit cards are accepted in most shops, hotels and restaurants. However, there are exceptions in some shops.

Media

Local Newspapers
The *Oxford Mail* is the city's leading evening newspaper. The *Oxford Times*, published on Friday, carries the week's news and the biggest coverage of property for sale. *The Star* and the *Courier Journal* are free weekly papers delivered locally.

Foreign Newspapers
Wendy News, 4 Broad Street, and W.H. Smith, 22 Cornmarket, usually have a reasonable selection of foreign newspapers.

Local Radio
BBC Radio Oxford, 95.2 FM, www.bbc.co.uk/oxford, tel: 01865 311444. Local news and talk programmes. When there are no local programmes, the channel reverts to BBC Radio 2.
Fox FM, 102.6 FM, www.foxfm.co.uk, tel: 01865-871000. An Oxfordshire commercial station with music and chat programmes. On air 24 hours a day.
Oxide 87.9 FM www.oxfordstudentradio.com. Oxford's very own student radio, which produces more speech-based radio than any other student station in the country. **Passion 107.9 FM**, www.passion 1079.com. Local pop station.

Local Television
Central Television, Unit 9, Windrush Court, Abingdon, tel: 01235-554123. Broadcasts local news in the central area of England, covering the Midlands as well.
SIX TV, 270 Woodstock Road, tel: 01865-314700, www.sixtv.co.uk. Oxford's own terrestrial television station, broadcasts 17 hours a day, featuring local information, local interest, lifestyle and music. Tunes into channel 6.

Parking

The one-way traffic systems and very limited parking in central Oxford make leaving the car at one of the Park-and-Ride sites around the outskirts of the city a very attractive option. Be aware that in residential areas you often need a resident's parking permit and that Oxford traffic wardens are vigilant. Parking in the city centre is much easier after 6.30pm. *For details on driving and parking see page 238.*

Parks and Gardens

Somewhere to sit on the grass is not easy to find in the immediate centre of town but take a short walk to one of the following: **Christ Church Meadow** to the south (entrances St Aldate's, Merton Street or bottom of Rose Lane); **Botanic Garden** *(see page 116)* and the **Deer Park** to the southwest, or **University Parks** to the north (main entrance Parks Road). The largest green space in Oxford is **Port Meadow** a beautiful open pasture along the Thames to the northwest of the city (entrance via Walton Well Road, Thames Towpath or Wolvercote village).

Further out from the centre are **Shotover Country Park** *(see page 207)*, west beyond Headington, and **Cutteslowe Park** *(see page 253)*, north past the ring road.

Near Wheatley, 7½ miles (10km) southeast of Oxford is the spectacular **Waterperry Gardens**, with nurseries, alpine and rock gardens, plus a Saxon church, museum, art and craft gallery, and tea-shop. Check website or call to check events (such as Shakespeare plays, apple tasting or morris dancing). Open Mar–Oct 9am–5.30pm. Nov–Feb 9am–5pm. Tel: 01844 339254, www.waterperrygardens.co.uk.

Postal Services

The main post office at 102–104 St Aldate's is open Monday–Saturday 9am–5.30pm. A currency exchange service and a shop selling a wide range of stationery is also available there. The last collection for nationwide next-day delivery is at 7pm, or midnight for local mail. Most post offices close at 5.30pm but those in shops may close for lunch and on Tuesday or Wednesday afternoons. For help or advice on all counter services call the Customer Help Line, tel: 08457 223344. For enquiries about parcels, try Parcel Force, tel: 08708 501150.

Oxford postcodes start with OX. OX1 is the City centre, OX2 is Summertown; OX3 indicates Headington; and OX4 is Cowley.

Public Holidays

The public holidays are:
New Year's Day (1 January)
Easter Monday
May Day (first Monday in May)
Spring Bank Holiday (last Monday in May)
Summer Bank Holiday (last Monday in August)
Christmas Day (25 December)
Boxing Day (26 December).
If 25 or 26 December or 1 January fall on a weekend the following Monday is a Bank Holiday.

For festivals and holidays, *see page 245, Calendar of Events.*

R eligious Services

Public services are held at Christ Church Cathedral on Sunday at 8am, 10am and 6pm, and on weekdays at 7.35am and 6pm throughout the year. There are also services generally open to the public in the college chapels of Magdalen, New College, Mansfield (United Reformed) and Manchester (Unitarian) colleges during the three University terms (Michaelmas: 1 October to 17 December; Hilary: 7 January to 25 March or the Saturday before Palm Sunday, whichever is earlier; and Trinity: 20 April or the Wednesday after Easter, whichever is later, until 6 July).

Anglican Churches
St Aldate's Church, St Aldate's. Services: Sunday 10.30am and 6.30pm; holy communion alternates between the morning and evening service during the week.
St Andrew's, Linton Road. Services: Sunday 8am, 9.30am, 11am and 6pm.
St Barnabas, Cardigan Street, Jericho. Services: Sunday 8am, 10.30am and 6.30pm.
St Mary-the-Virgin, High Street (University Church). Services: Sunday 8am, 10am (only during term-time), 11am (in winter) and 6pm; weekdays 12.15pm; Tuesday 7.30am Taize service (only during term-time); Lutheran service every fortnight.

St Michael-at-the-Northgate, Ship Street (City Church). Services: Sunday 8am, 9.45am, 11am and 6.30pm; Wednesday 1.15pm; Friday 12.15pm.
St Ebbe's, Pennyfarthing Place. Services: Sunday 10am, 11.30am (winter only), 6.30pm.
St Giles', St Giles. Services: Sunday 8am and 6.30pm; weekdays 5.30pm.
St Mary Magdalen, Magdalen Street. Services: Sunday 8am and 5.30pm; weekdays 11.15am, 5.40pm and 6pm.
St Peter and St Paul's, Elms Parade, Botley. Services Sunday 10am.

Roman Catholic
St Aloysius Gonzaga, 25 Woodstock Road. The Catholic parish church for the centre of Oxford and where Tolkien went to Sunday Mass. Services: Sunday 6.30am, 8am (Latin), 9.30am, 11am (Latin), 5.30pm (Vespers) and 6.30pm; Monday to Friday 7.30am, 10am and 6pm; Saturday 10am.

BELOW: the tower of St Barnabas.

Catholic Chaplaincy, Rose Place (off St Aldate's). Services: Sun 9am, 11am, 5.45pm, 8.30pm; Mon, Wed, Thurs and Sat 12.15pm; Tues and Fri 13:10pm.
Blackfriars Priory, 62–64 St Giles. Services: Sunday 8am, 9.30am, 11.15am (in Spanish) and community mass at 6.15pm; weekdays 6.15pm.

Baptist
Baptist Church, Bonn Square, opposite the Westgate Centre. Services Sunday 10.30am.
South Oxford Baptist Church, Wytham Street. Services: Sunday 10am, 6.30pm; Wednesday 7.30pm. There are also Asian Christian services held here.

Other Churches
First Church of Christ Scientist, 36 St Giles. Services: Sunday 11am (including Sunday school); Wednesday 7.30pm.
Orthodox Church of the Holy Trinity and the Annunciation, 1 Canterbury Road (used by Greek and Russian Orthodox communities). Services Sunday 10.30am, and 5.30pm.
Quaker Meetings, Friends' Meeting House, 43 St Giles. Services: Sunday 9.30am and 11am; weekdays 7.30am (Wednesday 12.15pm).
Salvation Army Citadel, Albion Square. Services Sunday 11am and 6pm.
St Columba United Reformed Church, Alfred Street (off High Street). Services Sunday at 10.45am.
Wesley Memorial Church (Methodist) New Inn Hall Street. Services Sunday at 10.30am and 6.30pm.

Buddhist
Thrangu House, 42 Magdalen Road, tel: 01865 241555. Oxford's Buddhist centre.

Jewish
Oxford Synagogue, 21 Richmond Road. Open: Friday 7pm; Saturday 10am.

Muslim

Central Oxford Mosque and Islamic Education Centre, Manzil Way, Cowley.

ecurity

Crime exists in Oxford, as anywhere else. Take special care in car parks. Don't leave any valuables in the car and secure it properly.

elephones

Almost all of the modern phone boxes still accept coins (taking 10p, 20p, 50p and £1 coins) as well as phonecards (sold by newsagents and post offices at £2, £5 and £10 denominations). The minimum call charge is 30p. Phone booths are located at the railway station, Gloucester Green, Carfax, Queen's Street, St Aldate's post office, and in many pubs and restaurants.

Numbers starting with 0800 are free, 0870 and 0845 are charged at local rate and 0990 at national rate.

Directory enquiries (local and national calls): 118 848 or 118 888. Websites: www.yell.com (businesses) and www.192.com (residential).

International directory enquiries: 118 449 or 118 866.

Operator (local and national calls): 100.

Tipping

Most hotels and restaurants automatically add a 10–15 per cent service charge to your bill. You are not expected to tip in pubs, cinemas, theatres or lifts, but it is customary to give hairdressers, sightseeing guides, railway porters and taxi drivers a tip of about 10 per cent.

Tourist Information

Oxford Tourist Information Centre
15–16 Broad Street
Oxford OX1 3AS
Tel: 01865 726 871

Email: tic@oxford.gov.uk
www.visitoxford.org
Provides information on accommodation, attractions, local events and guided walking tours and bus tours. A hotel and guest house booking service is also available. It is open Monday to Saturday 9.30am–5pm, Sunday (during the summer months) and public holidays 10am–4pm. You can find all kinds of useful information on their website. There is also the independent website at www.oxfordcity.co.uk.

Limited visitor information is also available from a kiosk in Oxford train station.

Walking

Oxfordshire is criss-crossed by a network of drover's roads (the tracks along which farmers drove livestock to market), bridleways (for riding horses) and footpaths. Notable routes are the Ridgeway, which follows the chalk uplands and is Britain's and possibly Europe's oldest road; the Thames Path, which meanders alongside the river; and the Oxfordshire Way. **Oxfordshire Countryside Service** has lots of information on walking and countryside access, including for those with limited mobility. Download or request printed maps of 12 attractive "Paths For All" routes across Oxfordshire detailing recreational routes for walkers, horse riders, and mountain bikers: tel: 01865 810226, www.oxfordshire.gov.uk/countryside.

Pub Walks in Oxfordshire, by Nick Channer, is also available from bookshops in the city.

ebsites

General

www.visitoxford.org – website of the tourist information centre.
www.oxfordcity.co.uk – local and tourist information.
www.oxfordshire.gov.uk – for the wider Oxfordshire area.
www.thisisoxfordshire.co.uk – including local news, movie list-

ings, pubs and restaurants.
http://oxford.openguides.org – a "wiki" (ie. edited by users).
www.chem.ox.ac.uk/oxfordtour/ - offers a virtual tour of Oxford with interactive maps.
www.oxfordrestaurantguide.co.uk –

Accommodation

www.oxfinder.co.uk – including camping
www.stayoxford.co.uk – the Oxford Association of Hotels and Guest Houses.
www.oxtowns.co.uk – for outside Oxford.

Museums

www.ox.ac.uk/museums
www.oxfordcity.co.uk

Leisure and Sport

www.oxford.gov.uk
www.inoxfordmag.co.uk

Transport

www.oxfordbus.co.uk – for London and local services and the Zone Freedom Pass.
www.citysightseeingoxford.com
www.parkandride.net
www.cyclemaps.org.uk

University

www.ox.ac.uk – information on the University of Oxford's colleges and their departments.

What's On

www.inoxfordmag.co.uk – the *In Oxford* magazine site.
www.dailyinfo.co.uk – good for what's on.
www.the-zodiac.co.uk – Oxford's premier live music and club venue.
www.ticketsoxford.com

Other

www.oxfordcity.co.uk/info/disability – disabled access.
www.tolkiensoxford.com – with links to the Oxford Tolkien Society.
www.ivu.org/oxveg/ – Oxford Vegetarians website.

TRANSPORTATION

ACCOMMODATION

ACTIVITIES

A–Z

FURTHER READING

General

Hugh Casson's Oxford, by Sir Hugh Casson (Phaidon Press). An illustrated guide to Oxford with watercolour drawings and pen and ink sketches by the author.

Oxford in Verse, edited by Glyn Pursglove and Alistair Ricketts (Perpetua Press). An anthology of poetry on the city of dreaming spires.

Oxford, by Jan Morris (Oxford Paperbacks). A brilliant account of the character, history, mores, buildings and much else by a top travel writer.

The Oxford Book of Oxford, by Jan Morris (Oxford Paperbacks). An entertaining, lively anthology, tracing Oxford's history back to its origins.

The Story of Alice, by Mavis Batey (Macmillan). By using diaries, newspapers and university records, this book tells the story behind Lewis Carroll's Alice.

Oxford: an Architectural Guide, by Geoffrey Tyack (Oxford University Press). A detailed description of buildings and features characteristic of Oxford's architecture.

Fiction

Inspector Morse Mysteries, by Colin Dexter (Macmillan and Pan). A series of crime novels set in Oxford, which achieved world-wide fame in their television adaption.

Zuleika Dobson, by Max Beerbohm (Modern Library). First published in 1911, this is a satirical story of the devastating effect of a beautiful adventuress on Oxford students.

Brideshead Revisited, by Evelyn Waugh (Penguin Classics). First published in 1945. Young aristo-

crats in Oxford living a sybaritic life of eternal summers.

Alice's Adventures in Wonderland, by Lewis Carroll (Puffin Classics). First published in 1865. The famous fantastical adventures of Alice.

Through the Looking-Glass, by Lewis Carroll (Puffin Classics). First published in 1872. The sequel to *Alice's Adventures in Wonderland*. Both Alice books were inspired by Oxford, its people and its sights.

Oxford Guides

Our Canal in Oxford, by Mark Davies and Catherine Robinson (Towpath Press). A guided walking tour along the towpath from Wolvercote to the city centre, with lots of keen historical details.

An Encyclopedia of Oxford Pubs, Inns and Taverns, by Derek Honey (Oakwood Press). A concise, alphabetical reference book of Oxford's pubs.

Pubwalks in Oxfordshire, by Nick Channer (Countryside Books). Thirty circular walks around Oxfordshire inns.

Oxford for Under-Eights, edited by Vicki Cullen and Dave Dalton (New Parent Network). Extremely useful information for parents with young children in Oxford.

Other Insight Guides

Nearly 200 **Insight Guides** and **Insight City Guides** cover every continent. In addition, a companion series of more than 120 **Insight Pocket Guides** provides selected, carefully timed itineraries for the traveler with little time to spare and include a full-size fold-out map. And more than 130 **Insight Compact Guides** provide ideal on-the-spot

companions, with text, maps and pictures all carefully cross-referenced and cover every popular tourist area of the British Isles.

Titles which highlight destinations in this region include:

● *Insight Guide: England*
● *Insight Guide Great Britain*
● *Insight City Guide London*
● *Insight Guide Wales*

FEEDBACK

We do our best to ensure the information in our books is as accurate and up to date as possible. The books are updated on a regular basis, using local contacts who painstakingly add, amend and correct as required. However, some mistakes and omissions are inevitable, and we are ultimately reliant on our readers to put us in the picture.

We would welcome your feedback on any details related to your experiences using the book "on the road". Maybe we recommended a hotel that you liked (or one you did not), or maybe there are interesting new attractions, or facts and figures you have found out about. The more details you can give us (particularly with regard to addresses, e-mails and telephone numbers), the better.

We will acknowledge all contributions, and we will offer an Insight Guide to the best emails/letters received.

Please write to us at:
Insight Guides
PO Box 7910
London SE1 1WE
United Kingdom
Or send e-mail to:
insight@apaguide.co.uk

OXFORD STREET ATLAS

The key map shows the area of Oxford covered by the atlas
section. An index of street names and places of interest
shown on the maps can be found on the following pages. For
each entry there is a page number and grid reference

Map Legend

Motorway with Junction	Airport	Motorway	Bus Station
Motorway (under construction)	Church (ruins)	Dual Carriageway	Tourist Information
Dual Carriageway	Monastery	Main Roads	Post Office
Main Road	Castle (ruins)		Cathedral/Church
Secondary Road	Archaeological Site	Minor Roads	Mosque
Minor Road	Cave		Synagogue
Track	Place of Interest	Footpath	Statue/Monument
International Boundary	Mansion/Stately Home	Railway	Tower
County Boundary	Viewpoint	Pedestrian Area	
National Park/Reserve		Important Building	

UNIVERSITY PARKS

0   50   100   150   200 m
0   50   100   150   200 yds

N

Cherwell

iversity Science Area

Hinkswood Rd

Slabuop Rd

E. Abraham Rd

South Parks Road

Linacre College

Pitt Rivers Museum of Ethnology

ersity eum

SPORTS GROUND

GREAT MEADOW

Holywell Mill Stream

South Parks Road

Rhodes House

Mansfield Road

Psychology & Zoology Faculties

St Cross Road

Mansfield College

Library & Law Facility

Manor Road

Manor Place

St Catherine's College

New College School

BALLIOL COLLEGE SPORTS GROUND

Savile Road

Mansfield Road

School of Geography

Wadham College

Harris Manchester College

Jowett Walk

St Cross Road

New odleian brary

The King's Arms

Holywell Music Room

Holywell Street

oad Street

Hertford College

Bath Palace

Holywell Buildings

MAGDALEN GROVE

DEER PARK

Clarendon Building

Bridge of Sighs

New

City Wall

eldonian heatre

Hertford College

College Lane

New College

ivinity chool

Bodleian Library

Queens

St Peter in the East (Library)

Longwall Street

Radcliffe

Castle Street

le Lane

Radcliffe Camera

All Souls' College

Lane

New Buildings

Brasenose College

Square

Queen's College

aln ge

University Church of St Mary the Virgin

St Edmund Hall

aints' reet

Rhodes Building

High Street

Magdalen College

University College

JP shop

King Edward St

Oriel St

Magpie Lane

Logic Lane

Examination Schools

Eastgate Hotel

ear Lane

Oriel Sq.

Kybald St

Oriel College

Merton Street

Rose Lane

High Street

Magdalen Water

Corpus Christi College

Merton College

BOTANIC GARDEN

Magdalen Bridge

D

E

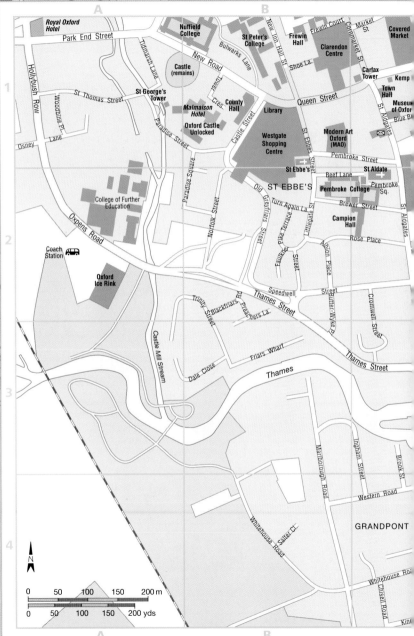

A

B

Royal Oxford Hotel
Park End Street
Hollybush Row
Tidmarsh Lane
St Thomas Street
Woodbine Pl.
Osney Lane
Paradise Street
St George's Tower
Malmaison Hotel
Oxford Castle Unlocked
Castle (remains)
New Road
Nuffield College
Bulwarks Lane
St Peter's College
New Inn Hall St.
Frewin Hall
Frewin Court
Cornmarket St.
Market St.
Covered Market
Clarendon Centre
Shoe La.
Carfax Tower
Kemp
Town Hall
Museum of Oxford
Blue Be
Queen Street
St Aldates
County Hall
Castle Street
Paradise Square
Library
Westgate Shopping Centre
St Ebbe's Street
Modern Art Oxford (MAO)
Pembroke Street
St Ebbe's
Beef Lane
St Aldate
Pembroke College
Pembroke Sq.
St EBBE'S
Old Greyfriars Street
Turn Again La.
Littlegate St.
Brewer Street
College of Further Education
Norfolk Street
Pike Terrace
Faulkner
Street
Campion Hall
Rose Place
St Aldates
Oxpens Road
Coach Station
Oxford Ice Rink
Albion Place
Speedwell
Street
Butter-Wyke P.
Cromwell Street
Thames Street
Trinity Street
Blackfriars Rd.
Preachers La.
Dale Close
Friars Wharf
Castle Mill Stream
Thames
Thames Street
Marlborough Road
Ingham Street
Brook St.
Western Road
GRANDPONT
Whitehouse Road
Salter Cl.
Whitehouse Roa
Chisnell Road
Kine

1

2

3

4

N

0   50   100   150   200 m

0   50   100   150   200 yds

A

B

coln
ege

ts'
street

OUP
okshop

Bear Lane

rch

Bate
Collection
of Musical
Instruments

Police
Station

University
University
Church of St Mary
the Virgin

High Street

Rhodes
Building

University
College

King Edward St

Oriel St

Magpie Lane

Kybald St

Oriel
College

Oriel Sq.

Corpus Christi
College

Merton
College

Merton   Street

Logic Lane

Examination
Schools

St Edmund
Hall

Eastgate
Hotel

Rose Lane

High Street

New
Buildings

Magdalen
College

Magdalen Water

Magdalen
Bridge

Christ Church
Cathedral

Merton Grove

Deadman's   Walk

★
James Sadler
Plaque

MERTON   FIELD

BOTANIC
GARDEN

Victoria
Fountain ★

Broad Walk

MAGDALEN COLLEGE
SCHOOL CRICKET
GROUND

St Hilda's
College

Boat
House

Cowley Place

Magdalen
College
School

CHRIST   CHURCH

MEADOW

SPORTS
GROUND

SPORTS
GROUND

Boat
Houses

D

E

1

2

3

4

STREET INDEX

ART & PHOTO CREDITS

Cartographic Editor: Zoë Goodwin
Map Production: Phoenix Mapping
©2006 Apa Publications GmbH & Co. Verlag KG, Singapore Branch

INDEX